From Brooklyn
I Saw Mountains *

* I also saw
Uncle Louie and Aunt
Minnie!

Jay

From Brooklyn
I Saw Mountains

Jay Freeman

VANTAGE PRESS
New York

FIRST EDITION

All rights reserved, including the right of
reproduction in whole or in part in any form.

Copyright © 1998 by Jay Freeman

Published by Vantage Press, Inc.
516 West 34th Street, New York, New York 10001

Manufactured in the United States of America
ISBN: 0-533-12570-7

Library of Congress Catalog Card No.: 97-91113

0 9 8 7 6 5 4 3 2 1

To my father, Samuel D. Freeman

Contents

Acknowledgments   ix
Preface   xi

Part I: Growing Up
   1. Earliest Memories and Memories Handed Down   3
   2. Childhood   25
   3. Adolescence   36
   4. College Years and the Single Life   61

Part II: The Responsible Years
   5. Patricia and Rachel   73
   6. Engineer to Entrepreneur   92
   7. FA Components   107
   8. Friendship   141

Part III: Internal and External Adventures
   9. My Human Body Adventure   157
  10. Vacations and Adventures   160

Part IV: Half Time Review
  11. Eulogy   229
  12. Endings and Beginnings   232

Postscript
A Young Traveler Writes Home   235

Acknowledgments

There are several people I would like to acknowledge. First, I wish to thank my editor, Claudia Strauss, who read and reread the manuscript, wisely suggesting necessary additions and subtractions so that my story could be told with greater clarity and logic. I also wish to thank my publishers, Vantage Press, for all their help in bringing my story to print. My elderly aunt, Manya Goodheart, was always pleased to search her amazing memory for facts and stories about my ancestors. With her help I was able to tell the Oxenhorn family story with accuracy and depth. And lastly, to my wife, Patricia, I acknowledge my deepest gratitude for a lifetime of loyalty and love. Countless times have I relied on her courage and good judgement.

Preface

In writing my autobiography I had to determine the limits to which I would probe and write about my inner self. I will describe many personal and revealing facets of my life and do so with all the honesty I can muster. Many of my vanities, conceits, insecurities and prejudices will be laid bare in a frank self-appraisal. However, other facets of my life will remain in shadows to preserve some privacy for myself and those I know. Writing an autobiography is by definition an exercise in self-indulgence. I have enjoyed the exercise and I hope that the experiences of my life, as set forth in this book, will be of some use and interest to the reader.

Great men are often defined by their work. Their autobiographies often reflect this. Their personal life, their leisure time are footnotes to the story of their achievements. Unfortunately, I am not in this class. My life is not defined by my work, though my career had moments of great importance to me. Therefore, this autobiography will give equal weight to the personal side of my life, the private experiences which defined and shaped my values and impassioned my soul.

To avoid potential litigation I had the choice of changing the names of a few "rogues" or simply eliminating events that I considered important in my story. I chose to use fictitious names for some individuals in Chapter 6 so that the truth, as I saw it, could be told.

From Brooklyn
I Saw Mountains

Part I

Growing Up

1
Earliest Memories and Memories Handed Down

The life which is unexamined is not worth living.

—Plato

The title of my memoirs, *From Brooklyn I Saw Mountains*, combines my origins with my aspirations. Brooklyn is a flat place with no physical mountains in sight. In fact, the name "Brooklyn" is derived from the Dutch word for broken land, broken and flat along its coast and lowland plains. Near my part of Brooklyn was an area called Flatlands and well-named it was, with its marshes, tall grass and junk yards. And in all directions Brooklyn was bordered by either the ocean, the East River or land just an extension of itself, devoid of undulations or texture.

No, there are no mountains near Brooklyn. But 250 miles from Brooklyn and to the north are the majestic Adirondacks, wild with old forest growth leading up to lichen-covered rocks and commanding granite summits. As a child of nine my father led me up one such peak, Whiteface Mountain and later, as a youth, I climbed others such as Algonquin, Marcy, Gothics and Upper Wolfjaw. What a challenge it was, to stand at the base and look up to the far-off peak. What a thrill to the spirit it was, to stand upon a summit after the struggle. For the mountain was a symbol of hope, challenge and conquest. There are many kinds of mountains, physical ones and those that only the mind's eye observes. From Brooklyn I saw all those mountains and, with the optimism of youth, aspired to conquer them.

My Roots

People will not look forward to posterity who never look backward to their ancestors.
  —Edmund Burke, *Reflections on the Revolution in France, 1790*

We enter this world with a genetic heritage and acquire a cultural heritage. What I know of my cultural heritage began around the turn of the 20th century. Both my father and mother were of Eastern European Jewish ancestry and the tale of their arrival to America is worth telling. Had two families, burdened by personal hardship, not chosen to emigrate, they and their progeny would probably have all ended up victims of World War II. My very existence and good fortune are owed to the saga of these two Jewish families.

First I will tell my mother's story.

Maternal Grandfather Elias Oxenhorn (aka Oxengorn)

My mother's maiden name was Oxengorn. The Oxengorns came from Bessarabia (now in Moldova). My great grandmother, whose maiden name was Raisa Goldenberg, was born in Rashkov, Podolski State, about 1844. Today, Rashkov is situated on the eastern edge of Moldova, less than one mile from the Ukraine. Raisa met and married my great grandfather, Sindel Oxengorn, about 1863 in the village of Kamenka about twenty miles to the northwest. Not much is known about my great grandfather but Raisa was considered a wise and educated woman. Her neighbors, both Jewish and non-Jewish, would seek out her advice. Kamenka was situated on a tributary of the Dnister River in Podolski State, about five miles from the present Moldova/Ukraine border. In the late 19th century, the authorities decreed that all Jews must leave these small villages and move to a few selected towns. These towns were called the "Pale of Settlements." Raisa and Sindel, with their five children, moved fifty miles west to the town of Beltci around 1878-79. Sindel died in 1880 before his fortieth birthday and Raisa was remarried, to Simon Millerman, whose spouse also had died. With his children and hers, my grandfather, Elias Oxengorn, grew up in a large household. Raisa died in Beltci sometime in the 1930s.

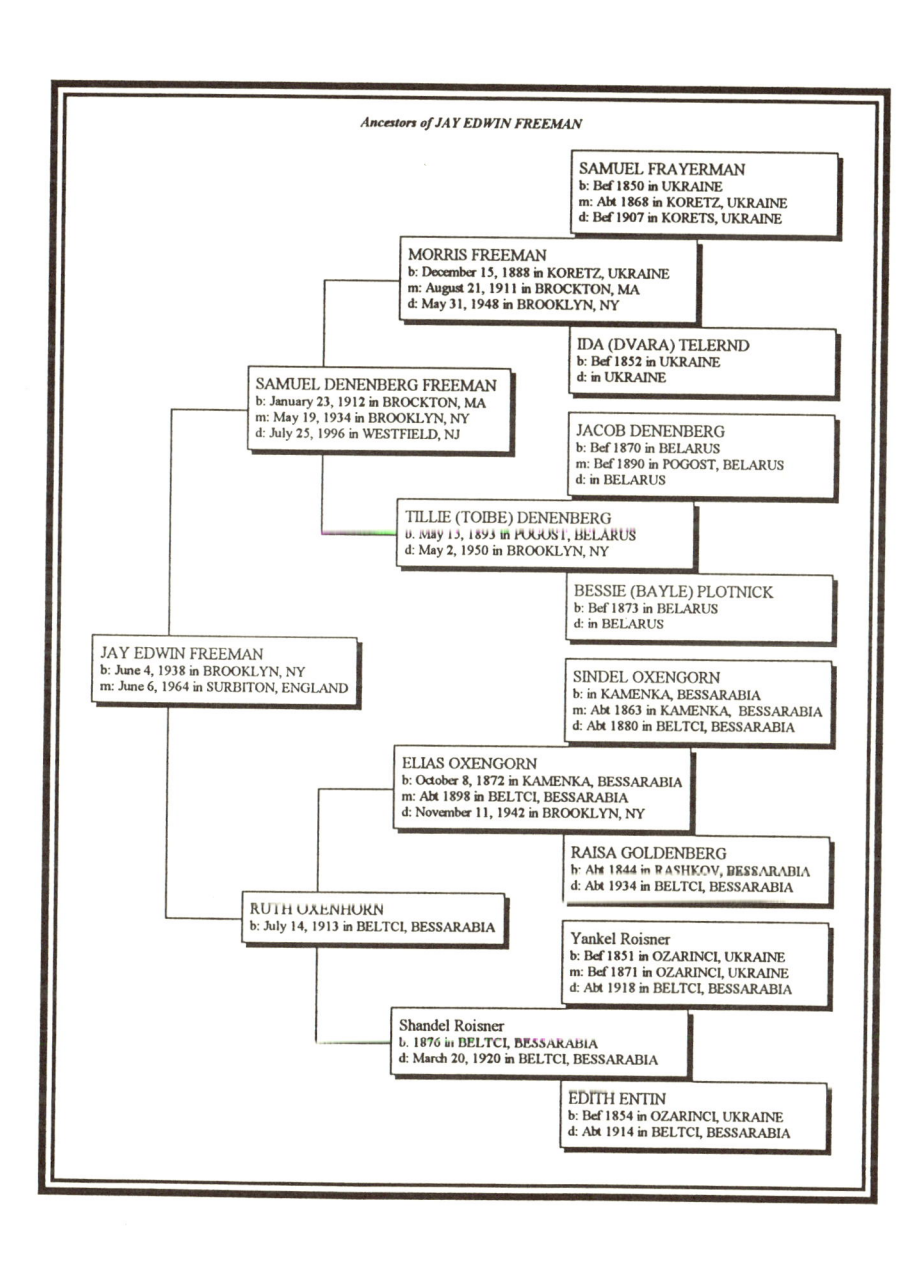

Ancestors of JAY EDWIN FREEMAN

- **SAMUEL FRAYERMAN**
  b: Bef 1850 in UKRAINE
  m: Abt 1868 in KORETZ, UKRAINE
  d: Bef 1907 in KORETS, UKRAINE

- **MORRIS FREEMAN**
  b: December 15, 1888 in KORETZ, UKRAINE
  m: August 21, 1911 in BROCKTON, MA
  d: May 31, 1948 in BROOKLYN, NY

- **IDA (DVARA) TELERND**
  b: Bef 1852 in UKRAINE
  d: in UKRAINE

- **SAMUEL DENENBERG FREEMAN**
  b: January 23, 1912 in BROCKTON, MA
  m: May 19, 1934 in BROOKLYN, NY
  d: July 25, 1996 in WESTFIELD, NJ

- **JACOB DENENBERG**
  b: Bef 1870 in BELARUS
  m: Bef 1890 in POGOST, BELARUS
  d: in BELARUS

- **TILLIE (TOIBE) DENENBERG**
  b: May 13, 1893 in POGOST, BELARUS
  d: May 2, 1950 in BROOKLYN, NY

- **BESSIE (BAYLE) PLOTNICK**
  b: Bef 1873 in BELARUS
  d: in BELARUS

- **JAY EDWIN FREEMAN**
  b: June 4, 1938 in BROOKLYN, NY
  m: June 6, 1964 in SURBITON, ENGLAND

- **SINDEL OXENGORN**
  b: in KAMENKA, BESSARABIA
  m: Abt 1863 in KAMENKA, BESSARABIA
  d: Abt 1880 in BELTCI, BESSARABIA

- **ELIAS OXENGORN**
  b: October 8, 1872 in KAMENKA, BESSARABIA
  m: Abt 1898 in BELTCI, BESSARABIA
  d: November 11, 1942 in BROOKLYN, NY

- **RAISA GOLDENBERG**
  b: Abt 1844 in RASHKOV, BESSARABIA
  d: Abt 1934 in BELTCI, BESSARABIA

- **RUTH OXENHORN**
  b: July 14, 1913 in BELTCI, BESSARABIA

- **Yankel Roisner**
  b: Bef 1851 in OZARINCI, UKRAINE
  m: Bef 1871 in OZARINCI, UKRAINE
  d: Abt 1918 in BELTCI, BESSARABIA

- **Shandel Roisner**
  b: 1876 in BELTCI, BESSARABIA
  d: March 20, 1920 in BELTCI, BESSARABIA

- **EDITH ENTIN**
  b: Bef 1854 in OZARINCI, UKRAINE
  d: Abt 1914 in BELTCI, BESSARABIA

My father's ancestors came from Belarus and northern Ukraine. My mother's side came from Moldova, that small region between Romania and Ukraine. The next two maps show these regions in much greater detail so that the exact villages and towns can be located.

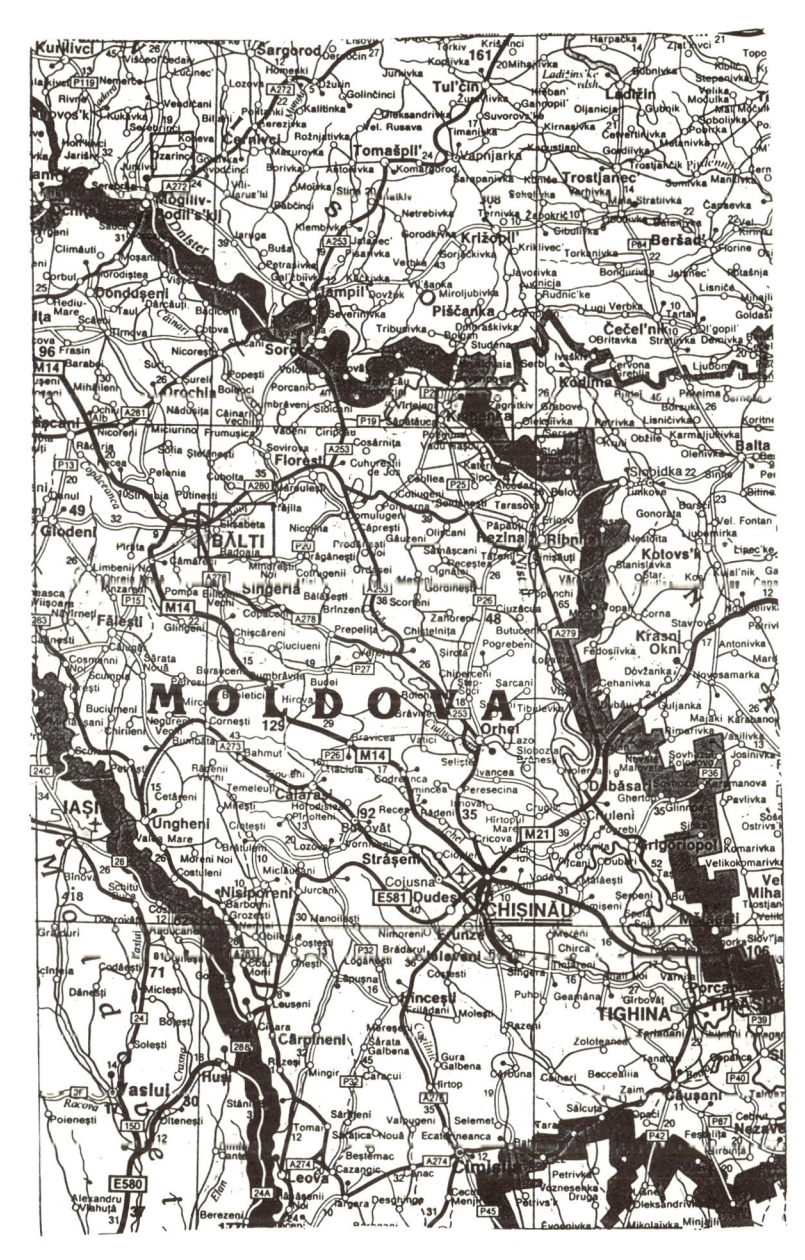

Moldova (Bessarabia)—My maternal great-grandmother, Raisa Goldenberg from Rashkov, married my great-grandfather, Sindel Oxenhorn from Kamenka. Around 1878 they moved with their children to Beltci (Balti). In Beltci my grandfather Elias married Shandel Roisner whose parents emigrated from Ozarinci. My mother Ruth was born in Beltci. Scale: 17 miles/inch or 12 km/cm.

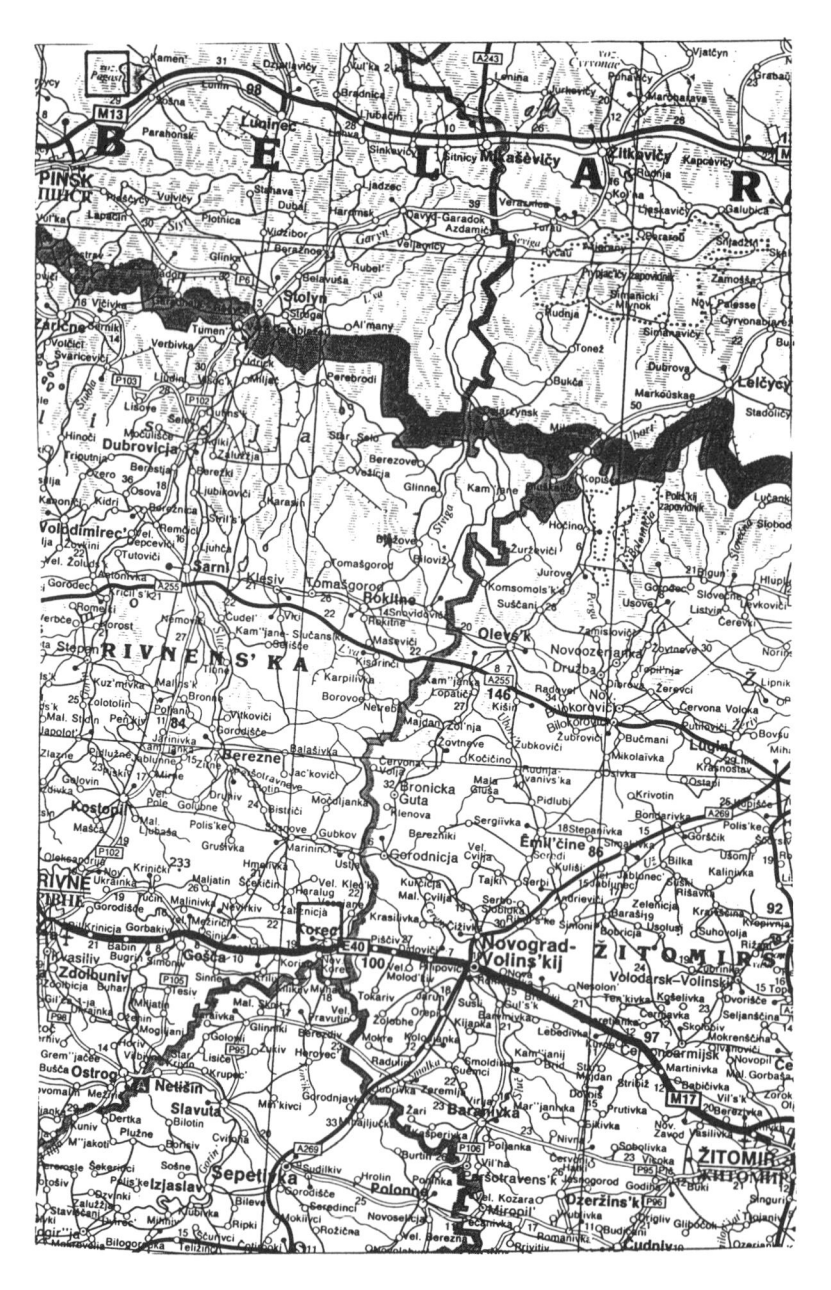

Belarus/Ukraine—My paternal grandfather, Morris Frayerman, was born in Korets (Korec) in Belarus. My paternal grandmother Tillie Denenberg was born in Pogost-Zagorotsky near Pinsk, Belarus. Scale: 17 miles/inch or 12 km/cm.

Maternal Grandmother Shandel Roisner

The Roisner family similarly had emigrated to Beltci from the small Ukrainian village of Ozarinci, approximately ten miles from the northern Moldova border. Eventually one of the Oxengorn sons, Elias, met one of the Roisner daughters, Shandel, and became engaged prior to his entering the army in 1894. Elias served four years in the cavalry and was stationed in Kiev. He fell off his horse, broke his leg and, after hospitalization, was sent home to Beltci. After his release from the army, Elias and Shandel were married about 1898.

Shandel gave birth to three sons and two daughters, all born in Beltci. One of the daughters, Ruchel Menea (Ruth), became my mother. To house their growing family the Oxengorns purchased a private home with a garden on Musikanskaya Ulitsa, where they lived from 1905 to 1910. The street was well-named since musicians would practice outside their house. The Oxenhorns moved again, this time to 8 Cuoa Voda, where they lived from 1910 to 1913. 8 Cuoa Voda was a small apartment house located between two churches. The larger church was on the main street. The smaller church was called "The Church of the Old Believers" or, in Russian, "Stare Obriatse."

By 1897 the Jewish population of Beltci had grown to 10,348 or 56 percent of the total population, largely as a result of the forced migration. In the early twentieth century the town had a total population of about 30,000, of whom almost half were Jewish. The Jews of Beltci engaged in commerce and crafts.

The Emigration to America

My great uncle Isaac, brother to my grandfather Elias, was the first in the family to leave Beltci for America. Our family folklore says that Isaac was in hiding from the local police. It should be noted here that in nineteenth century Moldova a Jew could be sought by the police simply for exercising what we today, in this country, consider legal personal rights.

Isaac changed his name from Oxengorn to Goldenberg, his mother's maiden name, and emigrated to New York in 1891. My great uncle became a citizen in 1893 and worked as a linotype operator for the newspaper *Der Taug*, and later as a furrier. He was also the first president of the First Belzer Sick and Benevolent Association ("Belzer") which was a support group for new immigrants arriving regularly from Bessarabia. The Belzer was established October 20, 1900.

9

My grandparents, Elias and Shandel Oxenhorn. Photo taken around 1900 in Bessarabia.

Grandfather Elias Oxenhorn. Photo taken in 1942, shortly before he died.

Uncle Isaac Goldenberg, the first of my mother's family to come to America in 1893.

Descendants of ELIAS OXENGORN

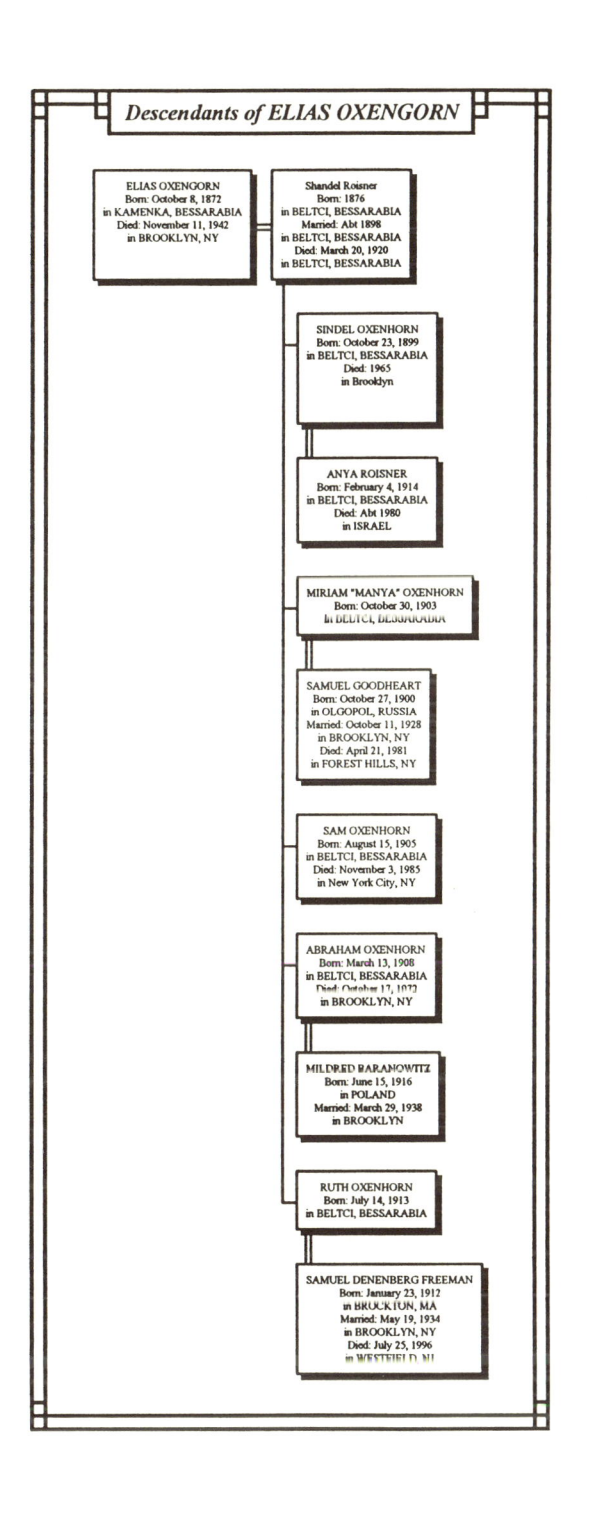

ELIAS OXENGORN
Born: October 8, 1872
in KAMENKA, BESSARABIA
Died: November 11, 1942
in BROOKLYN, NY

Shandel Roisner
Born: 1876
in BELTCI, BESSARABIA
Married: Abt 1898
in BELTCI, BESSARABIA
Died: March 20, 1920
in BELTCI, BESSARABIA

SINDEL OXENHORN
Born: October 23, 1899
in BELTCI, BESSARABIA
Died: 1965
in Brooklyn

ANYA ROISNER
Born: February 4, 1914
in BELTCI, BESSARABIA
Died: Abt 1980
in ISRAEL

MIRIAM "MANYA" OXENHORN
Born: October 30, 1903
in BELTCI, BESSARABIA

SAMUEL GOODHEART
Born: October 27, 1900
in OLGOPOL, RUSSIA
Married: October 11, 1928
in BROOKLYN, NY
Died: April 21, 1981
in FOREST HILLS, NY

SAM OXENHORN
Born: August 15, 1905
in BELTCI, BESSARABIA
Died: November 3, 1985
in New York City, NY

ABRAHAM OXENHORN
Born: March 13, 1908
in BELTCI, BESSARABIA
Died: October 17, 1977
in BROOKLYN, NY

MILDRED BARANOWITZ
Born: June 15, 1916
in POLAND
Married: March 29, 1938
in BROOKLYN

RUTH OXENHORN
Born: July 14, 1913
in BELTCI, BESSARABIA

SAMUEL DENENBERG FREEMAN
Born: January 23, 1912
in BROCKTON, MA
Married: May 19, 1934
in BROOKLYN, NY
Died: July 25, 1996
in WESTFIELD, NJ

Twenty-eight founding members contributed fifty cents each, thus raising a total of $14. Isaac Goldenberg wrote of that first meeting as follows: "Not with ink and pen and not with words can we express the joy and delight and the heartfelt pleasure that every founder experienced that evening." Their initial purpose was to buy land for burial plots but they soon provided financial and medical help as well. For at least fifty years, the organization served its immigrant members well but, in 1974, with most either dead or assimilated, the original purpose no longer existed and it was disbanded.

While Isaac was assimilating into American life, his brother Elias remained in Beltci. My grandfather Elias owned a gourmet food store. The store had tables outside where town folk would gather to eat and chat. One day Elias decided to sell the house where they were living and move to another location near his uncle, Nathan Roisner. A foundation for the new building was started but economic conditions were so bad that Elias decided to go to America in the hope of earning some money to improve his family's life in Beltci. However, Shandel did not want to leave her homeland. The year was 1912.

Elias sold the building foundation, paid off his debts and moved his family to Kishinevskaya Ulitsa. He then traveled to the German port of Hamburg. On February 7, 1913 Elias left Hamburg on the SS *President Grant* and arrived in New York harbor on February 22, passing through Ellis Island along with countless other Jewish, Irish and Italian immigrants. On the manifest Elias listed his occupation as "garment worker in shirt production."

For the next seven years, my grandmother Shandel struggled to raise her three sons and two daughters on her own.

Meanwhile, in Brooklyn, Elias worked to save money so that he could return to Beltci. He also sent money to his family. But in 1914 Europe was suddenly enveloped in war. This prevented any thoughts of return until after the Armistice in 1918. Furthermore, it was impossible to send money over during the war years. And Shandel was not well. She suffered from sciatica and rheumatism and took periodic trips to Odessa for treatment. Her health deteriorated and on March 20, 1920 she died of a kidney disease. Shandel lies buried in the Jewish Cemetery in Beltci. Elias made plans to return to Beltci to either stay or transport his children to America. Before leaving, he declared his intention to become a citizen at Brooklyn Supreme Court on July 10, 1920. At the Romanian border, customs searched him and found the money he had saved; it was confiscated. He arrived back in Beltci penniless.

When he saw the poverty his children were experiencing he decided to bring them to America with the help of his brother Isaac. First he moved his family back to 8 Cusa Voda, but into a smaller apartment. Since Elias did not want his son Sindel (named after his grandfather), to serve in the Romanian army, he decided they should return to America together. On January 8, 1921, Elias and Sindel sailed to New York on the SS *France* from Le Havre, France. And two years later, on March 24, 1923, his middle son Sam came over on the SS *La Savoie* from Le Havre, France. In August, he applied for naturalization, listing his occupation as "store keeper," and, in November, 1923, Elias became a United States citizen.

Finally, the remaining children, including my mother, Ruth, could come to America. However, although a quota applied to those over twenty-one, children under twenty-one could enter the United States to rejoin parents without quota restrictions. Since my mother's sister, Manya, would be twenty-one on October 30, 1924, it was a race against time. By traveling second class she could save eight days and board the ship for America before her twenty first birthday. In a last minute arrangement, my uncle Abie and my mother traveled 3rd class on the same ship, the *Mauritania*. The ship departed from Cherbourg, France on November 1, 1924 and arrived in New York harbor on November 6.

Elias, as mentioned earlier, owned a gourmet grocery store in Beltci. When he came to Brooklyn he opened a small candy store at 449 Stone Avenue. He and his five children moved into a five-room apartment on Powell Street but after a year they moved to a nicer apartment on Williams Avenue.

When my mother's family came to New York from Beltci the spelling of their last name was changed from Oxengorn to Oxenhorn. In Russian there is no letter "h," so a "g" was used in the Old Country. With the English alphabet this Russian phonetic simulation of the last name was no longer necessary.

Although the Oxenhorn children had little income after Shandel died, they owned beautiful possessions, including hand-made Romanian rugs, small hand-carved wooden furnishings, vases and frames purchased by Elias on his second visit in 1923. These possessions were brought to America and adorned their homes on Powell Street and Williams Avenue.

The story of the Oxenhorn emigration to America raises a question. How could Elias have left his family destitute and travelled alone to the United States? My Aunt Manya told me it was common in those times for families to be separated this way in order to make a living. Life was far harsher then. It was as if the family on a sinking ship had one strong one to swim ashore and throw a lifeline to the others still on the boat.

Seventeen years after my mother left Beltci, between July and August, 1941, the invading German army captured the town. With the collaboration of Romanians, Jews were murdered in the streets or transferred to concentration camps to die later. By September, 1941, the Jewish population of Beltci had been reduced to 28 percent of the 1930 census. This group was then deported to Transnistria, effectively destroying the entire Jewish community of Beltci.

The Freemans (aka Frayerman)

My father's family arrived in the 1890 to 1910 period, completing their emigration before my mother's side began theirs (1913–24). My paternal grandparents left what was then Poland as part of a massive migration to America to escape the brutal treatment they were receiving from the local population. As Jews, they were periodically subjected to pogroms which included murder, rape and property destruction. Jews were not permitted to engage in many occupations. They were forced to live in specified parts of selected villages. These came to be known as *shtetls*. Life was poor and the future uncertain. My grandfather's family came from one such village called Korets. My father's mother, Tillie Denenberg, arrived at about the same time from the small village of Pogost-Zagorodski, then part of Poland.

The *Encyclopedia Judaica* notes that Korets was part of the Rovno province and had a population of 4,600, of whom 76 percent were Jewish. The town was a center of Hasidic scholarship and claimed to be one of the oldest Polish Jewish communities, dating back to the 13th century. Today the village is in the Pinsk region, Brestskaya province of Belarus.

My great grandfather, Samuel Frayerman, worked for a Polish nobleman as a forest manager. He lived his entire life in what was then Poland. It was his children who made the decision to give up their homeland and culture for the long and risky journey to America. The first of Samuel Frayerman's children to arrive in New York was Aaron Frayerman, sometime in the 1890s. He worked in the garment business, cutting fur caps. His brother (my grandfather), Morris Frayerman, came to New York near the turn of the century. When my father's parents came to New York they brought virtually nothing of a tangible nature; they were lonely and isolated, but like so many immigrants before them, they believed they would return to their homes in the "Old

Descendants of MORRIS FREEMAN

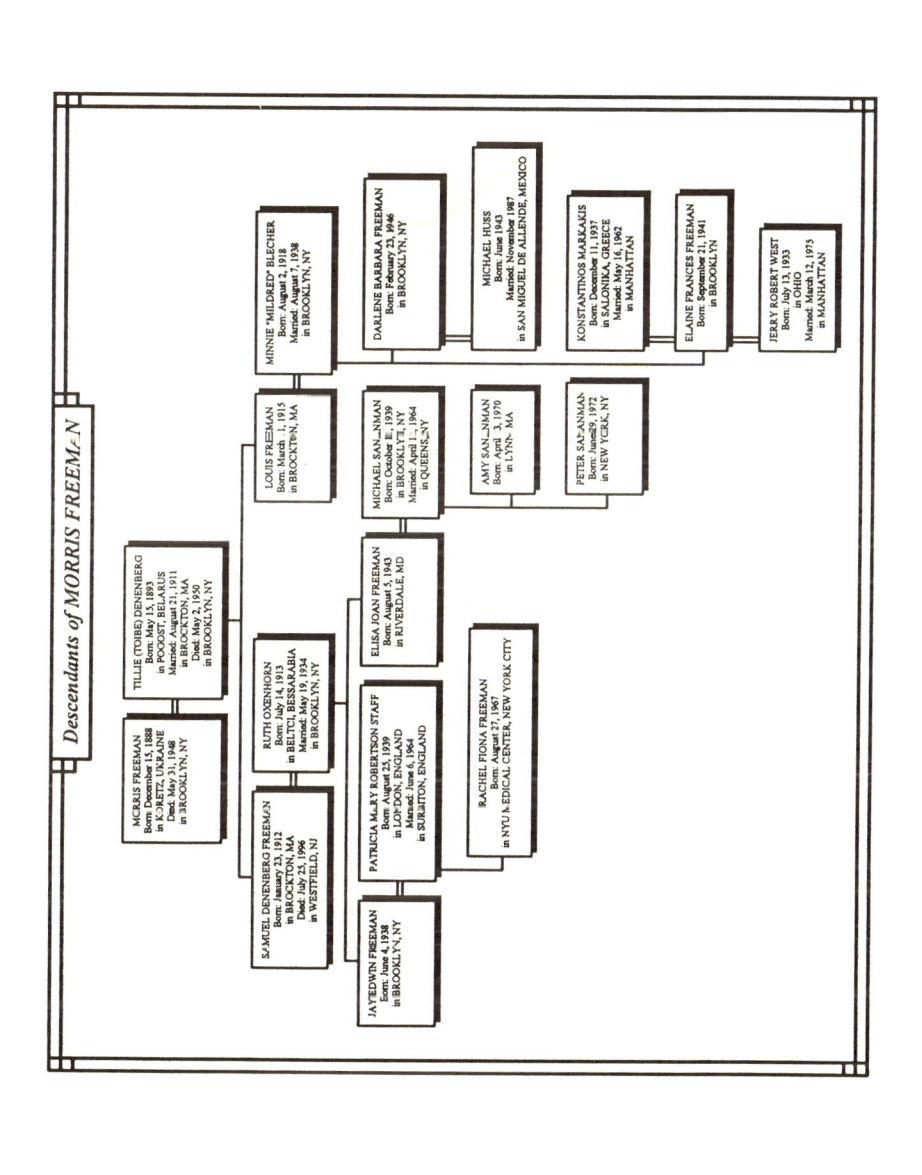

MORRIS FREEMAN
Born: December 15, 1888
in KORETZ, UKRAINE
Died: May 31, 1948
in BROOKLYN, NY

TILLIE (TOBE) DENENBERG
Born: May 15, 1893
in POGOST, BELARUS
Married: August 21, 1911
in BROCKTON, MA
Died: May 2, 1950
in BROOKLYN, NY

SAMUEL DENENBERG FREEMAN
Born: January 23, 1912
in BROCKTON, MA
Died: July 25, 1996
in WESTFIELD, NJ

RUTH OXENHORN
Born: July 14, 1913
in BELTO, BESSARABIA
Married: May 19, 1934
in BROOKLYN, NY

JAY EDWIN FREEMAN
Born: June 4, 1938
in BROOKLYN, NY

PATRICIA McKAY ROBERTSON STAFF
Born: August 25, 1939
in LONDON, ENGLAND
Married: June 6, 1964
in SURBITON, ENGLAND

RACHEL FIONA FREEMAN
Born: August 27, 1967
in NYU MEDICAL CENTER, NEW YORK CITY

ELISA JOAN FREEMAN
Born: August 5, 1943
in RIVERDALE, MD

LOUIS FREEMAN
Born: March 1, 1915
in BROCKTON, MA

MICHAEL SAN_NMAN
Born: October 8, 1939
in BROOKLYN, NY
Married: April 1, 1964
in QUEENS, NY

AMY SAN_NMAN
Born: April 3, 1970
in LYNN, MA

PETER SAN-NMAN
Born: June 29, 1972
in NEW YORK, NY

MINNIE "MILDRED" BLECHER
Born: August 2, 1918
Married: August 7, 1938
in BROOKLYN, NY

DARLENE BARBARA FREEMAN
Born: February 23, 1946
in BROOKLYN, NY

MICHAEL HUSS
Born: June 1943
Married: November 1987
in SAN MIGUEL DE ALLENDE, MEXICO

KONSTANTINOS MARKAKIS
Born: December 11, 1937
in SALONIKA, GREECE
Married: May 16, 1962
in MANHATTAN

ELAINE FRANCES FREEMAN
Born: September 21, 1941
in BROOKLYN

JERRY ROBERT WEST
Born: July 13, 1933
in OHIO
Married: March 12, 1975
in MANHATTAN

My paternal grandfather, Morris Freeman, shortly after arriving in America.

Descendants of MORRIS FREEMAN

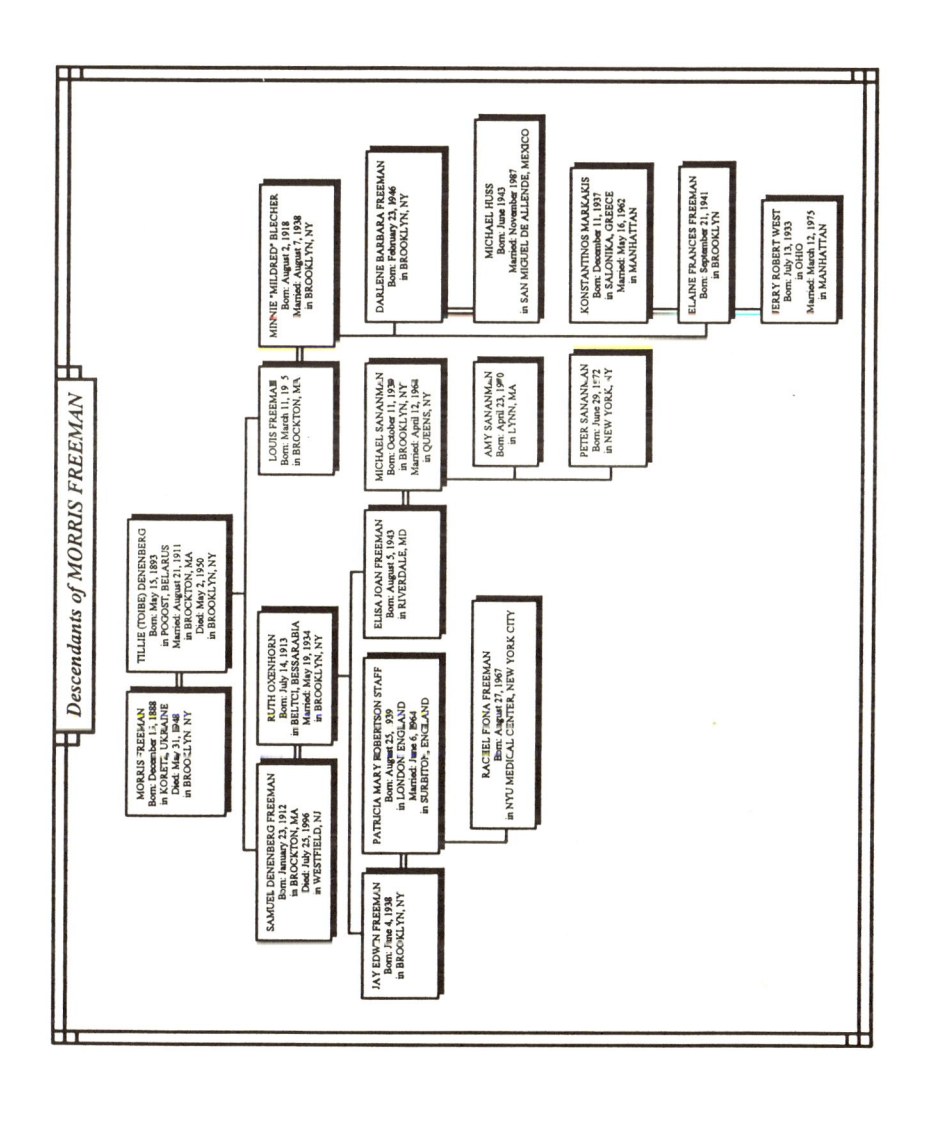

MORRIS FREEMAN
Born: December 15, 1888
in KORETS, UKRAINE
Died: May 31, 1948
in BROOKLYN, NY

TILLIE (TOBE) DENENBERG
Born: May 15, 1893
in POGOST, BELARUS
Married: August 21, 1911
in BROCKTON, MA
Died: May 2, 1950
in BROOKLYN, NY

SAMUEL DENENBERG FREEMAN
Born: January 23, 1912
in BROCKTON, MA
Died: July 25, 1996
in WESTFIELD, NJ

RUTH OXENHORN
Born: July 14, 1913
in BELTCI, BESSARABIA
Married: May 19, 1934
in BROOKLYN, NY

JAY EDWIN FREEMAN
Born: June 4, 1938
in BROOKLYN, NY

PATRICIA MARY ROBERTSON STAFF
Born: August 25, 1939
in LONDON, ENGLAND
Married: June 6, 1964
in SURBITON, ENGLAND

ELISA JOAN FREEMAN
Born: August 5, 1943
in RIVERDALE, MD

RACHEL FIONA FREEMAN
Born: August 27, 1967
in NYU MEDICAL CENTER, NEW YORK CITY

LOUIS FREEMAN
Born: March 11, 1915
in BROCKTON, MA

MINNIE "MILDRED" BLECHER
Born: August 2, 1918
Married: August 7, 1938
in BROOKLYN, NY

MICHAEL SANANMAN
Born: October 11, 1939
in BROOKLYN, NY
Married: April 12, 1964
in QUEENS, NY

DARLENE BARBARA FREEMAN
Born: February 23, 1946
in BROOKLYN, NY

MICHAEL HUSS
Born: June 1943
Married: November 1987
in SAN MIGUEL DE ALLENDE, MEXICO

AMY SANANMAN
Born: April 23, 1970
in LYNN, MA

PETER SANANMAN
Born: June 29, 1972
in NEW YORK, NY

KONSTANTINOS MARKAKIS
Born: December 11, 1937
in SALONIKA, GREECE
Married: May 16, 1962
in MANHATTAN

ELAINE FRANCES FREEMAN
Born: September 21, 1941
in BROOKLYN

JERRY ROBERT WEST
Born: July 13, 1933
in OHIO
Married: March 12, 1975
in MANHATTAN

My paternal grandfather, Morris Freeman, shortly after arriving in America.

My paternal grandmother, Tillie Freeman, at seventeen (right) with her older sister, Ida, shortly after arriving in America.

Country" when conditions improved. However, in deference to life in America, the family name was changed from Frayerman to Freeman. (The French branch of our family became Frajerman.)

My grandparents courted in Brooklyn. In 1911, Morris got a job offer from a shoe factory in Brockton, Massachusetts, and told Tillie she must come there or he would not marry her. She agreed and they were married on August 21, 1911, in Brockton. My father was born in Brockton on January 23, 1912. His parents named him Samuel Denenberg Freeman.

In July, 1941, German troops entered Korets. While some Jews managed to escape, most were murdered by the Nazis in the town or died later in labor camps. A monument stands in a forest near the town memorializing the event.

Personal Memories of my Grandparents

While I was very young both my paternal grandparents and my maternal grandfather were alive. They all resided within two miles of our home. I cannot remember too much about them now since they had all died by the time I reached twelve. However, I do recall, as a four-year-old, running into the arms of Elias Oxenhorn. He was a tall, slender man who died in November, 1942 at the age of seventy, from a heart attack.

I remember more of Morris and Tillie Freeman. They had one of those old Philco radios that looked like a bishop's hat made of wood. Morris had a shoe box full of leather working tools. He died on May 31, 1948, of a heart attack, and she on May 2, 1950, of cancer.

My Parents

My parents met through their activities in the Young Communist League. Many intellectual and rebellious young people joined left-wing political groups in those Depression years. My parents were married on May 19, 1934 in Brooklyn. My father had to take whatever job he could, though he had a degree in teaching. For a few months he sold shirts and dry goods on 14th Street in Manhattan. Around November, 1934, they moved to Washington, DC, and there my father applied for and accepted a two-year teaching assignment in Puerto Rico to teach English to children at schools in Naguabo and Caguas, PR. During the two years they spent there, both my parents learned Spanish. On returning from Puerto Rico, they again settled in Washington, DC where I was conceived in September, 1937. Soon after, my parents moved to 888 Montgomery Street, Brooklyn. On June 2, my mother went into labor. The family physician, Dr. Geshwin, was called and he drove her to Brooklyn Women's Hospital where I was born at 12:15 P.M. on June 4, 1938.

It was Saturday and the *New York Times* forecast clouds with temperature in the 60s. There were no big news stories that day. President Roosevelt planned to visit New York in late June to lay the cornerstone for the 1939 World's Fair. The Civilian Conservation Corps announced the closing of camps across New York State. Hitler decreed the confiscation of "degenerate art" displayed by museums. According to the edict, Hitler himself would decide what was "degenerate." And our Secretary of State, Cordell Hull, called on the nation to unite to restore, throughout the world, the principle of "order under law." The best tickets to the 1938 Pulitzer Prize-winning play, *Our Town*, cost $2.20 each. Other names in the news that day included Mayor La Guardia, Joe DiMaggio, Eleanor Roosevelt and Henry Fonda. It was just another ordinary day in America on the brink of summer, on the brink of global war. However, in June of 1938, Samuel and Ruth Freeman had more immediate preoccupations. They were now parents.

The Ashkenazi Jews of Eastern Europe name their children after deceased relatives. I was named after Jacob David Blinder, who was the husband of Rachel Oxenhorn, who was the sister of my maternal grandfather, Elias Oxenhorn. Jacob Blinder died in 1927 in Beltci. My Hebrew name is Yacov Dovid, or Jacob David in English. American Jews select the legal name based on some tenuous link to the Hebrew name. So in my case, Jacob became Jay, sharing the first two letters. My father decided early in my life to call me Jim instead of Jay. He felt it was a more masculine name than Jay. Only my father could call me Jim. It sounded wrong to my ears if anyone else did.

During World War II, my father worked for the USO, an organization that provided recreation for the troops. We moved to Laurel, MD and he worked at the military base there. My sister Elisa was born in Riverdale, MD on August 5, 1943. Soon afterward, my parents moved back to Brooklyn into an apartment at 196 Rockaway Parkway in the East Flatbush section. Then my father left for Panama to provide recreational and educational programs for servicemen stationed there to guard the Canal. Among other activities, he organized alligator hunts and bicycle trips across the isthmus. On returning to Brooklyn, my father left the USO and joined the Jewish Welfare Board (JWB). He remained with the JWB for thirty-five years, organizing educational and

My parents: photos taken December 1987.

entertainment programs for Jewish centers around the country. He was in charge of the Lecture Bureau until he retired in 1978.

My father was a dynamic optimist. For him the difficult was easy and the impossible would take a little longer. Two types of pursuits engrossed my father. The first was leading groups of people in some educational activity. He was a natural teacher and a democratic leader. As head of the Lecture Bureau of the Jewish Welfare Board he was constantly working with performers and rabbis to organize group programs for Jewish Centers across the United States. As if this were not enough, he would spend much of his vacation time leading groups around Israel. My father also enjoyed children. He would enter their world and encourage their interests. Because of this, he was much loved by my cousins, nieces and nephews.

His other love was making things, whether it involved carpentry, masonry or plumbing. This activity was solitary but he engaged in it with great vigor. It was the one-on-one meetings that were least interesting to him, and he felt most ill-at-ease in personal discussions. He would much rather talk about the impersonal than matters of the troubled soul. His kindness and love were expressed by doing, rather than speaking. Many members of my family have tables, cabinets and chairs built by my father, all physical symbols of the love he could not express with words.

When I was a child my father never hugged me, but I never had any doubt of his affection and pride in my achievements. In my adult years he began to shake my hand on departing. As the years passed, the handshake turned into a bear hug. In April, 1995, before I left for a four-month trip, as he said farewell to me, tears came to his eyes and he sobbed. A great sadness overcame me as a lifetime of unexpressed love suddenly found its voice. He was in his eighty-third year; two months later he suffered a massive stroke and our relationship was changed forever. I always wondered whether he had a premonition that a health catastrophe lay just ahead.

From my father I learned objectivity, democratic leadership, an analytical approach to problem-solving and the joyful pleasure of seeing to completion one's own handiwork.

My mother put all her energies into raising her two children. She always stood in the shadow of my father but nevertheless had a strong personality. After her children were grown, my mother returned to Brooklyn College and completed her BA degree at the age of fifty-five. That year at the ceremonies she was the oldest graduate. Although at times self-absorbed, she nevertheless showed great concern for her children's well being and could offer sound advice to friends and family

My father (on the right) with one of his lecturers, Nobel Prize winner Isaac B. Singer, 1960.

in time of need. My mother was a good storyteller and enjoyed center stage at family gatherings. Her favorite subjects were the Bible, Israel, politics and travel. My mother painted and tastefully decorated and furnished her home. Her cooking was excellent; I only came to appreciate it as an adult. My mother was much more practical than my father and would never indulge in extravagant spending or flights of fancy. From my mother I learned to boldly seize center stage in social gatherings, a sometimes useful skill. I noticed this tendency towards self-centeredness later in my own life while married to Patricia. Patricia tended to draw others out and get them to talk about themselves, just the opposite of what I would do. I began to admire that enquiring attitude, which she and so many of her British countrymen seemed to possess. On the other hand, it is unlikely I would ever have written this autobiography, the ultimate self-indulgence, without having inherited my mother's healthy ego. She also taught me, by example, to worry about the future and see the gloomy side of every uncertainty. Worry can be a powerful motivator and, later, while building my business, these characteristics kept me constantly vigilant regarding competition, new orders, cash flow and late-paying customers—all good subjects to worry about. In a perverse way it forced me to pay attention to detail which I might otherwise have overlooked.

After my father's stroke, my mother assumed the role of primary care-giver. Through inner strength, instinct and intelligence she found a way to keep my father in their apartment rather than a nursing home or hospital. My mother hired and fired a number of twenty-four-hour live-in aides before finding one from Eastern Europe who was capable of home care at the superb level she demanded.

Neither of my parents were interested in the popular culture of America. They knew nothing of baseball, football, Las Vegas gambling or rock and roll music. And these values were passed on to my sister and me, with the exception of popular music. It is impossible for teenagers to pass through life without the music of their age capturing their attention.

My Sister, Elisa

My younger sister Elisa was born when I was five. She is my only sibling. At first I was jealous of her. But as time went by we got on quite well. Elisa had red hair and developed a wonderful personality. She matured into an outgoing and warm woman. Elisa studied anthropology and later got a CPA in accounting. She and her husband, Dr. Michael Sananman, moved to Westfield, NJ and settled there, raising two children, Amy and Peter. Elisa is active in the community band and the emergency medical service. There is a lot more to say about Elisa, but that is for later.

2
Childhood

Sweet childish days, that were as long as twenty days are now.
— William Wordsworth, *To a Butterfly*, 1807

My Home

Until the age of four I lived on St. John's Place, a busy street in Brooklyn. Every so often a fire truck would race by on its way to some emergency. The sound of those clanging bells would get me very excited. I remember that once my father took me down the street to watch the firemen fight a blaze. My first aspiration was to become a fireman.

In those early years we had frequent family gatherings, mostly Oxenhorns, crowded into our small apartment, speaking animated Yiddish. Aunts would plant big wet kisses on my cheek and announce "*Kine anhora*, he's growing up!" *Kine anhora* is Yiddish and Hebrew for "no Evil Eye." The Evil Eye was a demon that just did not like good things happening to people. If something good was announced, the Evil Eye might hear the words and pounce on the prospective recipient malevolently. Therefore, it was prudent to precede any good statement with the prophylactic "God forbid the Evil Eye." You would think that such superstitious nonsense would be totally rejected by me, a logical man of the modern age! But as of this writing, whenever someone says something good about me, I am quick to respond with a self- deprecating comment.

In 1943, we moved to the small town of Laurel, MD. We lived on the main street. I would walk down a dirt lane to the nearby Patuxent River to splash in the water. I remember a fence around a church through which I caught a turtle. In my memory, the fence was six feet high. When I returned to Laurel as an adult, I located the church. To my surprise, the same fence was only three feet high.

One day a magazine salesman came around, gave me a test and

Oxenhorn family 1939.

said I was smart enough to receive a special children's magazine. In comic book fashion the magazine told of two boys, Gufus and Gallant (evil and good). When my mother wanted to scold me she just called me Gufus. It worked.

In 1944, when I was five, we moved back to Brooklyn and into 196 Rockaway Parkway, a six-story red brick apartment house. I lived there with my parents until I left home at the age of twenty-three. We first lived in a one-bedroom apartment on the fifth floor. One day, while listening to a soap opera on the radio, I heard that our President, Franklin D. Roosevelt, had just died. I ran in to tell my mother who immediately burst into tears.

After a few years we moved to a three-bedroom apartment on the fourth floor. Both apartments faced onto Rockaway Parkway, which was a wide street in a residential neighborhood. Across the street was a sandlot and on the other side was an elevated subway train, which made a loud screeching sound as it rounded a 90-degree bend in the tracks between Sutter Avenue station and the Livonia Avenue station.

In the period from 1944 until I left home in 1962, this building was my home. In our five-room apartment I had a bedroom facing Rockaway Parkway. Elisa's bedroom faced a center courtyard. My parents' bedroom was next to mine and also faced Rockaway Parkway. We had a living room and eat-in kitchen. All the rooms were off a foyer.

When we were children, Elisa and I would build tunnels and hide-a-ways in the apartment using sheets and blankets which we would stretch out over couches, chairs and tables. We would build these tunnels on Saturday or Sunday mornings and spend a few hours crawling about inside them.

My room was a center for my various hobbies. My father built a large workbench which faced my bed on the opposite wall. There I conducted my chemistry experiments, constructed model airplanes and operated my ham radio equipment.

Years later, 196 became a deserted structure. It was abandoned by the owner, taken over by New York City for unpaid taxes and eventually was renovated by developers as a low income project in 1988. I visited the building during this renovation with my niece, Patricia Ann Russell. The watchmen took us up to the apartment where I once lived. Then it had one bathroom; after renovation it would have two. The walls were stripped to the concrete and vertical steel studs were in place for a new plaster surface; a new look for a new generation of upwardly mobile tenants.

The author (age six), Elisa, and their mother, 1944.

Radio Soap Operas

In those years, 1944–48, there were many weekly soap operas and serial programs. I can recall the *Lone Ranger, Stella Dallas, The Inner Sanctum, The Shadow, Lorenzo Jones* (and his wife Belle). The *William Tell Overture* announced the start of the *Lone Ranger* who came "galloping out of the past from yesteryear with the pounding hoofs and the hearty yell, 'Hiyo, Silver!' " "Finiculi, Finicula" was the merry ditty that preceded *Lorenzo Jones*. And who could forget the creaking doors of the Inner Sanctum? Anyone who ever heard *The Shadow* will be able to answer the question "who knows what evil lurks in the hearts of men?" This mysterious prelude to the adventure program was followed by a sinister cackle. This wonderful age of radio storytelling ended quite abruptly with the coming of television.

Street Games of my Childhood

Rockaway Parkway was in the middle of a busy New York borough. However, in the 1940s and 50s there were many sandlots and even a small farm a few blocks away on Kings Highway. These areas have since been built up. But in those days the sandlots and sidewalks were wonderful places to play street games. Summers were spent refining our skills at baseball, stickball, Johnny on the Pony, Hide and Seek, Iron Man and Ring-a-Levio. We also flipped baseball cards, rolled marbles or nuts and shot "packs" to the nearest third line on the sidewalk.

Throwing packs was fun. Packs were objects such as a leather shoe heel or a stack of 50 baseball cards held together by rubber bands. Concrete sidewalks have square lines scored into them before they dry. The idea was to hurl these packs three lines away and get as close to the third line as possible. The closest after each round would win the prize, usually more baseball playing cards. These cards were much prized and came out of packages of Fleers bubble gum. Some cards were rare. Trading and bartering was fierce. You could also win cards by competitively flipping them onto the sidewalk and guessing correctly which side would face up.

In marble rolling the objective was to have your marble come to rest as close to an opposing wall as possible. You could knock away your opponents' marbles if they were already very close to the wall. During the Jewish holiday of Purim, we substituted round nuts for marbles. We really got involved in these games. The pleasure of winning was extreme, far beyond the value of the prizes.

In Johnny on the Pony, the first boy (girls didn't play these games) grabbed a lamp post low, so that he was bent 90 degrees at the waist. The next boy would put his head between the legs of the first boy. In effect a train of three or four boys lined up in this way. Then the rest of boys, one at time would run and leap onto the train. They would keep leaping and piling onto the train and when the whole squad was perched on the fellows below they would all shout "Johnny on the pony, 1,2,3." This was repeated three times and then the train would collapse into an hysterical jumble of legs and arms.

In Iron Man, one person would be chosen as "It." Everyone else would hold on to some iron. It could be a lamp post, a car, a metal gate. Boys would take turns running from metal to metal and "It" would have to try to tag them in transit. If he succeeded, the tagged person would become the new "It."

Street Talk

The friends of my childhood needed each other. Life was so much more fun when you had a friend to share it with. How will I ever forget that oft repeated expression of this need for companionship? "I'll be your best friend"—spoken in a plaintive and pleading voice, this offer was used to pry loose a secret or favor from another boy. "Walk me" was a request for company if you had some lonely errand to take care of. In context it might be employed as follows: "My mother asked me to buy some milk at the grocery store. Can you walk me?"

Our Summer Home in Carmel, NY

In the early 1950s my father purchased a summer home in Carmel, NY about 70 miles north of New York City. This modest one-bedroom wood-frame house sat on half an acre near the Croton Reservoir overlooking Shaft No. 9, the outlet of the 100-mile tunnel that carried New York City drinking water from the Catskill system. The house cost only $1500 and had no plumbing. We had an outhouse and a well for our water needs. There were three other homes nearby, so my father found three other families to jointly buy all the properties. The other families were Kagan, Oxenhorn (my uncle Sindel) and Fieffer.

We named our community the acronym KOFF for the first letter of the last name of each owner.

My father quickly set out to improve our summer home. He built a bathroom and a kitchen and we screened in the porch. We had to run a water pipe down from the well on the hill about 300 feet away. Each summer, from the age of twelve to seventeen, I would go with my parents to our Carmel home. I spent a lot of time helping my dad with his endless building projects. When we completed the major improvements on the home he decided to build a log cabin. This involved going each morning to the forest, about 1,000 feet up the hill, and cutting down trees. We trimmed away the branches and then turned the logs into rails which we used to roll other logs down the hill. Next, the twin rails of logs were rolled down to the bottom of the hill to the site of the cabin. Then we began sawing and hammering the logs into place. Finally we completed the one-room cabin which eventually served as a storage area.

I planted a vegetable garden near our summer home. By the end of the summer we harvested tomatoes, radishes, carrots and beets. I fished in the nearby reservoir and caught rock bass and sunfish. Once, while walking down to the reservoir, I stepped on a nest of yellow jackets. These are wasps that look like bees. They quickly attached themselves to my hands and legs and while I took off in a mad dash they just hung on and kept stinging me over and over again. This painful episode gave me a lasting fear of bees.

I spent many wonderful summers at KOFF but one day my parents decided that it was time to sell the place. My sister and I were getting older and my parents wanted to take us on overseas trips to expose us to foreign cultures. A very dignified couple, the Zampfs, bought our cottage in 1955. We left with many fond memories.

I revisited my old summer home a number of times after it was sold. It was nicely maintained by the Zampfs but subsequent owners allowed the house to decay. On one visit the log cabin was gone, burned down I believe. Next the cottage itself went up in flames leaving only a depression on the hillside with a few odd pipes sticking out of the ground. Weeds took over. My last visit was in 1992. By then the only cheerful sight was the original saplings we had planted around the property thirty years earlier. By 1992 they were huge graceful evergreens and maples, casting ample shadows over the empty field. Melancholy overcame nostalgia and I vowed never to return.

Hobbies and Interests of Pre-adolescence

One of my favorite toys was an Erector Set. With it I built derricks, trucks and other mechanical contraptions. The set was one of the larger versions that came with an electric motor. From this Erector Set I developed an early interest in mechanics and engineering.

My sister showed an interest in learning to play music and so my parents hired Mr. Botenberg to give her piano lessons. She also took up the guitar. My interests centered around the sciences rather than the arts. For me numbers held a greater fascination than words. From my hobbies I developed a sense of joy in the creation of order out of chaos.

A good example of this was stamp collecting, my first big hobby. At a Brownsville post office, a kindly clerk saved the corners of the stamp sheets for me. They are called plate blocks. I collected most of the commemorative plate blocks in the 1947–53 period. My father and I carefully mounted them in albums. I also had a world collection of used stamps. From this hobby I learned geography and the names of countries now long gone, such as Mozambique and Dahomey. The African colonies produced some of the most colorful stamps—completely worthless, but colorful. Once, my father gave me a partially-damaged set of early Israeli stamps. They were mint plate blocks but, unfortunately, as part of a touring exhibition, they had been mounted using rubber cement. Years later I sold this set for $1,500 to a dealer who was almost in tears looking at the damage. He told me they would have been worth ten times that amount in pristine condition.

Bikes and Skates

My father was a keen cyclist who had traveled by bike to Philadelphia and the end of Long Island, each in a single day. When I was about ten years old he bought me a bicycle, and I remember him giving me lessons until I finally succeeded in balancing myself. But I preferred my rollerskates. They had steel wheels and leather straps. A key was used to tighten clasps that gripped the front of your shoes. With these skates my radius of travel increased to over 2 miles. I could literally fly through the streets of Brooklyn, deftly avoiding cracks, potholes and other discontinuities in the pavement.

Elisa and I also ice skated, but I was no good at it. My ankles bent sideways as I tried to balance my feet over the narrow blades.

Pets

I did not grow up with a dog or cat. My mother said she once had a dog but it was run over by a car. She was so heartbroken she vowed never to own one again. Nevertheless, we did have two pet parakeets when I was a teenager. We also had hamsters for a while. I could provoke them into fighting by throwing a Ritz cracker into the cage; then I would watch with amusement as two hamsters tried to tear the thing apart. These little pets were fun, and I also enjoyed playing with other people's dogs, but I cannot say that pets were an important part of my early life.

Elementary School 1944–50

I attended public schools from kindergarten through college. I first went to PS 219, an elementary school about six blocks from Rockaway Parkway. PS 219 was a red brick building with a school yard behind the main entrance.

It took about fifteen minutes to walk to school. I was scared on my first day. My little world was being rearranged. There were new faces to deal with, a building with long corridors and many doors, rules to obey and orders to carry out. The kindergarten teachers, Mrs. McQuillan and Mrs. McKensie, asked that I bring in a notebook on the second day. Instead of the standard black and white notebook, my mother bought me a coloring book. I recall how upset I was at being the only one with this nonstandard notebook.

One of our class exercises was skipping around in a circle with each child following the one in front. I could not figure out how to skip and the class laughed at my clumsy attempts. The humiliation was profound. Then one day, while on the sidewalk in front of my house, it suddenly came to me. With a hop and slide of each foot I figured out how to skip. The next day I experienced a sweet victory by showing the class how well I could do it.

The vice-principal was, to my young eyes, an old battle-ax. Once, when I was in the second grade and misbehaving, she was called down to handle the matter. She told me I was being returned to kindergarten and would have to start all over again. Then she dragged me, panic-stricken and screaming, down to the kindergarten class and thrust me back into the room. I really believed I would have to start all over again.

Max Meyers was my most memorable teacher in those early years.

He was a gruff, charismatic extrovert who taught a sixth-grade class. Mr. Meyers was truly dedicated and held reunions at his home, years after his charges had left his classroom.

I went to PS 219 for seven years. While at the time those years moved by slowly, in retrospect it seems but a brief moment. Suddenly my elementary school years came to an end. In the spring before graduation it was the custom to buy an official autograph book. Students would run around to classmates and relatives to get them to sign a page and say something amusing or philosophical in the book. In my autograph book, I listed my closest friend as Howie Fox and the brightest student as Richard Witlin. According to this book, my favorite author in 1950 was Mark Twain, and my hero was Sherlock Holmes. I identified with Huckleberry Finn and Tom Sawyer. Both shared aimless days and youthful adventures of childhood discovery. Sherlock Holmes used clever scientific deduction and possessed a rational mind, something like my father, a quality I admired greatly and sought to emulate.

My father signed the book April 27, 1950 and wrote: "For my son Jim: May you set your goals beyond easy reach, Your daddy." On June 18, 1950, my mother wrote: "To my son Jay: Be successful in all your undertakings. Mommy." My Uncle Louie wrote: "To Jay: I wish you good fortune in greater amount than the comic books you've read (and that's a lot!), Your Uncle Louie."

Jewish Identity

My father came from a home with an observant mother and an atheist father. As my father grew older he became more observant. Working for thirty-five years with the Jewish Welfare Board immersed him in Jewish culture. My father attended an orthodox temple in Brooklyn and ate only kosher food; my mother was less observant. I do not remember her going to synagogue and late in life she admitted to me her atheistic beliefs. But she prepared kosher food and concerned herself with all the details on Passover and Hanukkah. Therefore, it was not surprising that my parents enrolled me in a Jewish school. Classes were held after the public school day ended. Students were given permission to leave an hour early for the purpose of religious education. I first went to a Socialist Jewish school on Clarkson Avenue, where the first thing I learned to say in Yiddish was "Hail to the soldiers of the Russian Army." My parents then enrolled me in another school on Winthrop Street where I studied Hebrew in preparation for my Bar Mitzvah. Most of the students, including me, found Hebrew school boring and could not wait for the classes to end. After my Bar Mitzvah, I pretty much left formal Jewish religious life behind me. However, this did not diminish my cultural identification with the Jewish people and, I can say with deepest sincerity, that I am proud to be a member of such an accomplished group.

3
Adolescence

Through our great fortune, in our youth our hearts were touched with fire.
—Oliver Wendell Holmes, Memorial Day Address, 1884

My teenage years encompassed the period 1951–57. These seven years of transformation seem in retrospect to be longer than any other period in my life. I suppose it was the kaleidoscopic pace of change, of awakening sexuality, of hobbies and schooling and friendships that made the years so eventful and important in my memory. But for all its stress and distress it was a wonderful time, a time when the future was bigger than the past, when the gates of hope opened wide.

Somer's Junior High School

I attended PS 252, Somer's Junior High School, for three years from 1951 to 1953. Somer's was located on Kings Highway, about 7 blocks from my home. In my first year at Somer's my homeroom teacher was Mrs. Sperling. My grades were average. Mr. Haskell was my second-year homeroom teacher for a while. I did not like him. Once he chased me around the room with the rest of the class in hysterics. I forget why he was so angry at me. Mrs. Tell was a math teacher I liked. She felt I could do a lot better. Once she announced in class the results of an aptitude test and said that I was the most underperforming student with the greatest potential. I had a woodworking teacher, Sam Weber. He was a philosophical gentleman. I recall him advising me to remove wood in small amounts because it is much easier to take more off than to add it back. It seemed like a lesson in life as well.

The class president in my final year, 1953, was my good friend Howie. He was still listed as best friend in this graduation autograph book but he shared that important place in my life with a second best friend, Sherman Zell. Some things, though, had changed in those three years: I listed my favorite authors as Jack London and Ernest Hemingway. I was fascinated by the vivid imagery created with simple language and the rugged adventures these authors portrayed. There was a place in the book for one's future profession; I put down "Science."

My father signed my book on May 23, 1953, writing: "To Jim: It's the little extra beyond the ordinary which makes the difference. Daddy." I think he knew, then, what a lazy son he had and was already dropping me hints!

My parents admired intellect, though their interests excluded many cultured pursuits such as ballet, opera and fiction. My father had an extensive book collection at home, mostly dedicated to education and Jewish life. I developed an appreciation for intellectual achievement though I did not have the discipline to devote long hours to study. Television was a major temptation and I rushed through my homework so I could maximize my TV time. And, in the summer, study was virtually impossible when I heard the voices of my friends in the street. However, reading books on astronomy, chemistry and electronics was fascinating and this I did on my own initiative.

My classical education was facilitated by reading every issue of Classic Comics joke books. I did not have to imagine what the Three Musketeers looked like. I actually saw pictures of them. One day my mother, angry at me for some transgression, tossed my entire collection down the incinerator. The greatest literary works of mankind, including carefully drawn illustrations, went up in flames. It was a sad day for the classics and for me. I have long since forgiven my mother in spite of the fact that these joke books are now valuable collectors' items.

Stuyvesant High School 1953–56

After Junior High School I attended Stuyvesant High School in Manhattan, from 1953 to 1956. Stuyvesant was a specialized science school and to be admitted one had to pass an examination. As a result of this screening process, this all-male school assembled the largest group of nerds in New York City with the possible exception of its major rival, the Bronx High School of Science. To get to Stuyvesant, I had to take the subway from Sutter Avenue to 14th Street in Manhattan and then walk east, passing under the 3rd Avenue elevated train line, to finally reach the school which was located on 1st Avenue and 15th Street.

The students were bright and competitive. At home, my father and I would work on the supplementary mathematics problems in trigonometry and geometry. I can still remember the great pleasure we had in solving these extra assignments.

During this period I read books on science, electronics and chemistry. History, foreign languages and literature did not interest me. This extreme focus brought me high grades in the sciences and lower grades in the arts.

Stuyvesant High School was built in 1904 and it seemed the equipment and some of the teachers were installed with the original structure. Our metal-working shop had lathes that were driven by long leather belts which ran up to the ceiling. By a series of wheels and belts on the ceiling, the power from a single electric motor was distributed to the many lathes in the shop. The place looked like a nineteenth-century sweatshop.

After School Activities

During this period I joined the amateur radio club and was elected to Arista, which was an honorary society for only those with high grades. The president of Arista, who interviewed me for admission, was the same Michael Sananman who years later would meet my sister Elisa and marry her. (They met by coincidence at the Wollman Skating Rink in Central Park.)

The Boy Scouts Circa 1949-54

At the age of eleven I joined the Boy Scouts, and this became a major activity and influence on my later life. The Scouts introduced me to hiking, camping and outdoor skills which stayed with me into later life. As a Scout I was a member of a troop and within that troop we had teams which competed in various scouting games, such as tying nine knots as fast as possible. Once we collected paper for recycling in a contest measured by weight collected. This troop of twelve-year-old kids collected tons of newspapers from around the neighborhood. Each week we had a "weigh in" session. We collected with a frenzy beyond belief. After a while a stack of paper was the most beautiful thing I could imagine.

In the Boy Scouts I found my inner circle of friends. They included Herb Schneider, who became my closest friend. The Scouts met in the

The author at eighteen.

The Old Stuyvesant High School Machine Shop, circa 1955.

basement of his home. The troop had four Patrols which were competing subdivisions. The Patrols were called Beavers, Panthers, Pioneers and Eagles. Herb was a natural leader and he was good in all his undertakings. He could tie the nine Scout knots in twenty-five seconds and place all the compass cards in order, faster than anyone in the troop. He was selected for the honored "Order of the Arrow" at the Scout summer camp, Ten Mile River. Herb earned enough merit badges to become a Life Scout. I achieved the next lower rank of Star Scout, but I was not selected for the "Order of the Arrow" and I never learned the secret password known only by its members. Compared to me, Herb was a much more successful teenager. He danced well, dressed in the latest fashions complete with tapered pants and slicked down hair, something like Elvis Presley. But Herb also had a sensitive and thoughtful side which in later years became the most salient part of his character.

Other fellow scouts included Todd Merer, Morty Steiner, Al Gennes, Lester Poris, Sherman Zell, Spencer Shaps, Paul Helfner, Eddie Stravitz, Eddie Katz and Harvey Bernstein, two of whom (Sherman and Al) would appear again later in my life. I had another good friend who was not in the Boy Scouts. I met Steve Maybar through my interest in amateur radio. Maybar, as we called him, was very bright with a sarcastic sense of humor. But under the bite he had a kind heart.

One day Maybar got hit by a car while crossing Rockaway Parkway. There were tire tracks running right across his back. I visited him at Brookdale Hospital and brought him a peg puzzle to keep him busy. Maybar eventually made a complete recovery.

Bar Mitzvah Parties 1950–53

During this time my friends were all approaching thirteen and having their Bar Mitzvahs. First the honor boy had to learn a section of the Torah and read it before the congregation at the synagogue, in the traditional "sing song" style. This was followed by the party. Very few guests went to the synagogue, but everybody went to the party! The Bar Mitzvah parties in those days were elaborate and costly. Parents spent $2,000 to $4,000. (Keep in mind that in the 1950s a house cost $5,000.) Food and drink were served in gargantuan proportions. The pastry table was greeted with adulation. These were monstrous feasts by any standard. The band was loud and exuberant, playing the old Jewish favorites for the adults and popular music for the young. The dancing was energetic. Toward the end of the festivities, the honored elders would come forward to light symbolic candles in honor of the Bar Mitzvah boy.

At the head table, the Bar Mitzvah boy and his friends frequently ended the meal by tossing food or rolled-up napkins at each other. The Bar Mitzvah religious ceremony marked the transformation of the boy into manhood. The party proved he still had a long way to go.

My Bar Mitzvah June, 1951

Then it was my turn. Since my father was head of the Lecture Bureau of the Jewish Welfare Board he had contacts with many entertainers. He arranged for a magician, a singer and a ventriloquist to appear at my party. Unlike other Bar Mitzvahs, which my friends had in large and ostentatious halls, ours was held in our home. I felt we had much better control over the event. I can still recall how wasteful my friends' celebrations were. The excess food that was thrown out could have fed an army.

During the party, relatives and friends gave me envelopes with gifts of money, as was the custom. I decided to consolidate all these gifts by putting all the money into a single stack of bills (just creating order out of chaos). When my mother saw what I had done she was horrified. Without knowing who gave what there was no way to reciprocate accurately, or know whom to thank for an especially generous gift.

As I mentioned, the religious part of the Bar Mitzvah was not as well attended as the secular part. But with my singing voice, who could blame the guests? I had a real problem getting a rhythm going as I made my awkward way through the text assigned to me that day. I believe it was the last time I actively participated in a synagogue service, though I would on occasion join my parents at services in later years.

Sports

I was not good at sports in my early childhood and this did not change in my teenage years. I even avoided spectator sports such as baseball and football. I had no feeling for which team won and to this day find it difficult to comprehend the extreme emotions people have if "their" team wins or loses. For example New York sports teams are made up of players purchased from other teams, men who were born and raised in other parts of the United States. These so-called "New

York" teams to my way of thinking do not represent New York if their players are from elsewhere.

In Brooklyn, in the 1950s, we had many undeveloped areas around the streets and buildings of our neighborhood. They were called sandlots, and many summer days were spent playing softball, hardball and stickball on those hot and dusty fields. The two best players by mutual consent became the captains. One captain would throw a baseball bat in the air and the other captain would catch it with one hand. They would then alternate in grabbing the bat, fist over fist, until the top of the bat was reached. The captain holding the top of the bat would have to swing the bat around his head three times. If he succeeded in not dropping the bat, he would have the first pick of the best players for his team.

The best were chosen first and so on down the line. I was poor at sports and therefore the last to be chosen. My captain would always put me in left field, the most inactive position in the game. I asked my parents to buy me a first baseman's glove because that was the position I dreamed of playing. So there I stood on those long summer days waiting endlessly for a ball to come toward left field, with my first baseman's glove at the ready. In the far distance I could just about make out the pitching, swinging and shouting going on in the infield. I was more a spectator than a participant. Once my father came down to give me practice and pointers. I recall he played as badly as I did. That is my memory of the great American pastime.

Teenage Hobbies

Because I was poor at team sports I pursued other activities. I took up chess and three other hobbies, besides stamp collecting: chemistry, model airplane building and amateur radio.

Chemistry 1952–53

Chemistry intrigued me. First, there was the science of how and why elements and compounds would react with each other. Second, there was the adventure of performing experiments that demonstrated these theories. Some of these experiments involved pungent and foul gases, explosions and danger. Of course, after the discovery of explosives, it was only a matter of time before I got into deep trouble. I invented a walnut bomb which consisted of potassium chlorate, red phosphorus and pebbles placed in an empty walnut wrapped in wire. The pebbles provided the friction to ignite the explosive ingredients. By simply hurling the walnut, it would produce an enormous explosion on impact. I threw these walnut grenades at stray cats. It really made them move. Windows in the neighborhood would shake and tenants would look out to see what happened.

One day my friend Howie learned about my experiments and asked if he could use my mixture. Why not? Howie sprinkled the explosive mixture in the stairwells of our Junior High School. As the students went from class to class, great bangs and pops could be heard, and the halls filled with smoke. The principal was furious and somehow found Howie. I sat in my class hoping against hope that Howie would not "squeal." Soon a school monitor appeared, whispered in the teacher's ear, and I was summoned to the principal's office. The principal said he was thinking of calling the police but decided instead to call my father. My father told the principal that he would punish me. I still remember the punishment. It could not have been worse. My father locked up my chemistry set for 30 days. Forty-five years later I can still remember the punishment and the suffering. The principal "punished" me by ordering me to read Jack London's books "The Call of the Wild" and "White Fang" and then write book reports. He wanted to suspend Howie, but my father told him that I would have to be suspended also since I gave Howie the chemicals. In the end, the principal was merciful. While the chemistry set was locked up I had time to read the Jack London books about the northern wilderness. It was a pleasant diversion, but eventually the chemistry set was unlocked and my attention returned to the molecular world. Howie went on to become the class president, to the consternation of the school authorities. He was a very popular fellow among his peers.

My chemistry mayhem was not finished. One hot summer day my friends and I went to a movie house to cool off. At the end of the film I took out a small bottle filled with dilute hydrochloric acid and dropped in a few pellets of ferric sulfide. This bottle I placed under my seat. Then we all beat a hasty retreat. Even before exiting we could hear the murmur of the patrons spreading like ripples in a pond, as the hydrogen sulfide gas drifted throughout the theater. The air conditioners helped and soon the entire movie house smelled of rotten eggs. Management had to fling open the doors to exhaust the putrid theater. This was a great success.

One day I brought metallic sodium into the science class to show my classmates. It was kept in a vial of kerosene since sodium is so active it reacts with the moisture in the air to form sodium hydroxide. My science teacher, Mr. Striker, asked what was going on. I showed him the vial and explained its contents. The remainder of the class time was spent hearing a lecture from Mr. Striker on the dangers of sodium and how I might lose a leg from keeping it in my pocket.

I recall the time Howie and I tried to make a zip gun. These were crude weapons that fired a twenty-two caliber bullet. We assembled a gun made of a small steel pipe tied to a wooden handle and used a nail and rubber band for a firing pin. I don't remember now if we were able to successfully fire it. Explosions and sudden bursts of chemical power were fascinating. The zip gun was just another way to demonstrate this power. Howie knew some tough street gangs in nearby Brownsville who may have had a more practical interest in our experiments.

In our Rockaway Parkway home I had my own room and my father built a large table for me to conduct experiments. Sometimes my gas generating experiments got out of hand. These generators are easy to start and hard to stop. I recall particularly the production of bromine, a brown heavy vapor, almost a liquid at room temperature. It oozed and insinuated itself along the floor of my room and throughout the entire apartment. My mother sometimes called to me from the kitchen to ask what was going on. I think the two-foot layer of brown pungent gas got her attention.

I got my chemistry supplies from the John H. Winn Company, a chemical supply house on West 23rd Street in Manhattan. The company required a parent's signature for the more dangerous chemicals. Since my father was my chief assistant in many experiments, I had no difficulty in getting his signature. With that obstacle cleared away I purchased concentrated nitric, sulfuric and hydrochloric acids plus one ounce of sodium cyanide. I planned to make aqua regia, the only acid that can attack gold. My father provided an old gold filling for this experiment. On October 28, 1952 I turned my father's filling into gold chloride. The sodium cyanide was intended for an experiment to produce hydrocyanic acid which can etch glass. But I knew the jar of sodium cyanide I purchased was so poisonous that a grain of it could kill you. The one ounce I had could kill an army. That fear was enough; I never even opened the jar.

I kept a notebook in which I recorded my experiments. The date of the first experiment was October 24, 1952 and the last was March 26, 1953, but I know that I was playing around with chemistry over a longer period than that. I recorded twenty-four experiments in my notebook. In each experiment I would indicate the problem, the materials, the procedure, the observation and finally the conclusion. For example, in the first experiment the problem was "What will happen when zinc and mercury nitrate are heated together?" I wrote out the chemical equation and then proceeded to heat the two chemicals in a test tube, using a Bunsen burner. In the conclusion I noted: "The more active zinc displaced the less active mercury in the nitrate salt, liberating nitrous oxide plus oxygen."

Model Airplanes

One day I put away the chemistry and took up building model airplanes. At first I made free-flight planes of balsa wood and special linen paper. Later I made heavier models that had small glow plug gasoline engines and were controlled by twin wires and a hand-held reel. My friend Sherman Zell and I shared an interest in this hobby and, later, amateur radio. Sherman lived on the third floor of my apartment building. He outdid me in both these hobbies. His planes were larger and he mastered acrobatic maneuvers that just made me gasp. He could fly a plane upside down, which is tricky because the controls are all reversed. Up is down and down is up. If you panic the plane just crashes into the concrete in total destruction. It was also bad for your ego because the place where we flew on weekends was jammed with fellow pilots. Realizing it was hopeless to try to compete with Sherman, I built smaller and smaller planes which struggled around at turtle speed. It was my way of avoiding direct competition.

Amateur Radio 1953-58

Next came amateur radio. Here, too, Sherman excelled. His transmitter was more powerful and his receiver was more sophisticated. To enter this hobby, the first step was to pass the FCC test for a novice class license, which permitted the operator to transmit Morse code but not voice. The next step was to take the test for the General Class license which permitted voice communications. The General Class test was more difficult and required passing a Morse code exam at thirteen words per minute. Sherman and I both got our General Class licenses at the same time though he could take down Morse code faster than I could; I think my speed was up to 18 words per minute at best. I logged my first voice communication on March 25, 1953. When we graduated to voice communication I found a place in which I excelled. I spoke more slowly and clearly than Sherman, and other operators would think I was the older, though it was he who was older by a year. His call letters were K2GYW and mine were K2GZE.

One day in 1955, my father came home and announced he too had passed the FCC license exam. His call letters were K2LDL. He logged his first voice contact on February 8, 1955. Years later he told me that he secretly had been practicing the Morse code at his office. He did not want to tell me in case he failed his examination, which he did once. But he passed on his second attempt. Now we were both "hams" and we began to build a large collection of QSL cards from all over the United States and a few from Europe. Every time you made a new contact on the air, you traded QSL cards. They were decorative postcards with information about the operator and his equipment. My Uncle Louie, the commercial artist, made up a unique design for my card.

One day I did a careless thing. To go from the 20-meter band to the 40-meter band, I had to change a coil in my transmitter. This coil consisted of a bare wire wound onto a ceramic cylinder. I forgot to turn off the power and grabbed the coil with one hand while resting on the grounded chassis with the other. Suddenly 600 volts, DC, ripped across my chest. I was thrown back violently to the other side of my bedroom. I began shaking and this continued for 30 minutes. That was as close to death as I had ever come.

The neighbors were a problem for us. Our amateur radio transmissions would break up their television pictures and they would hear our voices coming out of the speakers. The neighbors were not amused. Some went up to the roof and repeatedly cut down our antenna. I went so far as to put 18,000 volts on the antenna to stop them. I used a low amperage "Ford coil" so the shock would not be lethal. We tried to solve the problem with our neighbors by getting filters for their television receivers and my transmitter. But a solution was never achieved. One day I had an idea. Why not stretch a fine wire across Rockaway Parkway and place the far end high up on the chain link fence on the other side of the street? Perhaps the wire would not be noticed and it would make a terrific antenna. With the help of a friend I unspooled the wire down to the sidewalk from my bedroom window. Nonchalantly, I walked across the street holding one end of the fine wire in my pants pocket. Quickly I hooked it up on the chain fence. However, within hours, a neighbor spotted the wire running across the street. I could see the agitation from my window and felt the cops would shortly be knocking on my door. Deciding to bring down the antenna, I began to pull my end into the room. But the wire was very ductile and it simply would not snap. I just kept hauling away and the wire just kept getting thinner and longer. At last it did snap and all evidence drifted slowly away and down from my window to the street below.

Amateur radio continued to be my hobby when it came time to choose a career, and it was why I enrolled in a program leading toward a degree in electronic engineering. I logged my last communications as an amateur radio operator on September 1, 1958. This date also marked the beginning of my electrical engineering coursework at CCNY.

Chess 1955+

Although I learned to play chess when I was twelve or thirteen, I did not get serious about it until I was seventeen or eighteen. I began to read books by Fine and Reshevsky that dealt with openings, and with middle and end games. In the summer I would walk over to Lincoln Terrace Park to watch and occasionally play. Lincoln Terrace on a weekend afternoon in the summer was crowded with old men from Eastern Europe. They played hard and cursed harder, sometimes slamming the wooden pieces onto the stone chess tables with such force that the chips would fly off the pieces. *"Nem dem ferd"* the kibitzers would shout (take the horse). *"Drek kotch!"* the players would say to each other (you piece of shit). I never learned much Yiddish at home but the park players' Yiddish was really infectious. As evening fell, the old men would play on, struggling by candle and the dim park lights. Elderly Jews gathered nearby to sing, play the accordion and listen, perhaps remembering the "old country" and a shtetl long gone. Those were magical summer nights in a Brooklyn that is now my old country.

I continued playing chess in the park every summer, even during my early college years, but eventually I drifted away. Today, Lincoln Terrace Park is in the middle of a poor black neighborhood. My old country has disappeared as completely as the shtetls of Eastern Europe.

In the early years of my marriage I took up chess again and would spend weekends at tournaments in Manhattan. These contests were frequently held at the Henry Hudson Hotel on West 57th Street and anyone with fifteen dollars and nothing to do for two days could participate. I attained a United States Chess Federation rating of 1840, which was in the A class of players. After several years of engaging in these intense weekend chess battles I stopped. Eventually my favorite opponent became my computer, which was ready whenever I was and played a very strong unforgiving game.

Work 1952–58

As a teenager, I worked after school for the grocery store around the corner on Clarkson Avenue. I delivered groceries and stocked the shelves with canned goods stored in the basement below the store. A normal tip for delivery in those days was 25 cents. Sometimes the customer would pay me in returnable bottles; we had recycling even then. Once I got a five-cent tip and I was so annoyed I gave it back to the customer and told her "you need it more than me." For that rudeness I was sternly reprimanded by the store owner.

Between the ages of seventeen and eighteen, I sought summer jobs in Manhattan. One summer I was hired as an apprentice in a machine shop. The owner was Mr. Plenge. I told him I was available permanently, but I knew that in September I would be off to college. Anyway, I worked like a demon for forty dollars per week. The regular workers quietly told me to slow down because I was making them look bad. But I was having fun on the lathe, the drill press and the boring machines. As the summer came to an end it was time to give my notice. I told Mr. Plenge I'd decided to go to college and had been accepted. He was very understanding. He told me he wished his son had gone on to college and he then wished me the best of luck. I felt very guilty for my dishonesty.

The next summer I got a job as a draftsman working for Volt Technical in Manhattan, a company that produced instruction manuals for manufacturers. I worked in ink and used three- and two-point perspective. Lettering and executing explosion drawings were other skills I acquired. The regulars on the boards nearby were a funny and cheerful group and I enjoyed going to work each morning. One day there was a layoff and I was suddenly let go. Tears welled up in my eyes. My older colleagues were very sympathetic. My second job that summer was for a fire alarm company that needed a draftsman to draw the wiring layout for each client. I worked in pencil and the results were far less pleasing to me. At the end of the summer I resigned and began my next year's engineering education.

Learning to Drive 1956

When we were eighteen all my friends were learning to drive. I practiced with my father's car and took the test but failed. I got so nervous my foot started to shake and I could no longer control the speed. However, on the second attempt, with a kind examiner, I calmed down and passed. I had only one accident in those early years. One winter day I slid my father's car into the rear of another, damaging the fenders and lights. That lesson taught me not to tail-gate on ice.

My father bought a convertible car one year. My mother vowed never to ride in it. Elisa and I leaned out the window as we watched my father, on the street below, persuade her to just try one ride in the car. Reluctantly she agreed.

Our Home 1944–61

I lived with my parents on Rockaway Parkway from 1944 till I left for a job in Maryland in 1961. One block away was the New Lots subway line, which at this point was elevated. Every ten or fifteen minutes a train would roar by. We learned to tune out the noise but in the summer with the windows open the sound would block out the TV audio. It always seemed to happen at some critical moment like the punch line to a joke or learning "who done it." In the summer the women would sit on aluminum/vinyl chairs, and knit and gossip. Whenever my friends and I entered and left the building we knew they would start talking about us. On Sundays we would eat out, often at a Chinese-American restaurant on Utica Avenue. Elisa called Utica Avenue "the Nile of Jewish civilization." The street was filled with delicatessens, tailor shops and bakeries.

At home my mother prepared Jewish, Eastern European food. I appreciated it more as an adult after comparing it to the normal American diet. My mother made latkes, kugel, blintzes, chicken soup (of course), stuffed cabbage and many other wonderful dishes. She waged a never-ending battle to get Elisa and me to eat more and my father to eat less. It was a losing battle fought against metabolism and Mother Nature.

Pizza was as popular in the 1950s as it is today. A slice cost fifteen cents, a whole pie about $1.25. Also popular in Brooklyn in those days was a confection called "Charlotte Russe." A Charlotte Russe consisted of a small solid cylinder of sponge cake, upon which rested a generous cone of whipped cream capped with a red maraschino cherry. The sponge cake was contained in a white cardboard hollow cylinder, supported by a cardboard disk inside the cylinder. Charlotte Russes were stored in glass cases, row upon row. I bought them at a candy store near the Sutter Avenue elevated train station (the El).

The author with his parents and sister, circa 1958.

Television 1948–1958

The first television arrived in our building in 1948. On many evenings I would go down to our neighbor's apartment, where I joined other children, to watch Milton Berle's *Texaco Theater* or *Howdy Doody*. Around 1949 or 1950 we got our own television which was a small black and white set that sat in our living room.

We watched many different programs such as *Omnibus*, hosted by Alistair Cooke, who was a young man with blond hair in those days. *The Hallmark Theater* had excellent drama. Then there was *Captain Midnight*, a science fiction series, and the popular puppet *Howdy Doody*. Howdy's human partner was Buffalo Bill and another dumb character was Clarabell the Clown. The "Peanut Gallery" was filled with kids cheering on the mayhem. I also remember watching Jersey Joe Walcott lose to boxing champ Joe Louis.

But, for our family, the best of all the TV programs was Sid Caesar and his *Show of Shows*. He and his fellow comedians, Imogene Coca, Howard Morris and Carl Reiner, were so zany that our family went into hysterical laughter. I laughed so much at his comedy skits that my sides ached; I actually laughed myself onto the floor and rolled about on the rug. Never before or since have I laughed as much as during Caesar's weekly broadcasts. It truly was television's golden age of comedy.

Since I was not disciplined in completing my homework, I was easily drawn to the TV set. But all my father had to say was "I see you've finished your homework already" and the guilt would descend upon me like a dark cloud.

Music 1955-63

What a time it was to be a teenager at the dawn of Rock and Roll! It began with Elvis Presley and ended with the Beatles. In between were such favorites as "Earth Angel" by the Platters, which always brings back memories of slow dancing and young romance. All this new music created a generation gap. My parents' generation never appreciated this rock and roll sound. But I was plugged into the popular disk jockey Alan Freed and his top hits on the radio, and attended one of the big concerts he put together at a Brooklyn movie house. It was a mini Woodstock in its time.

I had trouble keeping with the rhythm on the fast dances; the slow ones were no problem. This would always prove embarrassing to me since I would ask a girl to dance when the music was slow. At the end of the slow dance a fast one would start and I would either have to sit down or make a futile attempt at trying to lead the poor girl through the next number.

Relatives

We had a large extended family. My mother had three brothers: Abie, Little Sam and Sindel, and one sister, Manya. My father had one brother, Louie. Add in wives, husbands and kids and a family gathering was a busy, noisy and exciting affair.

I loved Big Sam, Manya's husband. He took a real interest in my interests. He asked questions and listened to my answers. Once, on a long car journey, I was sleeping in the back of the car with my head on Sam's lap. I awoke and saw the moon set against a partly cloudy night sky. "Look how the moon is gliding by," I said to Sam. For some reason he was taken by that observation of mine and repeated it frequently to others over the years. You sensed his joy and lively personality. Later,

My sister Elisa and I. Photo taken 1997.

as a teenager, I would go to Sam and Manya's apartment for a light lunch of cottage cheese and cooked fruit, after a summer's day playing chess at Lincoln Terrace Park.

Big Sam died April 21, 1981 while giving directions to a taxi driver in Forest Hills. Manya was at his side as she had been all their married life. That day Manya telephoned and asked me to come to her house. I knew the news was bad without asking. Together we phoned their son Eugene who was on vacation in Paris. Manya could not tell him, so I broke the news that his father had just died. Along with the family I went through the ritual of "sitting shiva" and the burial. The realization that I would never see him again was too great to comprehend, especially mingling among other members of the family. A week later alone in our home in Fresh Meadows I started to recall memories of Big Sam. His kind face full of humor and good nature was gone forever. The sorrow and the grief welled up in me.

Eugene is the oldest cousin of my generation. He is also the scholar. Eugene received his Ph.D. in literature from Columbia and authored several books on literary criticism. He was head of the English Department at Boston University and a professor of English at

Brandeis University. I admire my older cousin. He has a terrific sense of humor and over the years I acquired my best jokes from him.

All my uncles had distinctive personalities. Uncle Louie was a commercial artist, with a philosophical disposition and a talent for cartoon drawing. Louie is also quiet and scholarly. However, his wife, Aunt Minnie, is talkative and exuberant with a hilarious nature. Her two daughters took after her. Darlene, the younger daughter, married in her 40s, not surprisingly to a quiet fellow named Michael. Elaine, the elder, married and divorced twice. Elaine has led an especially adventurous life, working abroad and marrying outside the faith, once to a Greek-American and once to an artist from Santa Fe.

My travels in Europe paved the way for Elaine. She persuaded her parents that if boys like Jay could seek adventure, why not girls? At one point in our teenage days, she tried to teach me to dance, a valiant but hopeless endeavor. For a while, Elaine dated my friend Herb Schneider and as adults they occasionally meet.

My uncle, Little Sam, was the bachelor in our family. He was a chain smoker, with a smoker's cough. Little Sam was a sun worshiper who, during the summers, would use an aluminum reflector to concentrate the rays on his face. As a result of this intense exposure he had a deeply weathered and lined appearance. After losing his hair, Sam wore a wig. From my mother and older cousins, I learned he was a true gentleman, considerate, well-dressed and, in his youth, very handsome. Little Sam did not show any obvious interest in me while I was growing up. However, toward the end of his life I had some fine conversations with him about working in the garment industry and about the union movement in which he had played a big role. I realized he had a great deal of wisdom, but only as an adult did I appreciate it, and by then it was late in his life. Little Sam died at Lenox Hill Hospital at the age of eighty, on November 3, 1985.

Uncle Sindel married his much younger first cousin Anya Roisner. They adopted a child, Emmanuel, who died at four of leukemia. A few years later, a Canadian family wished to conceal an out-of-wedlock birth. Through a rabbi in Connecticut, arrangements were made for the pregnant girl (she was only sixteen or seventeen) to live with Sindel and Anya till the birth. The baby became their second adoption and she was named Gloria.

Sindel was a natural leader. He was active in the Jewish community and helped many immigrants come over to America. As one of the cottage owners in Carmel, I saw him every summer. He was a hard worker and built many additions to his summer home. Sindel and Anya were very social and frequently hosted family gatherings. When I

Uncle Sam Oxenhorn (Little Sam), circa 1925. Lifelong bachelor, garment worker, union leader.

Aunt Manya Goodheart, 1994. Chief source for my genealogy research. Avid reader with a terrific memory.

was young, Sindel owned a bakery delivery truck. He would pick up the cakes from the bakery factory and deliver them to stores in Brooklyn. I recall riding on his truck as he delivered these cakes. Later he opened a toy store on Stone Avenue in a tough part of Brooklyn. This business turned out to be very successful and he made his fortune.

Sindel was a physically powerful man, but in the end it didn't protect him. A customer who refused to pay for merchandise that had just been put into his van got into a fistfight with him. That evening, Sindel had chest pains. He was hospitalized. I was asked to post a notice on his store explaining the closing. I visited him in the hospital; Sindel was having great difficulty breathing. A few days later he died at the age of sixty-six on June 12, 1966.

Anya and Gloria moved to Israel. After Anya died, Gloria married an Israeli, had three children and returned with her husband to the United States, settling near Seattle.

I believe Uncle Abie was my mother's favorite brother. They grew up together and he was a very gentle and kind man. Like Sindel, Abie tried to go into the toy business after losing his job in the garment industry, but he was not successful. Abie was ill for many years and died October 15, 1972 at the age of sixty-four, at Brookdale Hospital in Brooklyn. Mildred, his wife, moved to East Windsor, NJ to be near her older son. She had two sons who led very different lives. Melvin, the older, struggled financially in the difficult business of selling belts. The younger son, Eli, became president of Cheyenne Software and, after resigning in 1994 and selling off his stock holdings, became a multimillionaire.

Early Girl Friends 1953-57

Most girls from my neighborhood did not let the boys "go all the way." There was of course a great deal of kissing, hugging and necking. At first there were group socials. But in a year or so my peers paired off and went on dates. A date might include a film and then an ice cream parlor. If we were double dating and one boy had a borrowed car, we might drive to Jahn's, a popular ice cream parlor in Queens. Drive-in movies were especially popular because the privacy allowed for more necking opportunities. Nathan's hot dog stand in Coney Island was another favorite destination. And watching the "submarine races" in parking places along the Belt Parkway was a euphemism for even more necking opportunities.

My first contact with the opposite sex was at parties where we played kissing games like "spin the bottle" and "post office." I vaguely recall the oohing, aahing and giggling that went on. I was about fourteen years old at the time.

When I was fifteen I had a crush on a girl named Mildred in junior high. I took an unsolicited photo of her which I kept in my wallet and I would sit outside her house just waiting for her so I could say hello. She unfortunately took no interest in me.

Toby was the first girl I dated. I was sixteen and she was fourteen. This was more serious for me because it was not a blind date. I actually overcame my shyness, walked up to Toby, introduced myself and got her phone number. Toby was "Rubenesque" with curly blond hair. I remember telling her I was eighteen to impress her and then later confessing my true age. We went together for almost a year but then my parents took Elisa and me on a trip to Mexico and when we returned Toby was seeing a fellow boy scout, Morty Steiner. Toby's mother preferred me to Morty and phoned my mother offering recipes to fatten me up. I was six feet tall and weighed only 140 pounds.

After Toby, meeting girls became a little easier as my confidence increased. I went out with a girl named Lydia. She was statuesque and quite attractive. I took her to a big dance on my Vespa motor scooter; I was probably twenty at the time. Lydia had on a fancy, fluffy pink dress, and while en route to the dance I heard a scream. Lydia had been sitting behind me, sidesaddle, but her feet touched the pavement. In a moment she was flat out on the cement. It was very embarrassing but Lydia fortunately was not hurt. She got back on the Vespa and away we went.

I was "stood up" once. Upon arriving to meet my date, I saw a notice on the door. It said that she had to leave suddenly to take her sick cat to the hospital. I wrote below the note that "I hope your cat feels better than I do."

One of Elisa's girl friends, Eileen, liked me and, with some hesitation, I began to date her. There was a five-year age difference; I was twenty, she was only fifteen. It lasted only a few months.

I met Amy while at Brooklyn College. She was very attractive and self-assured. Amy would call me and come over to my home so we could study together. I really liked her but nothing romantic ever developed.

The House Plan 1956–60

My friends had graduated from the Boy Scouts to the Explorers, which was for older boys. But by age eighteen they were more interested in girls, smoking, drinking and other non-scouting activities. Our exploring had nothing to do with the forests. The Explorer Post was quickly transformed into a college social club. At Brooklyn College they were called House Plans and were the poor man's version of the fraternities and sororities at the posh Ivy League schools. At our House Plan, which met in the basement of Todd Merer's house, we held frequent parties with female House Plans. These parties were orchestrated by my friends to start with introductions and then progress to fast music, slow music, low lights, no lights—and lots of necking.

Frugal Freeman

My friends in the House Plan called me Frugal Freeman because I was careful about money. For example, I generally spent about $3.00 on a date. This budget included $1.00 for two movie tickets, up from twenty-five cents per ticket when I was a child. Included in my budget for the evening were two bus or train fares, and ice cream. All this seemed an appropriate amount to spend on a date; I was quite perplexed by the label "Frugal."

Learning About Sex

I learned about sex and reproduction from my friends on the street. I do not believe there was one particular moment when it was all revealed to me. Rather, I learned about it in stages. By the time I asked my father to give me an explanation, I already knew the details. I just wanted him to feel he had done the right thing as a father. I was not precocious about sex and it wasn't until my second trip to Europe, at age twenty-three, that I first engaged in intercourse. But I am getting ahead of the story.

My Parents and their Teenage Son 1952–56

I continued to have a good relationship with my parents while a teenager. Certainly they had to deal with problems created by my chemical experiments. But I did not get drunk, and I rarely stayed out late. There was no drug problem in those days. And I certainly did not get any girls "in trouble" though I tried.

I cannot remember my father ever striking me, though once or twice he was quite angry with me. My parents invited their friends and neighbors, Kurt and Ruth Lowe, to the Carmel summer home for a weekend. I was target practicing with my air rifle, shooting steel pellets at a tin can. What I failed to realize was that one hundred feet beyond the tin can, Kurt Lowe was sitting, chatting with my parents. I think after I shot him twice, my father came up the hill and he was pretty angry. He grabbed my air rifle, and it was quite a while before I saw the gun again.

Generally my father's approach was to reason things out with me. He was not authoritarian. This may have caused problems for me later on in life when I assumed everyone was as analytical, patient and reasonable as my father. In later life I would become bewildered by, and be unprepared for, the irrational or emotional reactions of others to comments or actions on my part. If my mother had a problem with me during the day she would simply say "wait until your father gets home!" But I cannot remember any serious arguments or family fights. If my parents had a disagreement they would settle it when Elisa and I were not around. I think my parents did an absolutely superb job of raising us. For this I shall be eternally grateful.

Goals and Dreams

I wanted to be an engineer ever since my days as an amateur radio operator. Electronics fascinated me. I spent my days wandering around Canal Street and the old electronics district in lower Manhattan where the World Trade Towers now stand. I would buy used components to build electronic gear for my hobby or just to experiment with. My parents, as most Jewish parents, wanted their son to become a professional which included medicine, law, engineering or teaching. Within that context my chosen course was perfectly acceptable. After graduation I worked as an engineer for ten years and then gave it all up to pursue very different work. My goals had changed.

I do not think young people should set life goals for themselves. The world changes too much during one's life and as a person matures his attitudes are likely to change as well. Because fate can lead one along unpredictable paths, education ought to consider this. First, education should prepare you for that initial step into the working world and second, education should train the mind to adapt to change over a forty-year period. This is a tall order. But when I think of my engineering education, completed in 1960, the principles of mathematics, physics and electronics still hold true and serve as a basis for understanding the revolutionary developments that I witnessed in my profession during my working life. Furthermore, the mental discipline acquired in my engineering studies helped enormously in grasping marketing and finance. So I was able to start and learn the distribution business 20–25 years after I graduated college.

Travel With My Parents

Mexico Trip, 1955

In the summer of 1955 my family took a vacation in Mexico; this was my first trip outside the United States. My parents rented an apartment at 131 Altamirano, Mexico City. This I am certain of because every time we got into a taxi to go back to the apartment my father would say *"Altamirano, ciento trenta uno, por favor."* Ultimately, this address was burned into my memory forever. It is one of the many useless facts that remains in your head whether you like or not.

The Mexican food disagreed with me and I recall spending a good deal of time in the bathroom. We saw a lot of the tourist sights during our stay in Mexico, including the murals of Diego Rivera, the University and the great central plaza with its ancient cathedrals. We traveled outside Mexico City to Taco and Acapulco, and visited an Indian village on an island in Lake Pátzcuaro where the natives used butterfly nets to fish. My parents had friends in Mexico City and they invited us to their homes for dinner and showed us more of the city. Herb Canerack was one friend and another was Julio de La Fuente, an outstanding Mexican archaeologist, who was married to my mother's friend Lubba.

Cuba, Guatemala and Mexico Trip, 1956

Following the success of our first trip to Mexico, my father planned a more ambitious journey which began in the summer of 1956. We flew to Cuba, which at the time was still under the rule of the dictator Fulgencio Batista. In Cuba we toured the island, saw the wealthy Jewish center and walked about Havana. Havana must have been quite a sin city in those days. I remember a pimp approaching my father and me and offering us two young girls. My father declined but asked if I was interested. Teenage life in Brooklyn had not prepared me for this; red-faced, I declined the offer also.

From Cuba we flew to Guatemala. We then took a bus north to Lake Atitlán, Quezaltenango, Huehuetenango and up to the Mexican border. The trip took many days and we traveled frequently at night across jungles, through rivers and over steep mountain roads. At one point the Pan American highway ended and we took a short flight to bridge the gap. In Mexico we reached San Cristóbal de las Casas. My father and I hiked up into the hills where we saw what the Catholics called "pagan ceremonies" performed by the local Indians. We continued by bus north through Oaxaca and Mexico City all the way up to Monterrey near the border with the United States. In Monterrey we were able to coax my mother onto a donkey to take her up a steep hill for a view of the city. From Monterrey we flew home. This was a big adventure holiday and instilled in me a curiosity about the world.

4
College Years and the Single Life

There is no time like the old time, when you and I were young.
    —Oliver Wendell Holmes, *No Time Like the Old Time*

Brooklyn College 1956–58

In September, 1956, I entered Brooklyn College's two-year pre-engineering program. Credits earned at Brooklyn College would be fully transferable to City College of New York (CCNY) where I would complete the last two years of my undergraduate engineering education. By enrolling at Brooklyn College I would avoid the long subway journey into Manhattan for two years.

Brooklyn College had a wonderful green campus in those days. Now those grassy quadrangles of spacious lawn are filled with buildings, but then it was almost like an out-of-town school. The coursework was easier than Stuyvesant High School's and the students were not as serious or clever. In some respects those two years were like a holiday. It was a time to discover the liberal arts. History was suddenly more interesting. The students worked from source books rather than pre-digested texts. From these source documents we drew conclusions about life in the thirteenth to nineteenth century and the forces that moved medieval and Renaissance Europe. The social science courses were a combination of sociology and anthropology. My narrow technical focus widened for the first time and I began to develop a respect for and curiosity about the humanities.

I sat in on a class in basic Russian for about six months. It was fun using my small vocabulary with my uncle Big Sam and aunt Manya. I volunteered as a lab assistant for my chemistry professor to learn what research work was like. Often, between classes, I played chess with fellow students in the comfortable lounges at Brooklyn College. I recall racing across the Quadrangle to get to class on time after playing chess just a little too long.

Students received their grades by postcards mailed from the college by the teachers. After the final exams I recall waiting apprehensively for the mailman each morning and, when I saw a postcard, I would cover the face with my hand and slowly slide it away to reveal the grade.

Brooklyn College Debate Society

I joined the Debate Society in my freshman year. The coach was Professor Parkhurst, a physically small man with a deep voice who enunciated each word with precision and clarity. The national topic for debate that year had to do with the union or closed shop. The next year the subject was foreign aid. Our team would prepare to debate the affirmative or negative and we had card desks of evidence for each position. When visiting other schools we might be asked to reverse our position with each round. This was good practice for aspiring attorneys. In fact, one debater, a year ahead of me at Brooklyn, was Alan Dershowitz, who later became one of the most famous American trial lawyers and a law professor at Harvard. On October 15, 1957, Alan and I were partners in a debate held before an audience at Public School 197. The subject was "Resolved: Testing of all nuclear weapons should be outlawed." We defended the negative, that is that testing should be continued.

Alan Dershowitz, in early 1957, was selected with another student to debate the visiting British team at an annual event held at Brooklyn College. I sat in the audience and was amused at the very different style of British debate. Making points with humor and wit was more important for the British debaters than reeling off boring statistics. They were far more entertaining for the audience of 500 than our own Brooklyn College team. The following year I competed to represent Brooklyn against the visiting Scottish team from Glasgow University. I put together some funny material and Mr. Parkhurst picked me and another student, William Earlbaum. The subject for debate was "Resolved: That the sun has set on the British empire." Our team took the affirmative. The Scots were champion debaters in their country and tied rings around us. Nevertheless, I was thrilled to speak before a large audience and hear them laugh at my jokes. Our opponents that day, April 25, 1958, were Ronald Bernard Anderson and Leonard McKenzie Turpi.

On June 9, 1958 I wrote the following essay to myself:

> Twenty years have passed since I was born. As I think back upon these two decades of life a strange mood comes over me. This is an awkward and uncertain period, one filled with exuberance and ambition for the future, an uncertainty as to how I shall fit into this future and how well, how adequately I shall meet the challenges of this future. Inevitably in questioning my motives and drives I ask what is the purpose of life. Is one to exist to be happy, to forge immortality for himself if he can, to be individualistic, to settle down and "raise a family," to travel, to build a home? These questions are so terribly important at this time. Till now I could go along my educational road unconcerned and quite happy, knowing that I was uncommitted in any phase of human endeavor. Up till [sic] this year in college, I could have become anything from an advertiser to a zymologist. I took varied courses such as history, physics, social science and mathematics. Quite suddenly though pressure began to work and there [sic] ever increasing force has been trying to mold me into a specialized cog to fit this complex world. I naturally have resisted and the result is a conflict. The world is so marvelous and fascinating that I think "specialization" is to the mind and spirit what blindness is to the eye or deafness to the ear. That my education, thinking and beliefs should be so limited to one area of concern in later years is a horrible thought to contemplate. So now I am in the engineering program. This coming year I shall take no more liberal arts or mathematics, only technical courses. The pressures are slowly gaining ground. What will the next few years do to me? What will the next twenty years do? Will I become so job centered that nothing but engineering in my field will interest me? Will people remember me after I am gone as the man who built a condenser that could handle ten more volts? I think there is one thing I am sure of. I don't want an uneventful life. If I have to be different to accomplish this then I will! If I must sacrifice convenience, success, "peace and quiet" then I will!

City College of New York, 1958–60

In September, 1958, I transferred to CCNY to complete the final two years of my electronic engineering education. At Brooklyn College I found the course work easy. My grade point average after two years at Brooklyn was 3.52 out of a perfect 4.0. However the engineering courses at CCNY were more difficult and the competition stiffer. The teachers were well-known in their fields and published the texts that were used nationally for teaching electronics or mechanics. For example, Professor Taub taught his course from the standard text written by Millman and Taub. And though I planned to work in electronics, half my electrical engineering coursework was in power engineering. Additionally, I had five courses in mechanical engineering and four in civil engineering. We studied advanced calculus, of course, but in addition tackled special mathematics such as discontinuous functions and Laplace Transforms. This math, though developed centuries earlier, had contemporary relevance in modern analog circuit design. We took courses in drafting and this was integrated into our civil engineering courses so that we could solve beam stress problems using either the drawing board or the slide rule.

The students were highly motivated. They included mature veterans on the GI educational program and poor and middle class students whose parents could not afford the tuition of a private school. The classes were filled mostly by Italian- and Jewish-Americans.

Once our teacher failed to show up for the class. One student rose, went to the front and said, "We can leave if we wish but why waste time? Let's go over yesterday's homework." The entire class then went over each problem we had been assigned and made terrific use of the time. The fast students helped the slow ones. I can still remember that class with pride. It was very much like the orchestra that performs without the conductor, to honor his memory.

CCNY was a commuter school. Every morning I would get up and take the 80-minute subway journey from Brooklyn to the uptown branch of CCNY at 138th Street. Then I would walk the steep hill to the gloomy neo-Gothic buildings of the Engineering School of North Campus. After the classes were over, I would reverse the trip and try my best to get a seat so that the time could be used for study.

In September, 1958 I wrote a short essay on my first impressions of CCNY:

> I got off the IRT at 139th Street station and walked up the steep street leading along the wall of a convent to the northern part of the College at the top of the hill. The buildings of this part of "City" are very old. The brick stones are about one foot by two feet long, black either by nature or years of Manhattan "air." They are set in grayish cement and the corner stones are also gray. Along part of the walls are ivy, feeble and trying very hard to survive. The buildings strike one as medieval castles grouped in a silent morbid atmosphere. Inside the years show equally well. The stairs, banisters, doors and hallway architecture simply reek with age. Students zip by and know exactly where they are going. I feel quite lost in a maze of new oldness. The room numbering system and where to go next are problems to be solved. I find my room. The blackboards seem to be placed without planning or symmetry. A few reach

higher than reachable unless City College has teachers over eight feet tall. This room is a lecture hall and the seats could get good prices in an antique store, especially with the historical carvings of forty generations of students. The room gradually fills with students coming to register. Up front on a raised wooden podium behind a large and embellished mahogany desk sit three students, one of whom calls out numbers and names. When I hear mine, I pick up the card and go to a room upstairs. I join a large mass of students seated before a movable blackboard. The room itself is much larger and this section is but a small area. We wait again for numbers to be called. Meanwhile on the blackboard classes which have closed down are noted. You pray that your number is called before a class which you want to take is put down.

Campus extracurricular activities played no role for most students. The football team was irrelevant, unlike the big private universities where the coach could be more important than the school president. However, I decided to get involved in some way, so I ran for office and won a place on the Student Council. Our weekly meetings were exercises in Robert's Rules of Order. I was surrounded by aspiring attorneys from the liberal arts college of South Campus. An engineering student was indeed a stranger on the council. We debated weighty matters such as whether the cafeteria should have a Coke machine. There was a strong Socialist bias on the Council, though I can't recall how it affected the Coke machine issue.

With every term at CCNY my grade point average dropped since I was now getting mostly B and C grades as compared to the A and B grades of Brooklyn College. However, my average was still over 3.3, qualifying me to enter Eta Kappa Nu (HKN), the engineering honor society. It is ironic that my liberal arts and basic science courses got me into HKN rather than the engineering courses.

During my college years I gave up my hobbies and focused on study, particularly during the CCNY years. Most leisure time was spent with my friends in the pursuit of girls. The exception was a minor role I played in campus politics.

Encouraged by my participation in the Council in my first year, I decided to run for President of the Council in my second year at CCNY. My Uncle Louie made up a snappy design for posters which my father printed up in quantity. These I plastered all over the campus. My opponent was David Burnheim, an extremely articulate and witty speaker. David was an interesting pre-law student. He had a part-time job selling pens in a department store. When he spoke he gestured with one hand as if he was holding one of his pens. His fluency was so astounding you felt he was reading text rather than composing sentences spontaneously. When the ballots were counted David had 55 percent and I had 45 percent. I accepted defeat gracefully and with some relief. At the graduation ceremonies, David delivered a brilliant speech to a vast audience of students, families and faculty. Afterward I congratulated him. He then told me he had planned to make a few off-the-cuff remarks before beginning the written text but, after a few moments, he decided just to complete all his remarks without notes.

Among my Brooklyn friends, the only ones to enroll with me at CCNY were Herb Schneider and Steve Maybar. For a brief period Herb considered medicine, but in the end he chose mechanical engineering. He went on to the University of Connecticut where he received a master's degree in mechanical engineering. Later Herb joined Grumman Aircraft and worked there till his early retirement. He was a specialist in heat transfer problems on the Lunar Landing Module, which was the spacecraft that first landed on the Moon. Steve Maybar received his master's degree in electronic engineering at CCNY and then went on for a Ph.D. I lost touch with him so I never learned if he reached his goal.

At CCNY, an engineering degree required taking 144 credits as opposed to 128 credits in liberal arts. Normally it took four and a half years to finish because of those 16 extra credits. But by assuming an extra heavy load of classes for four years, plus one summer session, I saved six months and finished in June, 1960.

Elisa as a Teenager

Because there were five years between us, Elisa and I did not share the same friends during my college years. The exception was that brief and uncomfortable romance with Elisa's friend Eileen. Elisa was a terrific student and had no problem avoiding television until all her homework was complete. It paid off. Elisa graduated from junior high in 1957 and was selected as salutatorian for getting the second highest grades in her class, a big achievement. She asked me for some suggestions on what to say before the large audience that assembled at the graduation ceremonies. Alexander Pope was my favorite wit and very quotable. I recommended some of his comments on education which Elisa used in her speech.

Elisa took piano lessons from Mr. Bottenberg who insisted that she cut her fingernails because they made tapping sounds on the keys. She also took up the guitar. My sister has always been good-natured and cheerful. Except for the normal sibling rivalry and squabbles, for which I accept all blame, we got on splendidly. This formed a solid foundation for a warm adult relationship, and we both look forward to seeing more of each other as the years pass.

Summer of 1959

In early 1959 I decided to apply for a summer job in Europe through a program called IAESTE (International Association for the Exchange of Students for Technical Experience). I selected three countries, and was assigned to work for the Danish Post and Telegraph in Copenhagen. From Europe I began to write letters home addressed to "Ma, Daddy and Elisa." These letters reveal my early affinity for the European experience. Now older and wiser, I cringe at some of the self-conscious and superficial observations which I penned so many years ago. However, this first trip to Europe, and the second one in 1961 which included North Africa and the Middle East, deeply shaped my future opinions and interests. These letters from 1959 reflect another world through the eyes of an impressionable young man tasting his first experience of independence in a foreign culture. [They are in the Appendix in the section entitled "A Young Traveler Writes Home."]

All too quickly my three-month summer in Europe was over. I returned to New York with all sorts of European affectations. I acquired a certain nod and a sucking of air which simulated the Danish habit of agreement. I felt more confident and worldly. My last year at CCNY could not end fast enough. The courses and professors were tough. By June, 1960, I took my last exams and received a BEE degree in Electrical Engineering. As with most of my class we interviewed the visiting employers and picked which of the numerous offers we liked best. I had five job offers.

Social Life 1960–63

In chapter 6 I will discuss how my work brought me to College Park, Maryland soon after graduation. Here, in this suburb outside Washington, DC, I lived in an attic apartment in a private home. During the day I worked at ACF Industries and in the evening and on weekends I spent time at the University of Maryland where I enrolled in a course on International Political Relations. I joined the Young Democrats and attended rallies in support of presidential candidate John Kennedy, and I had a busy social life dating some of the activist female students. For the first time in my life I got really drunk. It was at a Washington party. My date was scared to have me drive her home but somehow I managed. The next day I felt the misery of a hangover.

After six months I resigned from ACF Industries, packed up, left College Park and returned to New York. My parents urged me to study for a master's degree but I had my mind set on wandering around Europe and North Africa with a backpack. I left for Europe on February 28, 1961 on the S.S. *United States* bound for Southampton, England. I decided to head east for Israel. On my second trip to Europe I sent letters home to my parents and Elisa every few days for six months. (Excerpts are in the Appendix; one highpoint was my meeting with the author, James Michener.)

Summary of the 1961 Journey

Engineering was an exciting profession in the early 1960s, but travel and exploration of foreign cultures held a fascination for me not easily put aside. So, in 1961, I decided to take a break from my career and once again cross the Atlantic. This trip turned out to be a six-month odyssey. What follows is a summary of these early wanderings. The Appendix contains most of the correspondence with my parents during that trip. I was only twenty-three, and the impressions of Europe, North Africa and Israel accumulated during the 1959 and 1961 trips influenced my attitudes for the rest of my life.

The SS *United States* arrived in Southampton on March 3, 1961. I walked down the gangplank facing unknown and unplanned adventures. It was a moment of undiluted excitement. My travels took me south to Spain and into Morocco. From there I took a freighter, the Giovanni Tofolo, to France. Then, by train, I journeyed to Italy. From Florence I traveled South to Brindisi, took a ferry to Greece and another ship to Haifa. On the ship bound for Haifa I met a French student who invited me to join him on his way to a kibbutz.

We arrived, unexpected, at Ein Hachoresh, a very socialist kibbutz, and were soon settled in a small room with two mattresses on the floor. The same day we shed our clothes for kibbutz clothing from the communal laundry. The next day we were awakened by our boss who took us to a field full of rocks which we were instructed to put into wheelbarrows. Once filled, the wheelbarrows were rolled over to a flatbed truck. When the truck was filled it was driven off and when it returned empty we once again began to fill it up. After a few days of working like this in the hot sun I had enough and requested a transfer.

Soon I was working under the shade of plum trees picking fruit. This I found far more appealing. After work we showered and sauntered about before dinner in that relaxed state that comes from a day of physical toil.

At this kibbutz, the children lived together in a communal home and only visited the parents for a couple of hours each day. This permitted both parents to work outside the home and trained the children to cooperate within their peer group. Once we joined with other kibbutzim to sing and socialize.

Finally, my French friend and I bid farewell to our socialist employers and we set out to explore farther south. We parted in Beersheba and eventually, alone, I made my way up to Haifa. There I met a student named Ruth Rabi. Ruth had the dark olive skin of her Sephardic Mideastern ancestors and an intense personality. She was studying at Bar Ilan University. We really got to like each other and after I returned home we corresponded. She was ready for marriage but I was not. One day she could wait no more. I sometimes wonder what happened to her.

After leaving Israel I took a ship to Turkey and traveled overland west through Yugoslavia. It was in Yugoslavia that I finally lost my virginity. I rented a room on a ship/hotel anchored in the Morava River that runs through Belgrade. That evening I heard some tapping sounds on the wall of my cabin. I tapped back. There was more tapping. After a while there was a knock on the door. When I opened it a woman was standing there in a silk slip. She spoke absolutely no English. I invited her into my cabin and we made love. I was already twenty-three and accumulating some self-doubts. Probably the thrill of achievement equaled the physical pleasure. There were more romances on my return to England but now I was much more confident.

On a phone call home my parents informed me that the United States Selective Service had sent me a draft notice to join the army. I had to get back as soon as possible. It was September, 1961 and I had been away for six months.

I flew home from London in mid-September, 1961 and within two weeks found a job. On October 2, 1961, I began work at ITT Labs in Nutley, NJ designing defense electronics. My annual salary was $7,665. With this job, I was able to legally avoid the draft by receiving what was called a "critical skills deferment."

Now all I wanted was to meet European women. I found International House on the Upper West Side of Manhattan. At one of their parties I met Maria. Maria was twelve years older than I but she had a warm smile and jolly disposition. She was from Northern Ireland and worked as a secretary to one of the executives at International House. Maria shared an apartment with her girl friend Violet on West End Avenue near 73rd Street. For the next year and a half I saw Maria. We grew very attached. While I lived with my parents, I would spend weekends with Maria. I bought a Triumph TR3 sports car and Maria and I would go away on day trips. Once we took a long trip to Canada in the car. With my regular visits to Manhattan and my increasing independence I decided to move out of my parents' home. Maria helped me find a small studio apartment on East 51st Street. But as time went by I realized I was not going to marry Maria. I felt she was too old for me and with sadness and guilt I decided to end our relationship. First I tried a gradual approach. But this did not work. So one day I just ended it totally. There were lots of tears. A year and half is a long time when you are twenty-five.

After Maria, I dated a married woman who was separated from her husband but still sharing a house with him. She would drive in from New Jersey in her station wagon. When I called to speak with her, her husband answered the phone. It was all quite confusing and I was getting more uncomfortable with each date. That relationship soon ended.

After breaking up with Maria I did not want to return to International House where we might inadvertently meet. Instead I found the Midtown International Center where young foreign people also gathered. There I became a volunteer and soon had a small circle of foreign friends. There was Reggie from Jamaica, Arnon from Israel, Eliane from Belgium and others from Scandinavia and the U.K.

During 1963 I met an American secretary who was about three years older than I. She was sweet but nervous. Before I met her, she had once tried to commit suicide. While I was seeing her, I met Patricia. I wanted to break off the relationship with the secretary but she was hospitalized for an infection. I visited her at the hospital and, when she was released, I just stopped calling. Perhaps it was a cruel way to end it. The single life was becoming emotionally exhausting. Meeting new women was fun, but ending the relationship was not. Getting rejected, or doing the rejecting, was emotionally painful. I felt it was time to settle down with one life partner.

Part II

The Responsible Years

5
Patricia and Rachel

You know how it is: you're twenty-one or twenty-two and you make some decisions; then whisssh! you're seventy... and that white-haired lady at your side has eaten over fifty thousand meals with you.
—Thorton Wilder, *Our Town*, 1938

Early Days with Patricia

I first met Patricia Mary Robertson Staff at the Midtown International Center in October, 1963. The Center was then located directly behind Carnegie Hall and served as a social club for young foreigners working in the New York area. Patricia had arrived in Newark, NJ only two weeks earlier from England, to start work as a nurse at Beth Israel Hospital. She planned to work her way around the world. I was a volunteer at the Center. I would help out making the visiting foreigners feel more at home in New York. It was also a good way to meet foreign girls. That evening I was immediately attracted to this slim, blond young woman. After introducing myself and chatting for a while we agreed to see each other again. Patricia had a strong personality. Although quiet, her views were well-defined. She had this strong sense of what was morally right or wrong. I was very impressed. Our dates were modest. I was saving my money. Little did I know then, that my Spartan habits were exactly what appealed to Patricia. Showering her with extravagant dinners and gifts probably would have turned her off me. Without knowing it, my faults were assets. However, our backgrounds were very different. Patricia was Protestant, her mother Scottish and her father English. She had the good manners and consideration for others that I lacked. But she must have seen some good in me.

We decided to get married only three months after meeting. I suppose I felt the time was right and I was not likely to meet anyone nicer. Telesignal Corporation had just laid me off. So being unemployed made it even more convenient to leave for England. Patricia wrote to her parents, Sidney and Elizabeth Staff, and I told my parents. My father was greatly disappointed that I was not marrying a Jewish girl. My mother accepted the news much more readily and helped my father come around to the fact. Over the years my father's attitude towards Patricia changed remarkably. He began to see her strength of character and courage during the time we worked together at FA Components (a business we started some years later). He came to love her deeply and his efforts in Forest Hills in bringing together the Protestant, Catholic and Jewish communities were a demonstration of this wider world view.

We were married June 6, 1964 in Surrey, England. I recollect feelings of fear and doubt as I suddenly realized the big step we were both taking. Patricia and I had many differences and during our engagement period we were discovering some of them. She had a temper and moods which I was not familiar with. I had habits that annoyed her. We argued frequently. But something kept us together during that period and in the years ahead. I suppose we were drawn to each other by a powerful attraction neither of us understood. No argument, no matter how serious it seemed, could overwhelm this emotional attraction. I still can't explain it. Added to the differences in culture we had different interests. Patricia loved high culture, opera, ballet and concerts. She read widely, generally good fiction, biographies of performing artists, adventure travel and poetry. My interests were much narrower and centered around the physical sciences and technical subjects. But we had a convergence of interests, also, which included backpacking, walking and good films. That was luck since we only found this out sometime after we got married. And we had a convergence of values which was probably more important than either of us knew. Human chemistry—it's quite mysterious, really. Sometimes, after over thirty years of marriage, I look at Patricia and wonder who is this person? How did we manage to make our marriage work?

Before the marriage date we traveled up to Scotland together to meet Patricia's maternal relatives. This was when I discovered Patricia's natural athletic stamina. I challenged her to a race along a quiet Scottish road. I ran ahead and after about half a mile, puffing heavily, I looked back. There was Patricia keeping easily behind me. Finally, after two miles, I couldn't go any farther. Gasping for air I waited as Patricia soon came up to me. She was breathing normally as if we had just been standing still.

Back in Berrylands the marriage day was approaching fast. The wedding lunch was to be held at a nice hotel at Hampton Court on the

River Thames. I was meeting many people, future relatives. There was Peter, Patricia's brother. Peter one day told me to take off my shoes. I refused and we were soon engaged in a ridiculous mock struggle on the kitchen floor. Well, it was a good way to get to know about my brother-in-law. My father-in-law was a very traditional Englishman. He had a handkerchief tucked in his sleeve. He dressed up for dinner. Sidney has a quick wit and is a fine storyteller.

Dinner itself was more formal than what I was accustomed to in Brooklyn. Food was passed about in an orderly way. The eating utensils were placed in well-defined positions around the plate. There was a special knife and fork for fish. Everyone chewed their food very quietly. I could see I was going to have a lot of adjustments to make. Elizabeth, Patricia's mother, was Scottish, full of humor and a zest for life. She did her best to make me feel accepted and comfortable. The wedding itself went smoothly. I made a little speech thanking everyone and soon we were off on a 6-month honeymoon, backpacking through Spain, Morocco, Italy and Switzerland.

I was using up my savings and, without a job awaiting me in the United States, we finally returned to New York in the winter of 1964. We lived temporarily with my parents at Rockaway Parkway while I set about to look for employment. I soon had two offers. One was at RCA in Princeton, NJ and the other was Sperry Gyroscope in Great Neck. Since Sperry was closer to New York I chose it. Shortly thereafter we moved to a studio apartment on East 34th Street near First Avenue in Manhattan. I bought a Corvair automobile and commuted to Sperry via the Midtown tunnel which was right next to our apartment. Patricia began nursing at NYU Hospital after obtaining her New York State RN license. In those early days of our marriage we still had many of our single friends from the Midtown International Center. Gradually our activities and friends were changing as we settled into married life. One morning I walked to the Corvair only to discover someone had crashed into it overnight. The rear engine car was totally destroyed.

Since we were planning to have a family, the apartment would be too small. I made friends at Sperry and one of them, Al Lipsky, suggested we look at apartments where he lived in Fresh Meadows, Queens. We moved to 67-15 192nd Street, Fresh Meadows, in 1966. The apartment was a one-bedroom duplex in a garden community and much closer to work. We purchased a new gray Ford Mustang convertible. About this time Patricia became pregnant, but the baby was born prematurely and died after several hours. A second pregnancy produced our daughter, Rachel, born on August 27, 1967. Patricia's mother, Elizabeth, came over and stayed with us in Fresh Meadows to help Patricia before and after Rachel's birth. Rachel's first five years were spent at 67-15 192nd Street. But we soon needed a second bedroom. We moved to a larger apartment in Fresh Meadows. Then, in 1974, we bought a small home at 73-37 182nd Street, Fresh Meadows. We remained there until late 1983 when we moved back to Manhattan, this time to Park Avenue.

We went on holidays to Penobscot Bay, Maine. On a nearby farm we would sit at the feet of the guru of the "vegetarian socialists," Scott Nearing. This ninety-five-year-old gentleman pitched hay and worked a full day on his organic farm, and in the evening lectured visitors on the joys of disconnecting from the System. We stayed in a cottage owned by a Maine fishing family. The avuncular patriarch Father Venno would charm his guests while the huge family library provided ample reading material. During warm sunny days we would swim in the icy water of Penobscot Bay while seals randomly popped up to peer at our blue faces before submerging again. From time to time our hosts would organize a lobster party. Their fishing boat would carry us and other guests to a nearby island. Seaweed and saltwater would be added to the bottom of a fifty-five-gallon drum on top of which was placed a huge pile of live lobsters. They were soon steamed and consumed but long remembered. Those were sweet moments in our young married days.

Once we went to Mexico and once to Bermuda with Rachel. And we took long weekend trips to the North Fork of Long Island with my parents. There at the Sunset Motel near Orient Point we spent quiet times with my folks as we watched fishermen, the waves and the sea.

Rachel was sent over to England to spend several summers and holidays with Patricia's parents. Thus Rachel was getting a true Anglo-American upbringing. I also wanted Rachel to have some sense of her Jewish background and so we sent her to the Hillcrest Jewish Center for religious training. This did not last long as she soon got bored and I did not set a very good example by being almost totally nonobservant. I joined Hillcrest, but mainly for its sauna and the inspiring lectures of the brilliant Rabbi Moshowitz at his Sunday morning breakfast. The sauna was, for a while, my favorite place to be. There, in the basement of the Center and concentrated in a small very hot wooden room, assembled a most talkative and assertive group of Jews. I do not know which produced more heat, the 2,000-watt electric stove or the sound and fury generated by the occupants. Since the heat limited one's visit to about fifteen minutes, there was an urgency. To make your point within that period, one had to get the drift of the conversation and then somehow insert comments into the discussion.

During 1968 Patricia was asked by a gallery owner if she would consider photographic fashion modeling. She agreed as it seemed like fun, and he sent her to the Ford Agency. They immediately sent her to their photographers. Patricia followed up on only a few of the many offers she received during 1968–69. Most involved travel and, by the autumn of 1968, Patricia preferred to spend more time with young Rachel rather than take assignments away from New York.

During early 1968 I got restless and wanted to travel on my own. We agreed that I would travel for about three months while Patricia continued her photographic fashion modeling. So, during the summer of 1968, I took a leave without pay from Reeves Instruments and I traveled mainly in Europe and Russia, while Rachel spent two months in England with her maternal grandparents.

My travels took me through France, Switzerland, Italy, Yugoslavia and Romania. In Bucharest I met a lively group of Italians driving into Russia. They invited me along for what turned into a hilarious journey. Their high-powered Mini Coopers, modest-looking little vehicles, seemed to average ninety miles per hour as we raced towards Odessa. The stern Soviet authorities repeatedly confronted these charming exuberant young Italians who simply refused to take no for an answer. We varied our route from the official Intourist plan. Chickens flew in all directions as the Italian armada of Mini Coopers roared through peaceful Ukrainian villages. Whether in Odessa, Kiev or Moscow the Italians would quickly find their countrymen who would in turn advise them on where to get rubles at the highest black market rate and where to find the best restaurants. Whenever we sat down to dine, our leader, Mimo, would count heads in our group and order an equal number of bottles of champagne. Ten people meant ten bottles. We ordered food in similar quantities along with huge amounts of caviar. Black market rubles made everything cheap.

Finally we reached Moscow. Mimo and I went to an amusement park. "Look," he said, "isn't that strange?" I looked at the carnival ride whipping Russians about. "What is strange, Mimo?" I asked. "No one is laughing," he said.

The Italians were heading west from Moscow, but they would have to avoid Czechoslovakia which had just been invaded by the Russians. I missed Patricia. I called home and found out that she had gone to England to be with Rachel. I called Patricia in England and arranged to meet her in Stockholm.

It was thrilling to be reunited with Patricia. We spent a couple of weeks traveling around Sweden and Norway before returning to England. Rachel had grown and now had curly blond hair. After visiting

Jay and Patricia, wedding day, June 6, 1964, England.

Patricia, 1971.

Patricia's parents, Elizabeth and Sidney Staff, England 1977.

Rachel with her father, Bermuda, 1977.

Patricia's parents, we flew home to Fresh Meadows. I returned to my job at Reeves Instruments but did not stay there very long. I resigned after several months and began work at Litton Industries. Patricia stopped modeling and, once Rachel began first grade classes, resumed her nursing career at the Long Island Jewish Hospital and the North Shore Hospital in Nassau County.

Like many of our age in the 1970s, we experimented with marijuana. During this period we began to spend time with a cousin, his wife and some of their friends. Often we met in our home in Fresh Meadows. Reggie, our Jamaican friend from the days of the Midtown International Center, was our supplier. We had quite a few absurd gatherings. Being a nonsmoker, it took me some effort to inhale the marijuana smoke but soon the effects were apparent. Conversations seemed to be a series of unconnected statements. There appeared to be double meanings to what people were saying. Sometimes I would laugh and others wouldn't see the humor or it was the other way around. As if by some secret signal, the entire group would become hungry. Patricia would cook a huge amount of spaghetti or run out and buy large rich pies from the nearby "Four and Twenty Pies." The group would eat enormous amounts of food at these "pot parties." I recall how delicious the food seemed, how I savored the taste and texture as the food was chewed. I felt my throat muscles working to bring the food down to the stomach. The mind was very concentrated on these sensual experiences which we normally ignore.

One day Reggie came over in a foul mood. Patricia and I were hurt by his rambling and angry assertions about how we were becoming very middle class and typical. It was the last time we saw Reggie. That really ended our "pot parties." But it was all just as well. I am glad we had that experience; it was a part of the 1970s. After a while, however, the evenings under the influence of the drug seemed silly and nothing intelligent was ever said, in spite of what we might have thought at the moment.

In the mid 1970s I took the test for Mensa, a club for people with IQs within the top 2 percent of the population. I passed and we went to a number of social gatherings for a few years. Not only were the members bright, they were mostly eccentric underachievers. However, we had some stimulating and funny evenings. Since there were more literary types at these gatherings than scientific types, the conversation often turned to books. Patricia actually had more to contribute than I did.

We decided during this period to get a pet kitten. It was a small orange animal and we called him September after the month he arrived

Our Pet Cats: Very reluctantly I agreed to living with these animals. This uneasy co-habitation lasted seventeen years.

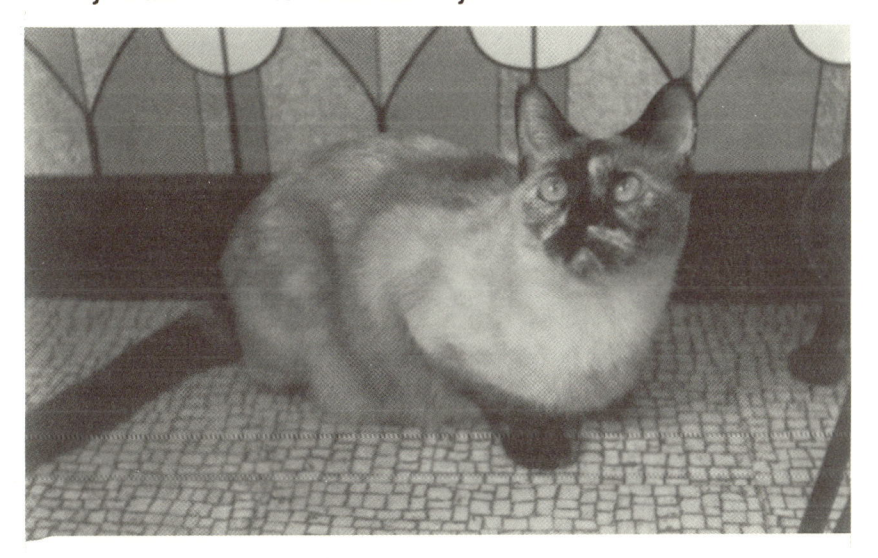

Thistle: Really quite a nice animal for a cat. She purred a lot and would rub up against your legs. Put some honey on your feet and she would give you a sensual tongue licking.

Clover: A neurotic animal with a well-developed paranoia. Specialized in hissing, skulking, and scratching.

We spent great weekends with my parents at Sunset Motel, Greenport, LI in the 1980s. Here my dad pulls raft from the Sound, tossing Patricia into the ocean.

Lunch at Sunset Motel, Greenport, with my parents, 1980s.

On trip to British Columbia we prepare to raft down some rapids, 1980s.

at our home. I liked September, but one day after scouting the neighborhood he came back very ill. We rushed September to the veterinarian but it was too late. September died from eating something poisonous. A few months later Patricia and Rachel came home with a cat-carrying box and out jumped two kittens. I objected, saying I had only agreed to one kitten when we got September and his replacement should only be one kitten. But they both pleaded with me, saying that the two kittens were sisters and it would be cruel to separate them. It was hopeless to argue. They were named Thistle and Clover, which are popular flowers in Scotland. Thistle was well-adjusted but Clover was a neurotic animal who saw threats everywhere. She hissed, scratched and bit at the slightest provocation. Clover lived about sixteen years and Thistle eighteen years. Both cats developed kidney disease and eventually each had to be put to sleep by the veterinarian. Patricia brought Clover down to the vet for the last time. When it was Thistle's last trip I went along. Thistle died quietly in Patricia's arms as the narcotic and heart-stopping drug was injected into one of her front paws. Once again I went into a state of depression. Too bad that cats and dogs do not live as long as tortoises or parrots; then they could mourn our passing.

In the 1980s, my income increased dramatically as my business flourished. In 1983, I earned more than in the all the years from 1960–82 combined. We bought a Fiat Spyder sports car, which looked great, but the engineering was so lousy it kept breaking down. We then leased the entrepreneur's favorite, the Mercedes 380SL sports car. In spite of this display of conspicuous consumption, we really lacked the imagination of true materialists. We bought no yachts, planes or villas on exotic shores. For us the thrill was being able to purchase a good backpack or a meal without worrying about the cost.

Rachel Grows Up

During these years Rachel grew up and so did we. When her public school did not meet our expectations we enrolled her in Lenox, a private junior high school on the Upper East Side. Rachel commuted from Fresh Meadows each day for two years. However, I felt she should be in contact with a normal cross section of students instead of just "rich kids" so she passed the examination and was accepted into the Bronx High School of Science. While her grades were high, we felt they were not deserved. Everyone at Bronx Science seemed to be getting high grades. Rachel was getting no personalized attention at this huge public school. So, under the advice of a guidance counselor, we enrolled Rachel at the famous sleep-away girls' school, Miss Porter's, in Farmington, CT, about halfway through her high school education.

At Miss Porter's, grades were not inflated and Rachel soon saw her first low marks on examinations and report cards. She cried when those first marks came in. But the teachers were highly motivated and knew each student in depth. The report card was in the form of slips of paper on which an entire paragraph described the strengths, weaknesses and progress Rachel was making. As she completed each term her grades improved and so did Rachel's spirit. The traditions and friends she made at Miss Porter's stayed with her into her adult years and it was probably the high point of her student days. I was so impressed with the school I gave them a large gift of equipment for their Computer Room. They offered to name the room after me or Rachel but I never followed up on the suggestion.

From Miss Porter's, Rachel applied to numerous colleges. She and Patricia visited them in Pennsylvania and New England but, finally, Skidmore College was chosen. Skidmore was once an all-girls' school but had converted to coeducation. Its large campus was located on the edge of Saratoga Springs, a town known for its race track and thermal water. Rachel enjoyed her four years at Skidmore. I must say I was

Patricia and me, Washington, D.C., May 1977.

Young Rachel, age four,
in Fresh Meadows.

A hairline fracture of the left fibula and neck sprain after careless step coming down Ben Nevis, Scotland, November 1989.

North Cape march begins, Honnigsvag, Norway, June, 1994.

surprised at the cozy and informal life in a co-ed dorm. The boys and girls shared the same bathrooms and constantly visited each others' rooms to chat. In her third year at Skidmore Rachel decided to participate in an exchange program with Edinburgh University in Scotland. So in 1988 she spent one year there. Rachel fell in love with Edinburgh and the students she met. After completing her final year at Skidmore she returned to Scotland, finding temporary work in radio programming and film production. In 1992 she began studies toward a Ph.D. with the objective of living there for several years. A problem developed. Rachel was an American citizen. Obtaining a work permit and permanent status in Britain is extremely difficult. She just did not fall into any category that would make it easy. We learned the following. If she were from a commonwealth country it would have been easy. If we had elected, before her 18th birthday, to become a dual citizen it would have been easy. We had overlooked this option. In spite of this oversight, if Rachel had a British father instead of a British mother it would have been easy. If Rachel was born after 1980 and either parent was British it would have been easy. The illogic of these rules all excluded Rachel from gaining the right to stay permanently in Britain. The rules on obtaining work permits were just as difficult as citizenship. It was necessary to show that her skills were so unique that no one in Britain could do the same thing. An employer had to prove this by advertising the position that Rachel sought, to first see if any British citizens would apply with those qualifications. As a young student, of course, she had no such exotic experience.

In the meantime, Rachel was permitted to remain in Scotland with a temporary student visa which was good until she completed her degree. Fortunately, or unfortunately, this was taking longer than anyone expected. The area of study Rachel selected dealt with the oral traditions and folklore of the people of the Hebrides and how it influenced their attitudes towards the environment in which they lived. Rachel made frequent trips to Lewis off the western coast of Scotland. Patricia and I, and my folks, had the pleasure of joining her on visits to this rugged rocky island. On Lewis, crofters sheep-farmed, harvested peat and lived a quiet, rural life. Rachel got to be well-known and liked by the local folk as she joined in the sheep shearing, cut the peat, interviewed them and studied their attitudes and recollections.

We visited Rachel in Edinburgh regularly and in 1994 we helped in purchasing an apartment for her near the center of Edinburgh. It was a large Georgian style flat on the second floor of a small apartment building. Rachel now came to know the joys and frustrations of property ownership. Extensive repairs were required before and after Rachel moved in. The walls needed plastering and painting. The floors were rough and had big gaps between the planks which needed filling. The kitchen and bathrooms had old or broken fixtures needing replacement. Patricia and I visited Rachel soon after she moved in and we spent about ten happy days buying, assembling and painting whatever it needed after the professionals had completed the bigger tasks.

In early 1995 Rachel's graduate advisor died suddenly. This was traumatic, especially as it turned out he had not been guiding her properly. New advisors reviewed her work and took a firm hand in refocusing her efforts on the thesis. This was a time of great distress for Rachel and for us. There were moments when we all believed that her years of work would be rejected by the school. Rachel felt as if she were letting us down. I told her that I had dropped out of my masters' studies at Brooklyn Polytechnic Institute when I found it had no relevance to my work. She might find the same to be true in her case. Rachel wanted to work in communications, which might include film production or writing and producing radio segments. Her studies had a rather tenuous connection to the work she sought after graduation. Both Patricia and I had only feelings of pride in Rachel's accomplishments. She had chosen a difficult path in life both in her studies and work plans. This took courage, independence and imagination. Patricia and I were pleased to help her at any point on this steep road and, if she faltered at any point, so what. The bravery was in the trying and in the struggle and this was the source of our pride.

The Empty Nest

Although Rachel lived at Miss Porter's School from the age of sixteen, she would come home during the holidays, many weekends and the summer recess. The same was true for her years at Skidmore. Starting in 1989, she lived in Scotland. Now Patricia and I were truly "empty nesters." The 1990s was a period of adjustment to my very early retirement. Patricia resumed nursing on a per-diem basis at St. Luke's AIDS unit in 1989 and stopped in 1995. She then began spending her Fridays at an AIDS hospice in Greenwich Village and Tuesday mornings at a shelter and soup kitchen in the South Bronx. We spent our time together going to films, eating in restaurants, reading, socializing with friends and planning our next adventurous holiday.

My tastes in film have always been eclectic. I enjoy high and low comedy, slapstick, sarcasm, cynicism and irony as long as it is well done. I enjoy historical films, romance, mysteries, psychological studies and science fiction. Although I once enjoyed films with lots of violence, they are getting repetitious.

As for restaurants, we eat out three to five times a week in New York. In the 1990s my favorite ethnic food changed from Italian to Japanese. Often I can be found at an East Side sushi bar consuming yellowtail, eel or salmon sushi washed down with hot sake. Since Patricia does not like sushi, she might be found at that moment consuming a grilled cheese on toast or pancakes at some local diner. I still enjoy Italian food, especially if I am very hungry. There is no shortage of good Italian restaurants in our neighborhood but my favorite is Mezzaluna, where the espresso and cappuccino are perfection. The Lenox Room and Daniel are fancier formal restaurants for special occasions. And the Pamir is a friendly Afghan restaurant on 2nd Avenue which we go to from time to time. Patricia and I also like Indian food and our favorite restaurant for this cuisine is Dawat. Food is one of the great pleasures of life. The older cultures of Continental Europe realize this, but most Americans are too busy rushing around to pay food the respect and attention it deserves. It is a privilege to live in New York where the European attitude towards food is emulated perhaps more than in any other city in the United States.

Patricia is a voracious reader. I read far less, although the preparation of this autobiography has increased my interest in reading the works of other writers. My favorite magazines are *Scientific American*, the *Economist* and *Backpacker*. We get the *New York Times* delivered daily to our apartment door.

After retirement I became increasingly drawn to my computer. I spend some hours each day surfing the Internet and watching the stock market. In the morning I rose and turned on the machine almost reflexively. I would then log on to Prodigy, a value-added Internet access provider. There I joined chat rooms where I could communicate with other addicts. The chat rooms had titles denoting the common interest of the folks who would gather there. The rooms had names such as Teen Chat, Over 20, Over 30, Over 40, Over 50, Trivial Pursuit, Lesbian Room and Meet Your Mate. There were dozens of these rooms. My favorite was the Over 40 room because, although I was older than most, it was always crowded with a lively bunch. Each room held up to twenty-five people and whatever you typed on the keyboard, all in the room could read it on their computer screens. After a while I got to know the regulars who gathered there each morning. While most of the chatter was banal, it was at least interactive banality as opposed to the passive variety on television. At times the exchanges could become

Rachel, 1995.

Patricia, 1996.

quite amusing and I found it a nice way to greet the day with a few familiar names and personalities for which dressing was not required.

We all had chat nicknames. Some of the regulars were called Arilove, Anne49, Clamette, Annie810, Sweetgator, Buttafli, Wildcard and Willow. I called myself Nerdbird and my motto was "better to be over the hill than under it." This was cyberspace, a community without a physical presence, dispersed geographically yet united by some common interest. Since communication is through the keyboard, a key stroke shorthand has emerged. LOL means laughing out loud. Or if something very funny happens then ROFL could be used to express "rolling on the floor laughing," or ROFLMAO for "rolling on the floor laughing my ass off." If you wanted to hug someone as they "entered" a room then brackets were typed around the name. For example ((((Nerdbird)))))) was often what I would see on my screen a few moments after entering a room. Typing in capital letters was the same as shouting. "Emoticons" were keyboard symbols that expressed emotions. For example a smile was expressed as :) and a frown was :(

The Internet and cyberspace were advancing at a revolutionary pace through the mid-1990s. The major technological limitation was the bandwidth of the communication line. Microprocessor power, memory size and speed had all progressed rapidly, but it was the phone line that limited the speed of data transfer. Images still took too long to paint themselves onto my monitor. On the horizon I could see clearly the joining of the television cable with the personal computer, permitting rapid transfer of not only still images but animated video. When that day arrives it will be the start of enormous changes in the way information is obtained and shared. I envy the next generation for the fascinating challenges that this will present to them.

From an empty nest one can have a pretty good view in all directions. This attraction to the Internet and the personal computer, during my retirement, was an extension of the path taken during my working life. In the next chapter I will discuss how I ended up in the computer distribution business. It took twenty working years to get there after graduation and seven years to succeed and exit.

6
Engineer to Entrepreneur

No one knows what he can do, till he tries.
—Maxims of Publius Syrus, 1st Century B.C.

Perhaps once in a generation, a new industry is created which transforms society. The personal computer industry certainly has had this effect. You could date its beginnings from the late 1970s when the Apple II was launched. Even the founders of Apple at that time could not have guessed the applications and markets waiting for their small computer and its successors. The early 1980s witnessed explosive growth in new products, applications and markets. The industry beckoned to a wide range of engineers, programmers, hackers, salespeople and entrepreneurs. They came from other more stable industries and entered a world of rapid change.

I was one of these individuals. Let me explain what brought me to personal computers, how I built a $50 million/year distribution business, the high moments and the low, and finally how I exited. I hope that through my experiences the reader will be able to understand not so much the technical changes in the personal computer industry, but the cultural changes. These are not so obvious but have a real impact on how business is conducted and who rises to leadership.

In the early 1960s most of the interesting electronic design work was in the defense industry. The Cold War was in full force and America's military budget was large and growing. While there was a modest need for engineers in commercial work such as TV and radio design, the costly leading edge of technology could only be funded by the U.S. Department of Defense or a few large technology companies. Complex radar, sonar and communications equipment with big development costs and short production runs required large numbers of engineers. I became a digital logic designer and quickly learned to use the new integrated circuits. My career was launched with idealism and enthusiasm. Electronic engineering can be highly absorbing work full of wonderful problem-solving tasks. However, the lack of recognition began to bother me. No one seemed to understand exactly what I was doing. If I came up with a smart solution to a design problem there was no one with whom I could share the excitement. Primarily, the supervisors wanted to know when I expected to complete the assignment. The real center of attention and power in these companies seemed to come from sales, marketing and top management. Engineers seemed relegated to being clever drones and best kept in the back room somewhere.

This situation frustrated me and my dissatisfaction grew. Changing jobs in engineering did not help matters. While I broadened my experience, the back room syndrome remained a constant source of irritation. It all began after graduation from CCNY Engineering School.

Engineering 1960-70

My first job was with American Cable and Radio at 60 Broad Street in the financial district of Manhattan. ACR laid and managed transatlantic undersea cables for telephone communications. The cables had amplifiers every thirty miles which used old vacuum tube technology. Along with other young engineers, I was hired to redesign these amplifiers using transistors. ACR in 1960 had some old engineers from another era. These fellows parted their hair down the middle and wore three-piece suits. Our department had to overcome the tradition and inertia of these older engineers who believed in vacuum tubes and did not trust the new solid-state electronics. Every day I got on my Vespa motor scooter and rode from 196 Rockaway Parkway into Manhattan. Once I skidded and fell off. Even though my suit was ripped and I had abrasions, I carried on to the office and put in a full day. Such was my early devotion and motivation.

However, after three months, the spirit of adventure called. I answered an advertisement placed by ACF Industries for a field engineering job. It would mean moving to College Park, MD and learning about radio back scatter. After six months of training, the employer would send me to a remote site in the Mideast or Northern Alaska. For eighteen months I would live in a trailer filled with electronic equipment. We would be listening for disturbances in the ionosphere caused by nuclear explosions. This was top secret work and I was thrilled with the idea. Living in College Park was fun. The nearby University of Maryland offered night courses and I enrolled in one on International

Political Relations. During the day I attended courses given by my employer on radio back scatter and ionospheric physics. They sent me for a battery of psychological tests to be sure I was stable enough to live in confined quarters with other field engineers. Afterwards the psychologist gave me his analysis. He said he would recommend me, but I would not last in the program. I would get bored. He also told me I had a dominant aggressive personality that was concealed. This came as a big surprise to me.

In any case, he was right about leaving the program. My employer assigned me to the remote North Alaska site and I wanted the Mideast. But because I was "of the Hebrew faith" he could not risk upsetting the local governments. So I resigned and gave two weeks notice. To keep me busy they gave me a pile of disorganized data on a super-heated steam rocket and asked me to sort it out. I really got involved and worked late at night on the project, finally delivering a detailed report showing that had the rocket ever been released it could have climbed to two miles. I used equations of motion refined by air resistance and diminishing weight as the rocket climbed. My employer liked the report and offered me another job in their research department if I agreed to stay. But I had set my mind on traveling overseas. "Well," he said, "you are free, white and twenty-one."

I returned to Brooklyn and soon thereafter left on an ocean liner for Europe. It was at this point that I took time off to backpack around Europe and North Africa. In 1961, travel by ship was about the same price as by air. For six months I wandered about Europe and North Africa. I got as far east as Israel. (This trip was summarized in chapter 4 and is detailed in the Appendix.)

Just as I was ending my European travels, my parents advised me by mail that the draft board was after me. I quickly returned home and got a job with ITT in Nutley, NJ. (See my correspondence from 1961). Since I was working for a defense contractor, I was able to get a critical skills deferment. But it was close. I had already received the famous "Greetings" letter with a subway token attached, inviting me down to the induction center for the one-way trip to boot camp. I moved to Nutley, NJ and lived in a rented room. The work at ITT was interesting but I got into trouble because I refused to wear a suit. Instead, I arrived at work each morning in a sports shirt, no tie and no jacket. My boss said he did not mind but the government customers who visited would think I was a technician rather than an engineer. It's hard to believe now, but I got fired over this dress code issue.

My next job I held for two years. I joined Telesignal Corporation in late 1961. The company was founded by a very urbane, sophisticated

European by the name of Anatole Minc. Telesignal manufactured communications equipment for the military. My assignment was to develop an error-correcting system for use in northern latitudes which are plagued by erratic ionospheric conditions. Without going into technical details, I came up with a very novel solution which greatly impressed my boss, the VP Engineering, Norman Neeson.

About the time the equipment was ready for testing I met Patricia and was seeing her once or twice a week. I was assigned to go to Goose Bay, Labrador, and another employee was assigned to the other end of the communications link, England. Not only was I going to be away from Patricia, I was being sent to a bleak air base at wintertime, in northern Canada. Reluctantly I packed. Patricia accompanied me late one night to McGuire Air Force Base. There I was issued a special cold weather parka, thermal clothing and mukluks (Eskimo boots). The Department of Defense issued me a Certificate of Identity for noncombatants, dated December 6, 1963, describing me as a Project Engineer with the rank of major. My listed weight on the card was 141 pounds, so I was still quite skinny.

Goose Bay Air Force Base was covered in snow. Each building had cots and emergency food for whiteouts and blizzards. In the morning the weather report would tell us if we could go outside. I lived in barracks with air force personnel. During off hours they took me fishing on the frozen Hamilton River. Inside an overheated shack, and through a hole cut in the ice, we hauled in hundreds of smelts in a couple of hours. Goose Bay was fun but I was missing Patricia. This was at a critical point in our developing relationship. The tests were dragging on for weeks. I phoned Anatole Minc and pleaded with him to let me go home. But in the end I did the right thing and stuck it out until the tests were completed.

In early 1964, Telesignal lost business and had a layoff. So once again I was out of work. Patricia and I decided to get married. Being unemployed meant I could take a long honeymoon in Europe.

Returning from Europe in late 1964, we temporarily stayed with my folks in Brooklyn. I began working for Sperry Gyroscope in Great Neck. Sperry was a large sprawling facility and the first home of the United Nations before the Manhattan site was completed. The plant employed 10,000 people and the central corridor, called Broadway, was over half a mile long. Workers would use large tricycles to get from one end to another. I was assigned to the Anti Submarine Warfare Group, which employed about 600 engineers, physicists, mathematicians, technicians, draftsmen and machinists. We were working on a project called PAIR (Performance, and Integration Retrofit). This sonar system would be able to detect friend or foe with greatly enhanced accuracy. Each system cost the U.S. Defense Department $5 million and, as my boss once told me, it only replaced a good pair of human ears.

At Sperry I lunched with a very nice group of engineers including Herb Gillis, Sol Rubin, Leon Sternick and Al Lipsky. Al became one of my best friends and it was he who suggested we move to Fresh Meadows, where he lived with his wife Sandy and their daughter Sharon. I also met Barry Rubenstein, a younger engineer. I helped teach him logic design and we spent a lot of time talking about the stock market which was really Barry's passion. Barry would reappear at a number of turning points in my life story.

I was appointed a reviewer of the other engineers' work. This was flattering recognition that I was competent but it was uncomfortable exposing the flaws in colleagues' work. We could not cover it up but had to report these errors to the engineer and his superior. In 1966, I submitted an electronic circuit to a contest run by a trade magazine. First I won Best Circuit of the Month, and then Best Circuit of the Year. *Electronic Design Magazine* sent me a check for $1,000, which Patricia and I used to buy new bedroom furniture.

I worked at Sperry till 1967 and then quit and joined Reeves Instruments in Garden City to work on radar systems. My boss, Tom Riley, was cheerful and outgoing and I enjoyed my time at Reeves. In 1969, Barry Rubenstein phoned me with an offer to join a new start-up company called Applied Digital Data Systems. This company was funded by a Wall Street "whiz kid" named Liam Lowin who wore braids and an Indian headband. Barry had some founders' stock and had helped put the company together. The president was William Catacosinos, the impressive former senior executive at Brookhaven Laboratories who later would run Long Island Lighting Company. I was promised shares in the new company in addition to my salary. I agreed and left Reeves Instruments.

ADDS later became a major supplier of data terminals, but at that time it had about ten employees. During a tour Catacosinos was giving to some investors, he referred to our small group of engineers as "good boys." Well, I was thirty-two years old at the time and getting sensitive about being considered a boy. Perhaps design engineering was for younger men. Perhaps it was time to get out and try to make a transition into marketing or planning.

My feelings must have communicated themselves to others. In any case, I had an argument with my boss, David Ophir, the Vice President of Engineering at ADDS, and was soon out on the street looking for work.

Product Planning and Business Experience 1970-79

This time I sent my résumé to firms seeking marketing or planning executives with engineering backgrounds. I got a job with a small "think tank" called Marcom in 1970. They specialized in futurology: forecasting and long-range planning for large corporations. I worked as a junior consultant on a project to forecast the communications needs for IBM ten to fifteen years into the future. The technique was based on the assumption that the only research and development to be commercialized is that which satisfies a societal need. Another assumption was that the time frame to go from the laboratory to the marketplace takes ten–fifteen years. To forecast we would link current trends, such as people's desires to communicate faster and at lower cost, to current laboratory work in satellite data transmission, fiber optics and microwaves. Ultimately, a picture of the future would emerge and out of this a recommendation to our client.

I assisted a creative, urbane gentleman named Dr. Smith. He and other members of the think tank were more sophisticated and possessed a wider educational background than my former engineering colleagues. Another colleague was Ed Kaufman, who would later become a friend. The work environment at times reminded me of the academic world, especially when we engaged in brainstorming the connective links that led to the future. This was heady stuff and I enjoyed it. Then a recession hit and I learned that the first thing major corporations do when it comes time to reduce costs is to stop using consultants.

All of us were asked to take a salary cut. I knew this was the beginning of the end for Marcom, so with only nine months of consulting experience I was once again in the job market.

This time I accepted a job as New Products Manager for Ideal Corporation, a manufacturer of hose clamps and auto parts, located in one of Brooklyn's shabbier sections. The company, which was founded about forty years earlier, employed about 1,000 people, and was managed privately and conservatively by the owners, the Rausch family. The Chairman was Phillip Rausch. The President was John Wenzel and my boss was the VP of Marketing, Len Wurzel.

Phillip Rausch was then about sixty-seven, John Wenzel about fifty-five, and I was thirty-three. This was significant: my experience in business had been very limited because I had worked primarily in the cloistered environment of engineering; these older men, however, had grown up in the business world. Phillip Rausch was a seasoned entrepreneur and the major owner of a $40 million/year manufacturing concern. He was gruff, direct and blunt. Although a millionaire, if he had to go to Manhattan, instead of taking a taxi or limousine, he would ride the subway. This is not to say he was cheap. In fact, the company Christmas parties were lavish affairs.

My job was to find new products that fit into the company's production capabilities and served their existing markets. I still wonder why they hired an electronics engineer who had no experience in new product management or the industrial and automotive markets. In any case I knew I had better start learning something about these areas pretty fast. I immediately purchased three or four books on new product searching, screening, commercialization and management. I sought ideas for new products from salesmen, engineers, customers and management and set up screening criteria and a rating system. A flurry of activity emanated from my office. Working in marketing exposed me to advertising, promotion and sales. New product management called for interdepartmental meetings which I organized. The idea was to get engineering, production and marketing working together in a coordinated way so that the new products would be launched according to a plan.

The new product textbooks helped, but Ideal Corporation was actually teaching me much more. I did not realize this at the time, but it dawned on me years later when my own business was expanding. At one meeting, my boss explained to Phillip Rausch that he had to terminate a sales rep organization. These are independent firms that make a profit on the commission for any sales made in their region. If they fail to meet quotas, manufacturers often terminate the relationship and seek other sales reps in the same region. At one point in the discussion Mr. Rausch said, "Len, be sure to pay them off generously when they are told. We want to maintain our good name." I was learning some good lessons in business which were probably not taught in MBA programs.

One of my best contributions in the five years I worked for Ideal Corporation was the addition of the automotive thermostat to their product line. The product was sold into existing markets and, like the hose clamp, was part of the engine cooling system. The thermostat was also made up of metal stamped components so that Ideal's familiar engineering and production know-how could be exploited.

The only problem was it used something called a wax element. This part was basically an enclosed copper cylinder, containing a special wax. As the temperature rose the wax would expand, squeezing a rubber boot which in turn forced a metal rod to push out of the cylinder. The rod was attached to a disc which, when lifted, would allow water to pass through the thermostat and thereby cool the engine. Most of the expansion would take place when the wax changed from a liquid to a solid. This component had rubber, wax and metal technology, unfamiliar to Ideal. So I began a search for a company that made these wax elements, and would be willing to sell to us; first the product, and later, the know-how to make the product.

All the U.S. manufacturers turned me down because they naturally did not want to set up yet another competitor. However, a foreign thermostat manufacturer would not be threatened. After I located firms in Japan, West Germany and France, our engineer selected the French, based on their design and pricing. On two visits to France I established the basis of a deal with the president of the French firm, Bob Frank, a man in his early thirties. The arrangement involved supplying Ideal with product in the first stage, and then selling know-how to permit us to make the wax elements ourselves. The deal was signed in Brooklyn in a spirit of great optimism. Then two months later the dollar began to weaken against the French franc. The contract was written so that we would pay for wax elements in U.S. dollars. Bob Frank contacted us pleading for relief. In a memorable exchange with Ideal's president I argued for sticking to the letter of the contract. "No," John said. "The deal is no good if only one side is making money. We must let Bob show us what his costs are and what he needs to make a profit. If he is losing money he will find some way out of the deal." I was learning.

But perhaps my biggest and most painful lesson did not come from top management but from some of Ideal's customers. This lesson cost me my job. When I first arrived at Ideal, the engineering department was completing a prototype of a band clamp. My job was to take charge of evaluating and coordinating the launch of this band clamp. Ideal's existing clamp contained a screw and a notched band. A screwdriver was used to tighten them. The band clamp was used in heavier applications, and two types of special installation tools were used to place them on large industrial hoses. The Ideal design was universal in that either tool made by the two competitors could be used on this clamp. Perhaps this was a small advantage but in mature products that is the kind of development they call a "breakthrough." Well, we made up some samples and went out into the field to test them. Many customers seemed to like the clamps. But a number of customers, particularly the larger installers with pressure testing equipment, did not.

Under increasing water pressure, Ideal's prototype clamp would burst open before the competitor's. What should I do, wave the red flag and tell everyone to stop? After all, I had just joined the company. On one side were Ideal's engineers ready to go into tooling and production. Top management was also eager to get rolling. On the other side was this collection of guys in dirty T-shirts with eighth-grade educations who happened to be our customers. How could they know more than the experienced engineers of Ideal Corporation? Well, we went ahead, built expensive automatic production machinery, created beautiful packaging, launched a wonderful promotion and advertising campaign. I concentrated on coordinating marketing, engineering and manufacturing with weekly meetings. I even introduced a computerized scheduling technique called PERT charting. Soon band clamps were pouring out of those relentless automatic production machines. The Ideal warehouse was brimming with band clamps. There was one problem: the customers did not like them. Many were returning their first shipments back to the Ideal warehouse. It was a disaster. Ideal's management, engineers and I were wrong. The guys in the dirty T-shirts with the eighth-grade educations were right. I should have blown the whistle. It sounds like all this happened quickly but in fact it took over four years for this sad tale to unfold.

It was already 1975. The Arab oil crisis had created a recession which hit the automotive after-market hard. Gas was expensive and people were driving less. It was layoff time at Ideal and a prime candidate was the fellow who led them into the band clamp business. It was a rainy afternoon and my new boss, Bob Ouellette, was assigned the unpleasant task of letting me go. He took me to a nice restaurant and told me the bad news over drinks. Bob said "Order anything you like. It's on the company." But my appetite had suddenly disappeared. Anyway, I did learn a very important lesson. Listen to your customers. Give them what they want and need, rather than some internally-generated creation. This is all basic advice found in many business texts and is mouthed by many executives who then turn around and do it their way anyway. For me this lesson was not just in my head. It was in my gut.

While depressed by this experience, I still wanted a career outside of engineering. Returning to this would seem like going back to a narrower occupation. On the other hand, I had a warm spot for my fellow engineers who were like grown-up kids playing with, and building, wonderful electronic toys. I enjoyed it too. After two months of fruitless searching, my old engineering friend Al Lipsky offered me a job working for his company, Hydrosystems, as a consultant logic designer. He was chief engineer there so he had no trouble getting me in. It was a favor I will never forget. The recession had made it tough getting a job anywhere and being a rusty engineer, five years out of the field, made it tougher. In the three months that I worked for Hydrosystems I caught up on all the new integrated circuits that had been developed. It was amazing how much more powerful these devices had become since the time I left the field in 1970. While the work was challenging, the longing returned to get back to the business side of business.

The résumés kept going out until I finally landed an unusual position with the Trade Office of the British Consulate in New York. My title was Commercial Officer and my job was to promote British exports. This involved visiting U.S. companies in the region and attempting to match their buying needs with British products. The Trade Office would also arrange cocktail parties to introduce British and American executives to each other. The Trade Office would rely on me and other commercial officers to produce the American executives. A computer in London would also assist in matching British exporters to American importers. It was one of my jobs to feed this machine with data on American buying interests. I worked for the Consulate for over three years until I found the bureaucracy too frustrating to bear. It was all heat and very little light. The commercial officers would furiously visit as many American companies as possible, racking up impressive monthly statistics. However, rarely did any of these visits result in an actual increase in British exports. The job did expose me to international trade and there was a social side which was novel. At the cocktail parties, I had to get used to being a good host, making introductions and cultivating contacts.

One British businessman made a deep impression on me. Ernest Rybacki was an export manager for Kane May, Ltd., and perhaps sixty years old. He was originally from Eastern Europe. We had lunch together on one of his U.S. visits. At one point in our conversation he advised me to always give myself choices in life and in business. "As long as you have choices you are free, otherwise you are like a prisoner. A prisoner lacks choices," he said. The challenge is to create options in your life. In my own life I could see that if my livelihood depended on the opinion of one man, my boss, I certainly had few choices except to please him. On the other hand, if I was self-employed I would have many bosses, namely my customers and my suppliers, but not one or even a few of them could control my livelihood. I could refuse; I could say no. That is a great freedom, the option of saying no if you disagree with a proposal or proposition. It would indeed be wonderful to be self-employed, but I was not ready.

The workload at the British Trade Office involved dealing with many companies and tasks simultaneously, rather than a few tasks carried out in depth. I admired the superior writing and speaking skills of the British career diplomats who were my supervisors. Farewell speeches given to departing colleagues were presented with a wit and fluency which I never saw equaled in American companies.

The commercial officers were given the opportunity to attend a one-week intensive marketing course at the Columbia University retreat at Arden House, Harriman, NY. I eagerly said "yes" and soon found myself in the middle of a forest preserve and fine old mansion. The study group was composed of middle managers from the Fortune 500 companies. We were separated into teams and given business problems to solve, using principles learned during the daily lectures and intensive studies at team sessions in the evening. One lecturer was especially memorable. A small, unimposing individual, he quickly got the class's attention by blowing a duck whistle. He then held up the whistle and asked a few students in the front row what each would be willing to pay for the whistle. One student said $4.00, another said $2.50 and yet another said $5.00. "You see," the lecturer said, "the price each of you is willing to pay for this duck whistle has nothing to do with what it cost to make. It has everything to do with your perception of its value. And your job as marketing executives is to maximize the perceived value of the product made by your company."

I learned that this is achieved by differentiating your product from the competition and finding the market segments that most value those differences. One student objected, pointing out that his company made some chemical commodity and it was exactly like the competition's product. The lecturer immediately asked if the product was really the same. Did the chemical have the same purity as the competitive product? What about speed of delivery, guarantees on quality, helpfulness of the sales department, etc. To each question the student would answer yes for some competitors and no for others. "So you see," said the lecturer, "your product is very different. It includes the package of goods and services which your company provides and which are unique." I was mesmerized. How could I use this stuff?

I returned from Harriman absolutely charged up with enthusiasm for creative marketing. But I also returned to the real world of government bureaucracy at the British Trade Office.

The locally employed, as opposed to London-appointed career diplomats, were largely on three-year contracts. These could be renewed once, we were told, so that this job from the outset was to last no more than six years. Shortly after my contract was renewed I began to realize that not only was this job a dead end, but the work experience was not applicable to any position back in U.S. industry. Furthermore, my résumé was beginning to look like a series of unconnected positions progressing nowhere. Was I an electronics engineer, a think-tank consultant, a new products manager in the auto industry or a commercial officer, whatever that is? It was 1979, and I was almost forty-one. Big companies do not like to hire employees over forty. They consider them "overqualified" for entry level positions and less trainable than younger workers. I know age discrimination is illegal, so let's just say being over forty is not a strong point when applying for a job.

I began to look for opportunities and perhaps open up a few choices for myself. I started with some of the British contacts I had made at the Trade Office. I had been told to use my contacts to help me re-enter industry. I went so far as to offer to represent personally one or two UK companies in parallel with my work for the Consulate. When my supervisor learned of this he was not pleased. I had overstepped my use of contacts and had to leave. I respected their concern about conflict of interest; however, I felt a pressure to get going and do something before I reached the end of the dead end.

My last job and certainly the most humiliating—was working for an outfit called Kettering Information Systems, which built point-of-purchase displays. These are countertop cardboard creations that promote products at the retail level. The company had some success with an electronic point-of-purchase device that asked women questions about their skin and complexion and then recommended make-up to match, based on the answers. My job was to interface with the engineering job shop which would design and build these displays and new ones which the company was hoping to sell.

Soon after joining this firm it became clear they had no idea where they were heading. They spent $100,000 building a prototype for an auto manufacturer to help consumers select the car best suited for their needs. A quick "no interest" from the auto manufacturer ended that venture. The next proposal was for a dress pattern company that sold designs to women who could follow instructions and sew their own clothing. The proposed point-of-purchase guide had questions printed on the front and buttons with choices for each question. Presumably, once the woman answered all the questions, the pattern best suited to her size, price range and personality would be recommended. A customized microprocessor would analyze the answers. However, the question "what type of man are you most attracted to?" had buttons with no wires connected to them. The answer to that question had no bearing on the recommendation. The woman was being duped into believing she would then have a dress that would attract the right kind of man.

My respect for this company was practically zero at this point, when they introduced me to a new boss named Barry. He had a small frame, short dark hair and wore pants that were too tight and ended above his ankles. Barry was a very insecure person. At our first meeting with the owner of the engineering job shop, Barry became upset because the owner was looking at me when he spoke, instead of at Barry. Barry demanded that the owner look at him when he spoke. With all eyes trained on my new boss the meeting proceeded. There were many other examples of insensitivity and stupidity which I endured from Barry while I clung to this miserable job.

Desperate Conditions Lead to Desperate Action

However, one thing made the job bearable. Most of the day I was left alone in my office while management tried to figure out what to do next with this division. This gave me time to figure out what to do next with my "career." One day I opened *Electronic News*, a trade weekly, and in the back I saw small ads offering to buy and sell integrated circuits, or "chips" as they are often called. This was the so-called gray market which lived on severe shortages that could shut down a production line. For want of a chip a factory might have to close its doors. In such a situation a manufacturer will pay exorbitant prices for chips, even if they have to get them outside the authorized distribution channels. Brokers would acquire stock from manufacturers, other brokers, or wait in line and buy from authorized distributors. Brokers could also sell off other brokers' stock without even owning the parts.

I decided to become a part-time integrated circuits broker. I also thought it would be interesting to see if I could export electronic components to Europe and Japan. I registered a company with the Queens County Clerk doing business as Freeman Associates. Next I ordered a separate business phone line and installed it in the basement of our home in Fresh Meadows with an answering machine attached. I found a telex service that, for a few dollars per message, would permit anyone to use their telex number. This firm would send or receive messages which could be telephoned in to them. It was the winter of 1979.

Now I had to locate customers. The international market intrigued me. The U.S. Commerce Department had a computer service which could provide a mailing list of foreign importers by country and product lines. I requested a list for Western Europe and Japan which included integrated circuits. Once I received this list I prepared a letter offering to supply these companies with hard-to-get electronic components. Within a few weeks I began to receive replies from England

and Japan, and one from Denmark. The Europeans were interested in getting prices and delivery dates for a range of electronic components. The Japanese firms, mainly trading companies, were offering to sell me electronic components. I put the Japanese replies aside and concentrated on responding to the Europeans.

In my Kettering office I spent most of the day searching for brokers and authorized distributors who could give me prices and delivery dates for what the European firms wanted. Then the inevitable happened. Barry and the company finally realized I was not doing much Kettering work and I was let go. My feelings were mixed. I had just been fired from a job which I hated. This job had lasted less than nine months, though in many ways it seemed much longer. I went home that day very confused. My little part-time business was not even off the ground. I had yet to receive my first order and it was far from certain that I could make a living by brokering integrated circuits.

Although I was terminated, I had developed a dialogue with one of the executives in the parent company. He asked if I could work on a consulting assignment to recommend a personal computer system for use in their office. Since I needed the money I agreed and was soon visiting one of the few computer stores which had just opened in Manhattan. The store was called Datel. The owner, Bill Barton, was very cooperative and turned me over to a patient salesman named Ray Simmons.

I spent some time with Ray, who explained what various computer systems could do for my client. And I spent some time trying to export. But mostly I was out looking for another job. My résumé by now was so confusing that it was impossible to develop a coherent story of who I was and where I was going. I sent out hundreds of résumés for a wide range of marketing and staff planning positions advertised in the *New York Times*. The responses were pitifully few. At one interview I was asked if I minded working for someone younger than myself. It was the first time anyone ever asked me that question. I gave the obligatory answer, "no, I wouldn't mind." But actually, in my heart, I knew I would, because it would have symbolized the slow progress of my professional life.

Let me explain where I stood financially in late 1979. As an engineer the most I earned was $18,000 per year. At Ideal and the British Trade Office I earned about $25,000 per year. At Kettering Information Systems I earned about $35,000 per year. The mortgage on the house was $40,000 and I had $5,000 in the bank. My wife Patricia helped out by working three to four days a week for the North Shore

Hospital in Manhassett. This added perhaps another $6,000 to our annual income. With both of us working we just made ends meet.

I had an interview with a manufacturer of electrical fixtures. It was for a marketing position and paid $42,000 a year. I would have accepted the job if it had been offered to me but it was not. In fact, when all the returns were in I had only two job offers. One was to work for a hospital supplies company called IPCO in Westchester, and the job paid $28,000 per year. The second offer was to work for a new magazine on Long Island, called *High Technology*, as a writer. It also paid $28,000 a year. So here I was at the age of 41, with a crazy work history and two job offers, each paying less than I earned in my previous job.

I know envy is not a feeling one should treasure but our good friend Bill Reilly was a Wall Street attorney and doing very well. My brother-in-law Mike was a neurologist and also doing very well financially. Both were my contemporaries. Putting it all together I would describe this as definitely one of the low points in my life. In twenty years of working for others I had many jobs, perhaps ten different employers. In some cases I quit by my own choice. However, the traumas of being fired make the best stories. This chapter has been about lessons taught to me by employers. When one quits a job he teaches his employer a lesson. The boss goes home and thinks "what did I do wrong to lose this person?" Conversely, being fired is a learning experience for the employee, who then is forced to reappraise himself. I went through more than my share of these traumatic reappraisals between 1960 and 1979.

7
FA Components

Circumstances rule men. Men do not rule circumstances.
        —Herodotus, *The Histories of Herodotus,* 5th Century B.C.

One of Patricia's qualities is optimism. Along with this positive outlook she brought courage and integrity to our marriage. Perhaps it is part of the British character. At any rate it was she who said I must try to start my own business and that if I did not do it now I never would. She would help out in any way possible.

"But I do not come from a business background. My father was not in business. What if I fail?" I said.

"Try," she said. "I know you can do it."

So one day I just stopped sending out résumés and told the headhunters I was no longer available. I recall being surprised at how curious the headhunters became when I announced my plan to start my own business. They did not just hang up but instead asked follow-up questions about the company.

Every day counted. With only $5,000 in the bank I figured we could last about two months. I decided that I would make a go/no go decision at the end of the sixty days. A desk was installed in our 800-square-foot basement. A telex machine was ordered and the business phone was moved downstairs. I could almost hear the sixty-day-clock ticking.

A Cottage Industry

Each morning Patricia would leave for the North Shore Hospital, Rachel would leave for school and I would head downstairs to my basement office. It was January, 1980 and the basement was chilly. I added an electric heater and opened the door to the unfinished furnace area to let in some warm air. It was also lonely, which only served to increase the tension and intensity.

I opened a business checking account with European American Bank in Fresh Meadows. I asked the branch manager, Edna Barry, for some guidance on letters of credit; she sent me into Manhattan to their headquarters for a brief education given by one of their L/C specialists. But as for getting a bank loan to help finance my business, this was out of the question for two years, I was told.

Knowing that I would also need a freight forwarder who could import and export goods for me, I found a company listed in the yellow pages called All Nations. Never having done anything like this before I must have sounded rather unsure of myself when I first telephoned them. I still remember my first conversation with Neil, the import manager who took the call. I was asking who would do this and who would do that. Neil said, "Don't worry, we will handle everything. We're on your side." It is hard to describe how consoling that sounded to me, at the moment when so much uncertainty lay ahead.

My ads in *Electronic News* generated some contacts among other brokers. I developed some phone contacts with authorized distributors such as Arrow, Lionex and Milgray. These companies would become sources for hard-to-get integrated circuits.

Some of the orders I had worked on in December came through. At the end of January I tallied up the results. Five of the six orders came from other brokers. One order came from Denmark. My gross profit was $2,455. I just about broke even after subtracting my living costs. What would happen in February?

The Danish firm was Peter Peterson Company, a European distributor that occasionally ran short of Texas Instruments semiconductors. Most of the domestic brokers were California-based and supplied Silicon Valley as well as the high tech firms in the Los Angeles area. They included Advanced Computer Products and TCC. These were all young companies. Often the salesman or buyer was also the owner. I was starting to enjoy the verbal exchanges over the phone and I think I was communicating the intangible feeling that they could trust me.

And if they did trust me to deliver as promised and pay my bills as promised it would never be misplaced trust. I vowed to myself in those early days that I would only feel comfortable by basing my business practices on keeping my commitments. What I aspired to was that level of business wisdom which I saw practiced by the owner and president of Ideal Corporation.

January had been nerve-racking. Six orders in twenty-one work days meant I was pacing the floor of the basement many hours between sales, wondering when the phone would ring again. Often days would pass after much quoting—but no order would result.

I recall wondering how often I would not get paid or how often a check would bounce. I did very little credit checking and offered mainly COD terms without certified checks. Receiving a bad check was a risk. Fortunately, in those early days, the business was on a person-to-person basis and few checks bounced.

The United Parcel Service truck was making repeated stops at our home. Bobby, the driver, was very helpful. He explained how to fill out the forms, attach shipping envelopes and labels and, when things got busy later, he would pitch in hauling cartons up from the basement. During the busy days before we moved the business out of the home, we would see Bobby every day at 5 P.M. It became a ritual that signaled end of play for that day's "adventure in business." But I am jumping ahead.

February, my second month, was better. Thirteen orders were receeived with a total gross profit of $4,896. Annualized this came to $58,000 per year, *if* I could equal the pace each month. I was getting very excited about this, though I still worried a lot between orders. Two of the orders came from Japanese trading companies, Kajima and Shintoa International. Kajima and other Japanese companies, however, were more eager to sell than to buy and I kept getting unsolicited telexes from them offering me memory chips. I suppose most readers are familiar by now with dynamic random access memories, DRAMS. Every computer has them and generally large numbers of them. For every microprocessor chip sold, perhaps 64 DRAMS were sold. I was soon to take advantage of this fact and make DRAMS the major part of my business in 1980.

February was really a natural extension of January. My ads and my phone calls to other brokers were increasing my exposure to this small community. I began to place orders with authorized distributors for hard-to-get integrated circuits for which I had no immediate order. Now I could offer my own stock as well as sell other brokers' stock. Integrated circuits have a very high value considering their physical size. You could store $1 million worth of stock in a closet. It was a great cottage industry.

I recall getting a call one day from a California broker seeking a particular part in some quantity. I knew another broker no more than ten miles from him, who had those parts. I quoted a price 30 percent higher and got the order. The product was shipped 3,000 miles to me from the supplying broker in California. I then replaced his shipping labels with mine and shipped it back to California to my customer, thus completing a 6,000 mile round trip and a tidy profit. This was one of the more amusing orders I received in those early days.

As we entered March, the go/no go decision was a "no brainer." Gross profits by the end of March climbed to $5,268. It seemed as if growth was slowing except for an unusual order I received in March for shipment starting in April. In early March I started to run advertisements promoting myself as a source for DRAMS. If I got any orders, I had a file full of Japanese trading companies eager to ship to me.

The head of purchasing of Dataram Corporation, a large systems manufacturer and a big user of DRAMS, read my advertisement in *Electronic News*, telephoned and asked if I could supply him with 5,000 DRAMS per month for six months. I almost fell off my chair.

"Well, do you want the order?" he asked.

Composing myself, I asked for a domestic letter of credit to guarantee payment for each shipment at the agreed price of $5.10 per unit. By the time I put down the phone I had a six-month order for $150,000 dollars which only a failure to ship could stop. Quickly I located my file on Japanese offers to sell DRAMS. Boldwin International in Tokyo had the best offer and I telexed them for their latest price on 5,000 DRAMS each month, with the price to be renegotiated with each order. Since prices were falling I did not want to get locked into the current prices.

Japanese trading companies work on letters of credit or prepayment by wire transfer. It can take years before they will consider giving terms. Boldwin asked me for an L/C amounting to $21,500. European American Bank required security equal to that amount before they would give me the L/C. My father, without hesitation, lent me $30,000 to cover this and other cash requirements. This was a substantial sum for someone living on retirement income and, after all, I had no successful track record. I was and still am grateful for the favor and the confidence he showed. I might add that, in a few months, profits were so large I was able to repay the full amount and the company would grow for some time thereafter on retained earnings.

April was a great month with forty orders. Including the big DRAMS order, my gross profit rose to $11,796. I was making more money than I ever dreamed possible. Increasingly my attention was drawn to DRAMS. In 1980 the maximum size of these devices was 16,000 bits of data. Fifteen years later the capacity of DRAMS had risen 4,000 times to 64 megabytes.

In early April I also received an order for DRAMS from a different kind of customer, a computer store. Harold Shair, the owner of Computer Corner in Westchester, called and asked if my DRAMS were the same as the ones Apple sold for upgrading their Apple II computers.

Neither of us knew for sure, so I sent 8 DRAMS to Harold who installed them and announced they worked just fine. The significance of this order was not forgotten. One aspect of brokering is the dependence on shortages. And shortages have a habit of disappearing. Very little good will is developed when a supplier, capitalizing on a shortage, charges much higher prices than the customer would normally pay. However, the reverse situation existed with Harold. He was being overcharged for memory chips from Apple. I could supply him the same devices for less. He would reorder continuously to fill a steady need. And if he wanted DRAMS from me, why shouldn't I approach all the other computer stores in New York, and why not the United States?

I knew magazines kept subscriber profiles and could produce mailing labels selected by class of reader. *Byte Magazine* agreed to supply me their list of 1,000 computer stores for $60. By the end of April my first simple postcard mailing went out to dealers nationwide. Through telemarketing, I already had received fifteen dealer orders for DRAMS, including such future heavyweight accounts as Computer Factory and numerous Computer Lands.

In those days, Computer Factory had one outlet and I doubt that the owner, Jay Gottlieb, envisioned the national network of stores he would assemble in the decade just starting. Gottlieb did his own purchasing and I recall with fondness and amusement the lengthy haggling sessions we would engage in. Jay would only place his order when he felt I was ready to walk away from the deal.

It soon occurred to me to add my computer store requirements to my scheduled monthly 5,000-unit order. Each month the computer store volume increased until it exceeded the scheduled order. This was just as well, since I had no assurance that this scheduled order would be renewed.

In May I had sixty orders but my profits had leveled off. It was getting busy in the basement. One day our daughter Rachel came home and asked Patricia, "When will Daddy get a job?" Five months earlier the question would have been disturbing. In May it was funny.

In June, profits widened as my DRAMS costs dropped faster than my average selling price. My dealer base was growing. I really enjoyed the friendly voices at the other end of the phone line. Most of these people were also just starting out and there was a comradeship that existed then which today is far less evident, having diminished as the industry matured.

Most of my computer store customers came from along the East Coast, though I was selling to some outlets in Denver and Texas.

In July, I could see that some secretarial assistance would be helpful. We had a friend and neighbor who lived around the corner. Eileen Abramson was once a legal secretary and accepted my offer to work part-time in my business. She was a great help typing invoices, answering the phone and doing record keeping. I was no longer a prisoner to the telephone. Now I could step out for hours at a time to deliver DRAMS to a computer store or just take a breather. By hand-delivering product I got to meet and cement personal relationships, at least in the New York area.

In July, gross profits hovered in the $12,000 range, but what made this significant was that it did not include the monthly 5,000 DRAMS scheduled order. Dataram had telephoned and requested that I postpone the July shipment and add it to the August and September shipments. This meant extraordinary profits would be made in those two months as my DRAMS costs had dropped further, down to $3.00 each. I simply could not believe this was happening to me.

For a while I had been frequenting the sauna at the nearby Hillcrest Jewish Center. I found it a good way to release tension. The sauna, as mentioned in a previous chapter, was always crowded with a loquacious group of regulars that included small businessmen, lawyers and accountants. One of them said what every business needs is a good lawyer, a good accountant and a good insurance man. The good lawyer I had, in my friend Bill Reilly. In the sauna I got my first insurance man, Elliot Waldman, and my first accountant, Abe Cohen. Abe was close to seventy and worked with his son. He told me to start thinking of the business as a separate financial entity. Later, in 1981, he advised me to get a good bookkeeper. He helped in making my periodic appeals to European American for a bank loan. Eventually they did give me a $200,000 credit line. He also advised me to incorporate rather than remain a sole proprietor. This would give me protection against lawsuits. At the time I could not imagine why anyone would want to sue me. Much later I discovered how quickly some people will sue. I believe some businessmen view suing as a profit center, especially if they are losing money in their primary activity.

I listened to the advice and asked Bill Reilly to incorporate Freeman Associates. We soon learned the name was already taken. I had to think up another name. I wanted to use the letters F and A in any new name since my advertisements and price lists employed a logo incorporating these letters. So Bill and I came up with FA Components, Inc. Later the name did not accurately describe what we became. Customers after a while just called us "FA" or "F and A."

In the last quarter of 1980 profits dropped back since the scheduled order was not renewed. This only confirmed my judgment about not basing a business on transient shortages. I now had 200 steady happy customers buying around 20–25,000 DRAMS per month. At that rate I would sell $1 million in DRAMS in 1981. My accountant, Abe Cohen, prepared my first annual financial statement. It showed I had sales of $600,000 and a gross profit of $106,000. My net income was $42,000. I finished the year overjoyed and took the family to Mexico for the Christmas–New Year's period. Eileen held the fort while we were away.

In January I learned that the personal computer industry was not for the complacent. Apple Corporation did not like all the dealers buying DRAMS from gray market distributors. They wanted to regain control of the situation. So in one announcement they brought the Apple upgrade market to an end. Henceforth, Apple would ship only fully-populated 48K machines. The partially populated 16K machines would no longer be shipped. Within a week my customers were refusing my shipments. DRAMS were heading the wrong way, back to me from my customers. I spent some sleepless nights trying to sort out this change.

One day I wrote down my three choices: I could return to exporting integrated circuits; I could try to find new customers for DRAMS; or I could try to find other products which my customers were still purchasing. It seemed to me that my greatest asset was not my stock of DRAMS but rather the 200 Apple dealers who liked and trusted me. Therefore, I had to find other products which I could distribute to them. In the meantime, I could fill in by finding some new outlets for the DRAMS. Calls to the Heathkit stores soon disclosed that they were still upgrading Heath computers. In the first quarter of 1981, I developed relationships with most of the fifty-five Heathkit stores. This helped to offset my loss of the Apple DRAMS market. However, the major challenge was to find out if Apple dealers would buy other products from me.

I located a manufacturer of printer cards. These plug-in boards permit the Apple II personal computers to send data to printers. The manufacturer, Tymac, was based in New Jersey and agreed to supply me at discount pricing so that I could resell profitably to dealers. My first mailing, offering the Tymac card, went out in February as part of a DRAMS mailing. When the first dealer ordered a printer card from me I knew an important strategic question had been answered. If I could sell printer cards to dealers then I could sell other peripheral cards and modems and monitors and printers to them just as easily. No longer restricted to memory chips, I could establish myself as a general distributor of computer hardware. The world had suddenly opened up.

The direction was clear and tactical. I must go West, to California, where the personal computer industry started and where most of the new suppliers were sprouting.

It was in Silicon Valley, that strip of land south of San Francisco and north of San Jose, that Apple was founded. All up and down the Valley engineers working in their garages built on the theme, expanded and improved the basic idea of a desktop computer in every home. I knew I must visit these suppliers and their trade shows and add their product lines to my price list.

While it all seems obvious now, these ideas came to me like revelations. In early 1981 there simply were no computer peripheral distributors on the East Coast and I was just starting to learn about some West Coast distributors that had recently begun operation. But I knew little about them at the time.

Each spring in San Francisco a computer show was held called the West Coast Computer Faire. I believe the exhibition started in the late 1970s. I flew out to San Francisco and attended my first show in early 1981. The attendees were mostly students, computer hackers and hobbyists, Apple worshipers all. The exhibition was a casual affair with guys in blue jeans selling to guys in blue jeans across cloth-draped card tables. I might note that very few women were involved in the industry at this point. The organizer whizzed down each aisle of the Moscone Center on roller skates to be sure there were no problems.

The show consisted of Californians selling to Californians. It was a provincial attitude and it would help me get started. I was from New York but, to these people, it could have been the planet Mars. I never met anyone from the East Coast during my four days at the show. When I introduced myself as a distributor from New York, the exhibitors were all happy to let me supply dealers in the East. The fact that I was operating out of an 800-square foot basement in a residential neighborhood in Queens, or the fact that I was in business just over a year with limited capital and one employee, was of no interest to them. In their view, I represented someone eager to sell to non-Californian customers in the "corrupt" New York market.

So now it just came down to picking and choosing which lines seemed most promising. I suppose my engineering background helped. Clever products that appealed to me probably appealed to the market. Later on I would develop other criteria for product selection since picking successful new products is not simply an engineering-oriented decision. I will explain later some of the other methods I used to select new product lines.

The West Coast Computer Faire and, later, the Comdex shows

were the big industry meeting places where all the start-up companies, dealers, distributors and end users met. During the next six months contacts made at the Faire were followed up and, by October, 1981, I had a one-page price list which included Apple computer peripherals from TG Products (a manufacturer of joysticks), Videx (a manufacturer of eighty-column boards) and CTA (a manufacturer of RAM expansion boards). I also added some word processing software from Information Unlimited. Since the Atari personal computer was selling well at the time, I also added RAM expansion boards for this machine from Axlon and Intec. The price list included DRAMS, but with each month it represented a smaller share of the total sales volume.

It is interesting to note that these new computer peripherals and software, which were becoming the backbone of my business, were all gone five years later. Obsolescence eliminated every product line I carried on my October, 1981 price list. The rule then and now is "change with the times or disappear." Adding the right product lines was instrumental in riding the market upward. Through each addition and deletion we would adapt to the advancing technology and market windows which were opening up.

The most important manufacturer I added in 1981 was Videx. The growth of this company was phenomenal. Videx was started in 1980 by Paul Davis, an engineer, and was based in Corvallis, Oregon. Videx's success was proof that Apple did not understand the biggest market for their machine. When Steve Wozniak, the founding engineer at Apple, designed the Apple II he gave it the ability to display only forty characters per line. He was designing the personal computer for fellow hackers and hobbyists and not for the much larger business market. A page of text has eighty characters per line. Word processing, spread sheets and other business applications all require, or work much better with, eighty characters per line. However, Wozniak fortunately included in the design, slots to add six plug-in boards. These boards could add features to the basic machine. Slots gave the machine the flexibility to adapt itself to market requirements and probably made the difference between a small success and the brilliant product it became. This flexibility literally unleashed the creative energies of hundreds of engineers, mostly up and down the West Coast. It seemed every week garage businesses launched new plug-in boards. The Videx eighty-column board corrected the forty character-per-line-of-text limitation and opened up the Apple II to the business market.

I first met Paul Davis at one of the early trade shows. We both had that low-key style common to most engineers and I think this helped in establishing a quick rapport. Paul agreed to let me distribute his product line. The deal was done with a handshake. In fact nearly all the vendor/distributor relationships established in 1981 began with a handshake between the owner and me. Those were the most personally satisfying deals. Sadly, such informality and trust between the early vendors was replaced by the lengthy contract of the new wave of professionals entering our industry.

I believed that news in the personal computer business travels not only through the obvious channels such as advertising and trade shows, but also through an underground that includes computer club meetings and word of mouth between dealers and end users. It did not take more than a few months for Videx to become a household name in the personal computer business and my largest vendor.

For every successful new product, I added three or four which went nowhere. ALF music boards, which permitted Apple users to compose music, flopped. QT clock/calendar boards, which permitted users to date their programs or turn things on and off at different times, flopped. IUS word processing software flopped.

In fact, none of my efforts to sell software were successful. Being a hardware designer seemed to give me a better feeling for "pushing iron." One problem I had with software was the enormous markup from its base cost. A software package might list for $1,000 and be sold to a distributor for $500. However, the materials, consisting of a looseleaf folder, printed paper, a floppy disk and pretty packaging, might cost the software developer or publisher only $20. It is easy for a large distributor to tempt the supplier to sell a large quantity for $450 or $400 or $300 each while the smaller distributor was still paying $500 each. There was no bottom. At least with hardware, the cost of goods was substantial. In theory, at least, this would work in favor of a level playing field.

Many of these comments are, of course, subjective. Some distributors became heavily involved in software and are now substantial companies. A series of these subjective decisions shapes the company around the personality of the owner. Eventually the company becomes an extension of all the owner's strengths and weaknesses. In my case, I felt uncomfortable purchasing unfamiliar software products and I found reasons to justify that bias.

One day, while doing some accounting, I noticed that one customer, Micro Center of Columbus, Ohio, was paying their invoices in five days instead of the thirty days I had given them. I telephoned the owner, John Baker, to make him aware that he had more time to pay. John responded by saying that he knew I was just starting out in business and felt I could use the money sooner. It was one of the kindest gestures I had encountered up to that point and since. A couple of years later John stopped by our exhibit at Comdex in Atlanta and introduced himself. I was surprised at his youth. I guess I associated wisdom with advanced age.

Micro Center grew to become one of the largest single location computer stores and eventually expanded to other regions of the country. I was always pleased to read in the trade papers about John's success. It proved to me that high principles and business success are compatible.

In March of 1981 I could see the need for more assistance. I asked my wife Patricia if she would be willing to give up her nursing career to help build the business. She agreed. For a while thereafter I needed Eileen less often, but soon the increasing sales volume required Eileen again. Patricia has a great memory and could remember customers' names, what they ordered and what happened when. She worked quickly, with competence. The customers, especially the Southerners, loved her British accent. Patricia quickly became a big asset.

In June of 1981 I could see that my father could play a useful role. I do not think either of us realized then how deeply involved and valuable he would become. My father, Sam, had retired from his position of Director of the Lecture Bureau of the Jewish Welfare Board. My father was very well-organized, creative, energetic and experienced in advertising and promotion. Sam was sixty-nine and, after four years of retirement, he needed a challenge. Initially, my father agreed to work two to three days a week, but it was not long before he was working ten hours a day, six days a week. By 1982 he was putting in more time than I was.

My father's first contribution was to improve the appearance of our price list and begin an advertising program. We needed more shelving in the basement for the inventory, so he built wooden racks. My mother, Ruth, joined in by collating and stuffing envelopes when we had to get out our customer mailings. Even our daughter Rachel was a help. After coming home from school, she would lend a hand by packing cartons with product, filling them with styrofoam chips and putting shipping labels on the outside of each box. This was turning into a real family business!

I decided to exhibit at the Comdex show which was held in 1981 at the New York Coliseum. Our booth was a small eight-foot-by-eight-foot affair but it had an excellent location near one of the entrances. Comdex in 1981 was much smaller than the huge industry trade show it is today. I recall an enormous man named Tiny who rode around the hall on an electric vehicle helping the exhibitors get set up before the show was opened to attendees. The unions created a problem for exhibitors. You could not use a hammer to set up your stand. This required union help at very high rates of pay. Special assistance required a tip or bribe. The Comdex people had enough and the following year the show was moved to Atlantic City and then, finally, its permanent fall home in Las Vegas.

Our booth was very modest with a sign listing the product lines we carried and a table with our price lists, to be handed out to prospective customers.

During one of my Manhattan visits to the Datel computer store, I met Larry Kerrigan, who worked for the owner, Bill Barton. Larry took an interest in my business and over lunch one day gave me a lot of good advice. Later on he left Datel and went to work for Exel, a Connecticut computer store. Following his advice, I tried to become a distributor for Hayes modems, but I could not get the Hayes VP of Marketing, Glenn Sirkis, to decide yes or no. Larry said he would take care of it. Within a few hours Mr. Sirkis called me and gave me the Hayes modem line. I called Larry back to thank him and ask him exactly what he had done. Larry said he called Hayes and, speaking as a dealer, asked Mr. Sirkis to recommend distributors he could buy from. With each name Larry said they were terrible and he would not buy from them. Finally in frustration Mr. Sirkis asked who Larry would buy from. At that point he began to praise us wildly. "That does it. I was not sure, but now I will definitely put them on as our distributor," said Mr. Sirkis. Fortunately, Mr. Sirkis never visited his new distributor in New York, or he might have been surprised to see a modest private home located on a residential tree-lined street.

In my first letter to Glenn Sirkis I thanked him for the line but spelled his name "Circus." A few days later he phoned me to say that if I wished to remain a Hayes distributor I had better learn to spell his name properly. Sirkis was an interesting fellow whom I only met twice. After a couple of years he had a disagreement with Dennis Hayes, the owner of Hayes Microcomputer Products, and he left the industry. He purchased a movie house in Atlanta and rebuilt it. At one of the Comdex shows in Atlanta, Sirkis stopped by our booth and said he was happy to be out of the business. It wasn't fun anymore. Then he disappeared down the aisle. The comment stuck with me.

Hayes Microcomputer Products was to become our strongest line and at one point represented 40 percent of sales volume. Hayes soon replaced Videx as our strongest product and forced us to move the business out of our home. Their product is modems, which are used to transmit computer data over telephone lines. Hayes would ship these modems in lots of seventy-two per carton. Each carton weighed over 200 lbs. Every two weeks a huge eighteen-wheel tractor trailer would negotiate the narrow streets of Fresh Meadows, driven by an incredulous trucker attempting to find a commercial warehouse. Finally arriving at our home, he would deposit the Hayes cartons on the sidewalk. It was now our job to somehow get these modems into our home. First we freed the 6-packs from the overpack and carried these smaller cartons up the driveway to a small window which let air, light, and now modems into our basement. My father built a wooden slide and down this slide the modems would descend.

Everything purchased was sold. A sale would reverse the process. At around 5 P.M., product would be carried up the stairs from the basement to our kitchen. There the orders would wait until Bobby, the UPS driver, arrived to pick up the goods. An area in the basement was set aside for shipping. After picking and checking the product against the invoice, we would put the goods into a larger carton and add Styrofoam chips, which we called popcorn. My father built a popcorn dispenser so that gravity would allow it to flow out of a tube that could be directed toward the carton.

With a growing inventory and a new shipping area, we were rapidly running out of space. I asked my father to look for a small warehouse in Queens.

I was reluctant to move out of the basement. I had had a "staircase commute" to work for over eighteen months and liked the convenience. On some days I worked straight through in my pajamas. That was, of course, before Eileen joined us. I recall a subway strike which produced enormous traffic jams in the New York area. As usual I went to work each day totally unaffected by the urban chaos the strike had created. Now I would be giving up this easy life for a commute.

However, there were advantages to moving. I would be leaving my work behind me at the end of the day. This physical separation might release some of the tension inherent in building the business. In our Fresh Meadows area, each house was separated by only a driveway, so the neighbors were close to all the comings and goings of large trucks and merchandise. The narrow streets were for residential traffic and not zoned for commercial activity. Yet my neighbors never complained. The move would ease my conscience and end the imposition on their tranquillity.

In late 1981 my father located an 1800-square-foot warehouse in Corona, Queens. Corona is an old Italian-American neighborhood. The landlord, Tony Melita, an electrical contractor, worked next door. The warehouse itself had a roll-up door that fronted on to the sidewalk. The space behind the door was only about eighteen feet wide. Still it was more than twice the space of our basement and should have been adequate. Little did I know then that our sales within twelve months would leap from a run rate of $1.5 million per year to $10 million per year and we would be desperately seeking larger quarters.

Tony was a fine landlord. I still recall, though, how an overzealous attorney almost blew the deal with due diligence overkill. I met this fellow in the sauna at the Hillcrest Jewish Center. Before I signed the lease the lawyer made elaborate demands on Tony, treating the contract as if it were some huge real estate deal. Tony, in desperation, threatened to just walk away. I finally used some common sense, ignored the complex one-sided proposals of my lawyer, signed on the dotted line and FA Components had a new home. My father immediately began building wooden walls inside the warehouse to separate the office area from the inventory and shipping areas.

While this construction was going on, we were still operating the business out of our home in Fresh Meadows, four miles away. It was time to hire a bookkeeper. The advertisement was placed in the *New York Times* and soon the phone was ringing with applicants calling to be interviewed. I set up about ten interviews, each of which was held in the basement. Many applicants were older women who were motherly types. Since I was planning to put accounting on a computer I wanted someone who was very bright and able to adapt to this change. I hired Nancy Tellis, a young woman in her early thirties. I was lucky, for she turned out to be intelligent, hard working, dedicated and loyal. Those were a combination of qualities, I found later, to be rarely held by the same person.

Later Nancy told me she felt I had misled her at the interview. She saw a nice little family business with the daughter packing product, the wife on the phone and the father talking about his disorganized record keeping. Nancy concluded that this would be a simple and temporary position. She would just get our books in order and be on her way. Why didn't I tell her about the distribution madness that was about to descend on us during the next twelve months? I do not think she was ever convinced that I was as surprised as anyone. In 1982, FA Components made a rapid change from cottage to warehouse. Nancy would start work, not in the basement of our home, but in Corona at our new location. I remember at the end of the interview, just after I offered her the job and she accepted, I said "I will do my best to be a good employer." What a challenge that was to become.

By late 1981 I was well aware of the competition. Micro D was a hardware distributor established in 1979 by Lorraine Mecca and her husband. Softsel started in 1980 and specialized in software. Both of these outfits were expanding rapidly but for some reason avoided the New York area. Later I learned that many Californians considered New York to be a special market based on price and shady practices. For a few years this prejudice kept them away from my stronghold and allowed me to grow without serious competition. Finally, they did open warehouses in New Jersey and Connecticut.

My first local competitor was Straitline, based in Queens. They had been around for many years, selling electrical appliances and other consumer products. In 1981 they entered the personal computer business in a big way, having resources and experience which I did not possess. I was surprised when Larry Kerrigan visited our home one evening and, over dinner, forecast that Straitline would be out of business and my company would become the major distributor in New York. I was astonished, but that is exactly what happened. Straitline's accounting got out of control. Other mismanagement exacerbated the problem. They did not know who owed them what. Then one day they were auctioning off the business.

All over the country regional distributors were opening up. They included Price Electronics in Chicago, Micro America in Boston, Micro Distributors in Maryland, Crystal Computers in Kansas, Vitek in Southern California, Sigma Distributing in Seattle and Tech Data in Florida. Business fills vacuums. The market growth taking place was so rapid in 1982, and later, that all these new competitors seemed to have no effect on FA Components, nor did seasonality or the recession of 1982. Each month exceeded the one before it.

Abe Cohen prepared my second annual financial statement for the year ending December 31, 1981. Sales had risen from $600,000 to $820,000. This sales increase was not impressive. However, the slow growth masked a significant transition which had taken place. FA Components was not just shipping DRAMS but had redefined its goals and broadened its range of products. The foundation was established to capitalize on the personal computer market of 1982. The business's net worth stood at $106,000. Profits were the same as the year before.

Corona Warehouse

The five of us: my father, Patricia, Nancy, Eileen and I, moved the inventory and ourselves into the warehouse in Corona. My father had arranged for a new phone system; purchased and assembled the racks to hold the goods; and taken care of a host of other details. It was strange in those first few months, getting up and going someplace else to work.

My father also hired an assistant named Ahmed. He was originally from Pakistan and the brother of my father's physician. While Ahmed had no experience in the computer business at that time, he was very bright. In the beginning Ahmed was just doing odd jobs and helped set up the office in preparation for the move. Later he helped my father in the numerous advertising campaigns and promotional tasks the company was launching. All the while Ahmed was learning about the technical and sales side of computer distribution. Ahmed was a rising star and within two years would become our most valuable and troublesome employee.

I attended another West Coast Computer Faire and another Comdex show, widening my contacts among the manufacturers. By September of 1982 I had assembled twenty-six product lines and our price list was four pages long. Apart from selling some RAM cards for the Atari computers, every other product was used on the Apple II. We had monitors from Amdek and Electrohome, memory expansion, music and multifunction cards from Mountain Computer, printers from Anadex, printer buffers from Practical Peripherals, modems from Hayes and Anchor Automation, eighty-column cards from Videx, printer cards from Tymac, Joysticks from TG Products, disk drives from Rana, accessories from Kensington and RH Electronics, and floppy disks from Control Data. I had not yet given up on software so we also carried Microsoft, Stoneware and On-Line Systems.

Apple announced that a new machine called the Apple IIe would replace the Apple II and the IIe would have built into it memory which previously had been part of a 16k memory board. This eliminated one of our product lines and three of our vendors who made this card. Changes like this caused some concern but they did not hit us across the board the way the DRAMS announcement had. We were no longer a one-product company, but we were a one-machine company and, by that definition, we were still vulnerable.

As sales and product lines increased we could see that five employees were not enough. In mid 1982 we hired six more people. First, we hired a shipping and receiving person named Jim Wiley. What a relief it was not to have to stuff boxes any more. We added three young computer-trained men—Ramon Ferrerez, John McGuiness and Vinny Corda—and we hired two secretaries, Angie Gonzalez and Miriam Moreno. By the end of the year our eleven employees were working overtime to keep up with the orders. As Christmas approached it seemed we could not get product out fast enough. We were selling thousands of joysticks (used in computer games). This was a great gift item for the home market.

Microsoft and Videx had teamed up to sell something called a Premium Pack, consisting of three products. The Premium Pack was sold to dealers for about $500. However, if each of the three products were sold separately, the total sale would be about $600. We could make extra profit just by tearing apart the outside packaging and selling each item separately. In November and December we rarely had time to do this. The UPS delivery trucks would arrive with merchandise and we had no room in the warehouse. So we just unloaded the goods on the sidewalk, repacked and re-labeled the goods for our customers and awaited the return of the UPS truck to pick up our day's shipments. One day it snowed and the UPS truck arrived late. That evening the whole company formed a bucket brigade carrying the goods out to the truck. The driver could only get to within 100 feet of the warehouse en trance because of the snow.

When Amdek monitors arrived we had the worst time. These cartons were almost two feet on each side. There was no way we could fit 100–200 monitors in our warehouse. Somehow we survived the last quarter of 1982. We were shipping almost $1 million a month, more than we did for the entire 1981 period.

In those early days we had high morale and few personnel problems. We all worked in one large room and each knew what was going on just by the physical closeness of the environment. If anything, the hard work and activity raised spirits. Everyone could see something exciting was happening.

IBM Enters the PC Market

In the spring of 1982 I returned to the annual West Coast Computer Faire. IBM had recently announced its decision to enter the personal computer business. Within a few weeks some enterprising peripheral companies had purchased the first few machines, analyzed them and designed plug-in cards. Some of these companies were already exhibiting prototypes at the Faire. Immediately I could see the threat to our business. If IBM was successful, it might replace Apple and thereby eliminate the peripheral business we depended on. A defensive strategy would therefore require us to add IBM peripherals also, so that no matter what happened we would have products to sell. However, IBM had decided to sell their new machines through only two outlets, Sears Roebuck and Computerland headquarters. All the peripheral companies then believed that their products also would be sold to these two customers. Who needs a distributor if you have only two customers? At the Faire and at later Comdex shows, I tried to persuade the peripheral manufacturers that it was only a matter of time before IBM widened its dealer network and when that occurred they, too, would need their own distributors to reach all those dealers. However, by the end of the year the only IBM peripherals sold by us were those added by our existing Apple vendors. The leaders in the IBM peripheral field, Tecmar, AST and Quadram, were as yet unconvinced that they needed distributors.

The first IBM computer compatible machines were already being produced by mid-1982. These were disparagingly referred to as "clones." All the dealers who were cut out of the IBM market, because of IBM's limited dealer network, were interested in adding clones. It was a lot better than nothing at all.

We added a line of IBM computer clones to our line but it turned out poorly. Soon we learned through the rumor mill that the computer salesman had set up a relative in New Jersey as our competitor and he was receiving favored treatment. Additionally, we faced many problems with this supplier involving lack of product and quality control. Once you get suspicious in a business relationship one quickly thinks the worst, even when an innocent problem arises. Call it business paranoia. We did not keep them long afterwards.

Early Growing Pains

I decided during 1982 that it was time to computerize our own operation. After all, it was somewhat hypocritical to sell computer equipment to others and still do your accounting manually. Nancy was concerned. She liked her little card files and ledger sheets. Nancy insisted on running a parallel manual system for months after we began using our computer. We began with an Altos and graduated to a faster IBC system. The software was a distribution accounting package from a developer on Long Island called Trac Line. Unfortunately, the software need constant attention. We had to purge data repeatedly and clean up the data files. Frequently the system would lock up and getting it running again was not always easy. Vinny was the most knowledgeable and I relied on him to sort things out. On a few occasions we had to carry the computer, containing all the records of our business, out to Long Island for the experts at Trac Line to examine. Even our back-up tapes would have corrupted data on them. We had some very tense moments using that system until 1984, when we installed an IBM 36.

We were beginning to get credit problems with some of our customers. Rubber checks were becoming too common. Nancy started a credit procedure using D&B and bank references. One day, she identified two bounced checks from the same person using two company names. When we stopped shipping to one company he simply ordered using the other company. That is about as close to fraud as one can get. We took this personally. Nancy and I went to his Queens address, knocked on the door, and a seedy looking character presented himself. We asked him if he was our customer. He said he was a relative. We doubted this but left a strong warning about a lawsuit and left.

When we returned to the office we told everybody about the problem. I said it would be great if we had a "personal collection agent." Vinny said he had a friend named John McLeod who would be great for the job. One day the office door opened and there stood John McLeod. He literally filled up the entire frame of the door. This guy was huge. He was interested in becoming our personal collection agent. I had two problems. First, John had such a gentle personality I could not envision him frightening anyone once he started speaking. Second, I felt we were pushing close to the edge of legality. So we decided to use the normal route of a professional collection service. They generally receive 20–25 percent of whatever they collect. That is expensive but it's better than never getting paid. We hired John anyway, as a salesman. His was a voice of integrity which was well received at the other end of a phone line.

While in Corona a homeless dog attached himself to us. He was brown and dirty and we called him "Flea Bag." Flea Bag, our mascot and guard dog, was loved by us all. But he could not distinguish a mugger from a vendor. Anyone who was not a regular FA employee received the same surly and threatening growl from loyal Flea Bag.

But the vendors came anyway in a steady stream. I would often take them to the Parkside Restaurant, a landmark Italian eatery. Across the street from the restaurant was a small park with a *bocci* ball court and a large brick fireplace for barbecuing which the local residents would use in the summer. The Parkside had eye-level mirrors running around the dining room. The story was that this permitted Mafia patrons to see who was approaching them if they faced the wall while eating. I am sure it was just a joke but the visiting vendors seemed to enjoy hearing it.

Sales were climbing rapidly during 1982 and, as we approached year-end, we were all stretched to the limits. We held our first year-end company party at a hotel restaurant in the neighborhood. Our landlord, Tony Melita, attended. I made a speech regretting that he did not have a larger warehouse to accommodate our growth. He was a wonderful landlord.

Sales continued at a rapid pace past December into January, 1983. Abe Cohen prepared our financial statement for 1982 with sales of over $9 million, and this was for an 11-month year. It was clear that in less than a year we had outgrown the warehouse. Some quick arithmetic showed that our rate of sales had increased tenfold in less than 12 months. My father went forth to look for a 15–20,000 square foot warehouse in Queens. We were really committed to the area because our employees all came from Queens and used public transportation to get to work each day. I knew we were forgoing the lower state taxes of New Jersey and the modern warehouses of Long Island, but I just did not want to lose employees because of the move.

Around this time we did face the emotionally difficult experience of terminating our first employee, Eileen. What made it more difficult was that she was a good friend and neighbor. Further, she was loyal, honest and dedicated. However, the office work pace had quickened substantially. Eileen was extremely thorough which led her to take a long time to do certain tasks. The evening we told her, Patricia, Eileen and I were all in tears. In retrospect, I believe letting her go was a mistake on our part. Subsequently, as the company grew, we could have found a place for Eileen. To our surprise and pleasure, Eileen did not feel bitterness after she left the company and we kept our friendship intact. This was a credit to her maturity more than to ours.

Elmhurst Warehouse

My father located a number of warehouses and finally we selected one in Elmhurst, Queens. It was located in a mixed residential and commercial area just off Queens Boulevard, a major thoroughfare. The warehouse was only 13,500 square feet but it had balconies which increased its effective size. We had to build extra office space. This we expected. Most of the warehouses we visited had only 10–15 percent of their area set aside for offices. In our industry, 30–40 percent was required. This was because of the unusually high value and small size of the merchandise in the personal computer business.

This location would give us a stepped loading dock, which would eliminate lifting heavy pallets and cartons up to or down from truck level. It would also mean the breaking up of our one-department com-

Entrance to Elmhurst Warehouse, 1984.

pany into geographically dispersed departments. We would no longer be in sight of everyone. It would mean using memos and the phone to communicate within the company. I believe this is one of the big changes a growing company must pass through. Morale problems can develop as some of the personal rapport and recognition is lost when employees are dispersed through a large building. Nancy sensed this change and made it clear, soon after we settled in, that she was happier when we were a smaller operation.

My father took care of the entire move. He handled the phone installation, the landlord's contract, the movers, the purchase and assembly of additional storage racks and the interviewing and hiring of additional employees. The move was completed over one weekend and I don't think we missed a beat in shipping goods on Friday or Monday.

With physical separation of people comes the need for specialization of responsibilities. Previously we all wore many hats. Now it was no longer practical. My father focused on advertising and promotion.

Patricia ran the Purchasing Department. Nancy did only bookkeeping. For a while the customers missed talking to them and vice versa. We now needed employees dedicated to nothing else but sales.

Just prior to moving to Elmhurst we hired Mike Polowe to assist Jim in shipping and receiving. We also hired Louis Ortiz specifically for shipping. Mike and Louis turned out to be very loyal and honest employees. Mike was a large powerful man, awkward in manner and speech, but he had a marvelous memory for numbers and detail. We soon relied on him to check received goods and count inventory. Patricia eventually assumed a protective attitude towards Mike and brought him into the Purchasing Department to handle expediting. Mike was concerned about how he would sound to others over the phone. With patient insistence, Patricia finally got Mike to use the phone and speak with our vendors. It was the first desk job that blue collar Mike ever had. One of the genuine joys of running the business was helping people learn new skills. We brought Mike from a shipping clerk to an expediter where he could use his mental ability with numbers and detail.

Another success was Danny Alvarez, whom my father hired as a shipping clerk. Here was a young man from the Puerto Rican minority of New York, without any marketable skills whatsoever. What a great pleasure it was to recognize his brightness and give him a chance to become a computer salesman. After a year of vendor training classes, on-the-job learning and an eagerness to help customers, Danny became one of our best salesmen.

At Elmhurst I began to realize that I needed top management assistance. Up to that point we had been hiring salesmen, secretaries, clerks and technicians. Nancy, the bookkeeper, was our most highly trained and professional employee. But we needed someone who knew the industry from a marketing and sales perspective. Larry Kerrigan had left Datel and was now working for another computer store in Connecticut. For some time he had expressed an interest in joining our company, but I had felt we were too small for someone with his plans and goals. Now I felt we could use him. Larry was very different from me. He was a large man, overweight with a round face that lit up when he smiled—an extrovert, with a lot of "street smarts." He presented his ideas forcefully and persuasively. The industry noise level was rising. Perhaps Larry could be the gladiator I needed to do battle against the growing competitive forces. I hired him in early in 1983 as our Director of Marketing. Later I would promote him to VP of Marketing.

I remember at our first outing together we visited a trade show in Boston. Larry listened to my conversations with each vendor. Then

Larry began to engage the vendors in conversation. He quickly reached a conclusion which overjoyed him. "They love aggression," Larry announced to me.

Larry made no secret of the fact that he had mood swings and took lithium to regulate them. He also used it to regulate his energy level. Larry could work round the clock for days in this way and then collapse from utter exhaustion. At the Comdex show he would employ this questionable technique and, like a tornado, visit and impress every vendor on his agenda. Larry was charismatic and his enthusiasm soon spread around the company. However, some were concerned. At various times Nancy, Patricia and my father had problems dealing with Larry. Sometimes employees, on arriving to open the warehouse, would find Larry snoring away on the lobby sofa after an all-night binge.

It was soon clear that I had employed an individual possessing complexity and personality extremes which I had no idea how to handle. I could give him marching instructions to persuade a vendor to give us their product line. At this he was excellent. We began a series of dealer round tables which we held monthly at restaurants in different cities. Key customers were invited. Larry was master of ceremonies and he could lead and hold the group for hours. As a former school teacher, he loved these events. Our customers could discuss dealer concerns, market changes, new products and business strategies. The problem was how to harness Larry's impressive talents and limit the damage his personality could unleash.

Among the regional distributors I was looked upon as a leader with a good reputation. At least that is what a number of my competitors told me. One day the president of one of these distributors phoned me and suggested we form an association to share information on customers with bad credit history. He suggested that, because of my prominence, I should be the one who ought to call together all the computer distributors at the next Comdex show in Las Vegas. With my father's help we invited about thirty distributors to a conference room during the show and nearly all of them came. We formed the Association of Microcomputer Distributors, AMD, and soon our controllers were exchanging information on non-paying customers. My father became very active in the organization and really enjoyed the company of all our competitors. He shared none of my fears that we were just a group of sharks warily circling and eyeing each other with a mixture of respect and suspicion.

I made a number of trips to England, both to visit my in-laws and for business purposes. On one such trip I decided to take the supersonic

Concorde back to New York. I struck up a conversation with the man next to me who turned out to be the president of Brown and Williams Tobacco Company. I asked him many questions about the problems of running a large company. I was very eager to learn what I could from this experienced executive. "You must surround yourself with people who know more than you do or you are dead in the water," he said. After a while he asked about me and I gave him a copy of our latest catalog. About two weeks later, back in my office, I received a call from the director of the Purchasing Department of Brown and Williams. He told me that his boss, the president, requested that he place an order with us for computer equipment.

Single to Multi Location Distributor

In early 1985 I could see that our growth was slowing. The big West Coast distributors had at last decided that the New York market, though filled with "sharp and seedy" operators, was too lucrative to avoid. Micro D, Softsel and Micro America were now in our region in force. In addition, our customers further away could buy locally since regional distributors and nationals now had warehouses in nearby major cities.

I had two choices. We could focus on a "vertical" market. For example, we could select a narrow high support segment such as CAD/CAM (computer aid design/computer aided manufacturing) and control the New York region. This would mean differentiating ourselves from the national distributors by the products and services we offered. It is difficult for a large distributor, established to sell commodity products, to follow this path. The second choice was to fight the competition head on by opening warehouses in other parts of the country and become a "horizontal" distributor, handling a wide range of personal computer products.

Had I to do it over again I would have gone "vertical." It would have suited my own personality better. The company would be easier to control and would be technically oriented, thus shaped around my own strengths and weaknesses. Unfortunately, I did not know my own limits as well as I do now. So I opted for the ego trip and decided to create a national distribution network.

Where should we place our second warehouse? The Midwest seemed like a good place to start. It was not too far away if we had trouble. And it was far enough so as to provide true incremental business.

But in which city should I locate the warehouse? Chicago was too obvious and too competitive. Every national distributor was already there. The UPS one-day shipping zone gave me the answer. From Fort Wayne, Indiana, overnight, we could ship to more major cities than from Chicago. These included Cleveland, Detroit, Louisville, and Chicago itself. My father traveled to Fort Wayne to scout the region and locate a warehouse, a local attorney and a newspaper in which to place employment ads.

My father returned from his mission with everything accomplished. We soon had a 2,500-square-foot warehouse with an adjacent unit we could grow into. We placed advertisements and soon had a stack of résumés to go over. From New York we set up a series of interviews in Fort Wayne to hire a regional manager. Patricia and Larry joined me as we flew out to Fort Wayne for the interviews.

Larry's interviewing style was unusual. For example, he would ask each candidate what credit card was closest to the driver's license in his wallet. Larry then asked the candidate to recite his telephone number backwards. He would ask if they had brothers and sisters and the occupations of each. These "under the skin" questions gave Larry clues as to the management potential of each candidate. Patricia and I were asking more straightforward questions. In the end we differed on who was the best candidate. Back in New York Patricia and I selected a warehouse manager who had worked for the local International Harvester plant. He was excellent at arranging the warehouse but knew nothing about sales and, ultimately, we had to replace him.

Soon after opening Fort Wayne, Lee Mannheimer contacted me regarding the acquisition of a warehouse near Seattle, WA. I had met Lee at the first AMD meeting during the Comdex computer trade show in Las Vegas and we liked each other. When Lee was told by his employer, Vivitar, to sell the Seattle warehouse, Lee thought of me. The deal was on very favorable terms. Basically, Lee told me to make any reasonable offer and he would accept it. I bought the inventory at cost, excluding obsolete goods, and the fixed assets at their depreciated cost. For example, a $20,000 lift truck was valued at $400. Lee assumed the task of collecting the balance of the accounts receivable. So for about $100,000 I got a functioning warehouse with eight trained employees. My attorney, Bill Reilly, quickly drew up a contract and the deal was done.

In 1985 Steve Owings, from Greenville, SC, contacted me with a proposal. He and his colleagues wanted to buy out their employer's business, a small computer distribution company. But Steve felt they needed a larger distributor to be affiliated with. As a result, Steve and I made a deal where I would buy 44 percent of the South Carolina business, he and his colleagues would own the remainder. The new com-

President of FA Components, 1985.

pany, Freeman-Owings, would use our name, FA Components, get our product lines and benefit from all our advertising, catalog mailings and promotion. Later Steve and I agreed that opening a Florida warehouse would be a good idea. By 1986 we had a business consisting of five warehouses, with 100 employees and annual sales of about $50 million. This was personally very satisfying; however, clouds soon appeared on the horizon.

An emerging problem was the growing power struggle between Larry and Ahmed. Ahmed's rapidly growing knowledge could not be ignored. He outgrew the assistant role under my father and became Larry's assistant where he learned marketing and sales techniques. Ahmed became more assertive and Larry gave him more responsibilities. Eventually a competition developed as Ahmed sought to protect his growing domain. Terrible arguments developed between the two men, who were together the driving force of the company. I was happy to let them take on responsibility and both were self-driven to control and achieve. But these arguments were upsetting other employees who could hear the shouting and foul language emanating from the thin walls of Larry's office. Larry said on a number of occasions: "I've created a monster." Ahmed shouted at Larry: "I will destroy you." In hopes of easing the conflict I separated the responsibility of sales and marketing. Larry would handle marketing. Ahmed would report to me, instead of Larry, and he would run the sales department. I wrote two job descriptions which separated out who did what, explained it to them both at a meeting and crossed my fingers. But it didn't work and conflict arose again. This time Larry got very depressed and with his depression came a long period of nonproductivity.

He always told me he was a two-year man who would stay just long enough to solve problems and then move on. Larry said he was bad at "maintenance." I recall insisting that I would keep a steady stream of problems coming, to keep him interested. Perhaps I could have, but solving the disagreement with Ahmed was beyond me. Larry lasted just over two years with FA Components before we both agreed it wasn't working anymore. There is more to tell about Larry Kerrigan, but that comes later.

Ahmed had emerged as the winner in this contest. He was now in charge of marketing and sales and, because of his technical knowledge, I released to him what I considered the most imaginative responsibility, the addition of new product lines. Ahmed also had the technical department reporting to him. His conflicts were now with other departments, such as Accounting and Purchasing, which still reported to me.

My father played the role of peacemaker and instructed me on how to handle employee conflict. Generally this involved calling each party in separately to hear his side but without taking any position. Then I would call in both parties together to have a three-way meeting and try to work out a compromise, again without partiality. I did not enjoy this procedure because of its unpredictability and my lack of training in management and personnel techniques. The meetings helped for a while but soon the same disagreements would erupt.

How did Ahmed get all this power? He was clever and aggressive. He worked sixteen hours a day. I believed that promoting him to greater responsibility would lessen his anger and discontent. It only got worse. Ahmed brought in some good product lines such NEC monitors and he spearheaded the establishment of our own house brand. The idea was to purchase little-known Asian peripherals, put our brand name "Varsity" on the boxes, and sell these products to price-sensitive customers. In this way we could escape the fierce competition developing in the well-known U.S. brands. It was an attempt to take control of our margins rather than have the vendors control them through overproduction, over distribution and direct selling.

Ahmed made good headway in this effort and made it a personal challenge. However, in the process, he offended a number of existing U.S. suppliers who were upset at all the Taiwanese clones coming in at very low prices. Hercules, a graphics card manufacturer, was especially upset. The President, Kevin Jenkins, finally called me and told me we would not get any of his new products as a result of our selling a Taiwanese copy of his graphics card. He further said that he felt Ahmed did not like Hercules. All in all, the profits coming out of the Varsity line were simply not enough to justify the ill will being created among our established suppliers. And Ahmed's single-mindedness in developing the line was creating more problems than I wished.

Ahmed sensed my reservations about his efforts and his behavior became more difficult. He decided to throw a fishing boat party the same day we were to hold our company picnic. He began to invite a great many people in the company to his outing, basically trying to sabotage the picnic. A few days before the company picnic I asked him to call off his fishing trip. Many of the employees were confused about which event to attend, especially those who worked directly for him. But Ahmed went ahead with his event, pulling about seven or eight people away from our company picnic. Some others decided to avoid either event. I was furious and the next day I called Ahmed into my office and asked why he was engaging in this power play and splitting up the company into two camps. Ahmed lost his temper, complaining that I had not praised him recently for all his hard work. I don't recall whether I fired him or he quit. It was almost simultaneous, as he stormed out of the office. I was literally shaking with rage. How could someone so bright as Ahmed do something that I considered so stupid?

After the angst of dealing with Larry and Ahmed, both unpredictable stars, I was ready for more stability and less "brilliance" in my Number Two. Enter John Brandon, a sales manager for one of our suppliers. John had the appearance of a conservative senior executive. He was calm and mature. This I felt was what we needed. We hired John and later he became president and I kicked myself upstairs to CEO.

Prior to Larry's departure, Nancy came into my office and announced she was resigning and taking her husband, belongings and relatives to Florida. She was tired of the politics and the fights with Larry and Ahmed. Though I wanted to try to change Nancy's mind I could see it would be futile. I knew I was losing a most dedicated and loyal employee, one who had been with FA almost from the very start. Nancy gave us four weeks' notice and the rush was on to get a new controller. My father knew a young accountant in his synagogue. I'll call him Arnold. We hired Arnold before Nancy left, so that she could train him. The decision to hire Arnold turned out to be the worst one I made.

The Problems Begin

By 1986 both Patricia and I were losing interest in the daily running of the business. Patricia felt that nursing had more purpose than petty office bickering. I found managing people to be stressful. I was simply no good at it; soft when I should be tough, impatient when patience was needed. So I started to delegate responsibility and back away from daily involvement, as did Patricia. We took long vacations to remote places like the Antarctic, Baffin Island and Greenland. The company, increasingly, was on autopilot.

By the time Arnold came on the scene I was eager to turn over all financial responsibility, including check signing. On first meeting the new controller I was uneasy. Arnold was about thirty-five years old, had a fleshy flabby appearance, curly hair and a weak chin. There was something insincere and sly in his manner. But I never trusted my first impressions and so I put aside these feelings. I even ignored warnings of both Nancy and Patricia. As the months went by we seemed to be running out of cash. Vendors were calling and complaining of slow payments. Still each quarterly report was showing profit. Arnold said we needed a bigger credit line. Since our bank, Bank Leumi, had a loan limit of $3 million, he brought in Citibank, which offered a $5 million limit but required daily reporting of our sales figures. After months of accounting scrutiny Citibank agreed to give us the loan, but the need for additional cash kept increasing. Arnold said we were growing and that was the problem. We did not have an audit for one year since we had terminated the previous accountants. So I called in the big eight firm of Coopers and Lybrand. The senior auditor and partner, Bob Fish, took charge. Soon they found the problem. Arnold had been putting checks to vendors in a filing cabinet and holding them there for weeks. He did not reduce the checking account when he wrote the checks, but did reduce accounts payable. The controller was creating phony nonexistent assets and producing quarterly statements which showed a profit when in fact we were losing money. It turned out that he was not trying to steal but felt the job was getting over his head. Fish told me not to fire him immediately since they needed more information from him. When the time came I unleashed a fury of invective at Arnold calling him incompetent and directly responsible for the crisis the company now faced. "This is some exit interview," said the unrepentant Arnold who then scurried out of my office to pack up and leave.

With each day the financial crisis faced by the company grew worse. We were severely undercapitalized. Since I had been under the impression we were making money, I had transferred some "profits" into my personal assets. Now much of that money had to be returned. But even that was not enough. We had been losing money for five quarters because of rising expenses, smaller margins and a badly managed credit and collections department. Citibank was, of course, extremely upset. Their auditors had not uncovered the problem and we were a new account for them which might now go bankrupt. Since bank loans are based on assets such as accounts receivable and inventory, the auditors had not looked at our liabilities, namely accounts payable, which is where the biggest problem lay. In an attempt to reduce their exposure, Citibank began to reduce our loan. This exacerbated our cash flow difficulties. John Brandon felt the best course of action was to level with our suppliers. The suppliers, almost without exception, panicked. The Japanese suppliers reacted worst by withdrawing our credit lines immediately, demanding full payment of all outstanding debts and requiring cash on all future orders. At the other end of the spectrum was AST Research. Their chief financial officer expanded our credit line after learning of our problem. His view was they did not want to lose a distributor and would help us through the problem.

Well, with Citibank and most of the suppliers cutting down their lending to us, things began to deteriorate rapidly. Steve flew up from

Greenville with his secretary, extremely upset that my problems would also pull his company down. I was in a state of despair and unable to make decisions. He occupied my office and tried to sort out the financial problems. We had an emergency meeting during which Steve offered me a deal which would leave me with one or two warehouses and almost certain bankruptcy but might allow him to survive with the remaining parts of the company. Since I owned 44 percent of his firm this offered me some hope. But then his southern company might also fail since our suppliers, not realizing these were separate companies, might cut him off as a customer if my northern operation failed. Also, Steve's company would no longer get sales and marketing support from us. It was a less than perfect offer but I accepted. The next day I changed my mind. Steve was angry with me for backing out of a handshake but I saw a better solution which was worth risking Steve's rage.

Selling the Company

During this period I was looking for a buyer to rescue our company. The first group that came in were slick operators with gold chains and bracelets. Steve felt I was wasting time talking to people like that. The second offer came from my cousin Eli Oxenhorn and Barry Rubenstein. I talked to them about my problems at a bar on Long Island where Eli was celebrating his fortieth birthday.

Barry and I had worked together as engineers for Sperry Gyroscope in 1964. We again worked together for a while at ADDS. He eventually left engineering and become a very wealthy financier. He founded Cheyenne Software and, coincidentally, met my cousin who was looking for an entrepreneurial opportunity. Barry hired Eli to be President of Cheyenne Software in 1983. Now Cheyenne had $8 million dollars in the bank and was developing software for large clients. They wanted to invest some of their excess cash in a computer distribution company. Barry, chairman of Cheyenne, was interested. Trying to get Steve to meet them was a problem. He had enough of gold chains. After pleading with him, he reluctantly went out to the Cheyenne headquarters in Roslyn, Long Island, where I introduced him to Eli and Barry. Fortunately, Steve liked them and, after a long and stressful negotiation, we closed on the sale of our two companies, FA Components and Freeman-Owings, to Cheyenne Software on July 7, 1987 for stock valued at $13 million. I received some of this Cheyenne stock and cash to pay company tax liabilities.

My attorney and friend, Bill Reilly, had at first urged me to roll up my sleeves and rescue my company. But my heart was not in it. Bill then applied his legal skills to defend my position during the long negotiations with Cheyenne. Because of him I had a seat on the Board of Directors of the future FA Computer Technologies and Bill won other guarantees which never would have occurred to me.

Patricia was planning to leave the company anyway to resume nursing. Telling my father that he would have to leave also was not easy. But he understood that these changes were now beyond my control. It was no longer a family business. My father soon obtained consulting assignments from our advertising agency, ACS. We always had a close relationship with the owner, Andrew Shupack, and his wife Rita. Clearly, working for Andy was not as enjoyable for my father as helping me. He wanted me to find a new work challenge that he could participate in.

Steve Owings became President of the new company, FA Technologies, and I served for a while on the board of directors. But my days were numbered. It was no fun playing a minor role in the company after having had total control. And the new management was not happy with my appearing every morning at the New York headquarters where the remaining employees still considered me the boss. I showed up less and less and one day I simply stopped showing up. Steve was commuting up from Greenville to the New York headquarters frequently. I suggested, and the Board agreed, that moving the headquarters to Greenville was best. Ultimately Cheyenne engineered another acquisition, Gates Distributing, on the west coast. The combined company, Gates/FA Distributing was, by 1994, the fourth largest distributor of computer hardware in the United States, employing hundreds. This company was then acquired by Arrow Distributing and renamed Gates/Arrow Distributing. By 1996, this company had sales in the $1 billion per year range.

FA Retrospective

In spite of the heartache and trouble, it is a permanent source of satisfaction to me that I started FA Components. Instead of forever executing someone else's vision, I had the opportunity to execute my own. I made some good decisions and some bad ones but at least they were mine. "I did it my way," as the song says.

In 1985 *Inc Magazine*, read by entrepreneurs nationwide, made a list of the 500 fastest growing private companies in the United States. FA Components placed 59th that year and 69th the following year. In

New York City we were the second fastest growing company in 1986. Mayor Ed Koch invited the owners of the New York top 10 to breakfast. It was a great honor to join that small group for orange juice and croissants at City Hall. Significantly, all of us at the table were service companies. Manufacturing did not appear to have a future in the Big Apple.

Who at Gates/Arrow today would know that part of their company started in a small basement in Queens with Patricia, Rachel and me stuffing cartons with computer products and Styrofoam chips, picking up the phone and scurrying to meet Bobby, our UPS driver.

Having power as I did was intoxicating. I can easily understand how the owner of a company can become arrogant and authoritarian. I resisted these temptations and discounted the flattery. The lower the employee was in the organization, the more I felt the need to be deferential and respectful. We established a medical and disability insurance plan for all the employees which was as good as any in the much larger firms. I would not want to ever face a situation where an employee, unable to work for health reasons, had to be terminated without substantial insurance benefits. We also established a generous defined benefit and defined contribution retirement fund. To my way of thinking, it was a bargain if I could purchase a benefit for an employee that cost me $1.00 but would cost the employee $2.00 to replicate it. So I tried to run the company in a humanitarian and enlightened manner yet pursue profits aggressively. It was with mixed emotions that I passed the helm to a new captain.

A great disappointment to me was the sudden loss of personal contact with the suppliers, employees and customers. No longer relevant, no longer writing the big checks, I felt suddenly outside the industry and its marketplace. I attended a few more Comdex shows in Las Vegas and Atlanta, wandered about saying hello to old faces, but there was no real purpose to it, except nostalgia, a pale substitute for a purchase order.

Because the Cheyenne stock was restricted, I could not sell it for two years. By then Cheyenne had changed from a developer of customized software to a developer of Novell utility software. This was significant because the utility software were standard products that could be packaged, marketed and sold in quantity. I had confidence in Cheyenne's products and cousin Eli's competence. In spite of mutual bad feelings between Steve and me, I knew he was hard-working and capable. So I held the Cheyenne stock for years afterwards. Both Cheyenne and FA Computer Technology prospered and the stock reflected that success.

So reluctantly, at the age of forty-nine, it occurred to me that, like it or not, I was retired. To keep my mind and body busy I needed a challenging substitute, something more than watching the price of Cheyenne stock every day. Patricia and I went on some unusual vacations before we sold the business. We expanded that activity during my retirement and our world travels are described in Chapter 9.

Between 1987 and 1990 I made some feeble attempts to start a new business. I knew my father and others wanted me to get back in harness. However, traveling the world, hiking, climbing mountains, going to films anytime, watching the world go by at a sidewalk cafe almost anywhere—well, it would take one hell of a job to equal that in my view. Sometimes I missed the challenge of running my own business, but then I remembered the stress, the personality conflicts, chasing people for unpaid bills, the tedium of many tasks. As a wit once said, "no one ever lay on their deathbed saying they should have spent more time in the office."

With the need to earn more money no longer a priority, the use of time becomes the preoccupation. What is a billion dollars to a person who has only five minutes of life left? I have far less than a billion dollars and an actuarial life expectancy of more than five minutes, but the principle is the same. Our values, rather than the necessity of work, become the determinant in choosing what to do with time. Values determine what is enjoyable, meaningful and worthy. Certainly my leisure time is enjoyable. But I have found pleasure also in sharing with, giving to and helping friends and family.

I find I am giving more and more thought to a trust fund of some kind that will support good causes after I am gone. I find a growing desire within me to leave an enduring living monument to my values that will give back to humanity what I received from it.

8
Friendship

Friends are born, not made.
—Henry Brooks Adams, *The Education of Henry Adams*, 1907

With self-employment came a break with my past. Not only was my working day radically different but so were my leisure time, my interests and attitudes. There came a growing self-assurance, a liberation from dependency on employers and bosses. I looked both at the past and the present with the confidence that accompanies financial success. I formed new friendships and sought to re-establish old ones.

Reunion 1983

In January, 1983 I took my family to Copper Mountain, Colorado, on a skiing holiday. One evening, after a day of skiing, I was sitting in the Club Med hot tub on a dark and steamy outdoor deck. The woman next to me was speaking to her husband sitting in the tub with her. I heard her call him Sherman. Now that is not such a common name and I asked him if he came from Brooklyn. Well, it soon was apparent that he was the same Sherman who was my childhood friend. Later our families joined for dinner and a lot of catching up on the past twenty-five years. Sherman left Brooklyn around 1960 and disappeared. He went West, settled in California and worked for IBM until an early retirement. Then he started a real estate management firm in San Jose and was evidently quite successful. After the dinner I made a proposal to Sherman. If I organized a reunion of all our old friends from Brooklyn would he join us? Sherman was willing and so upon my return to New York I began the detective work necessary to find friends I had not seen for twenty-five years. Using the telephone directory and networking from friend to friend I found almost everyone. Todd had an unlisted phone but I learned that his father still lived in Brooklyn. After

In 1984 Alvin Gennis and Sherman joined me for a weekend at Mohonk Mountain House.

locating the father I got the unlisted phone number of his son. Morty I guessed might have moved to Long Island. This is a large area covering two counties, but there was only one listing for Morty. Sometimes calling a former employer led me to an old friend. What a thrill it was to introduce myself on the phone after all those years. I set the date for May, 1983 at a hotel near JFK airport. There were Steve Maybar, Al Gennes, Herb Schneider, Harvey Bernstein, Eddie Stravitz, Lester Poris, Eddie Katz, Spencer Shaps and others from the old boy scout troop. Even our scoutmaster, Marty Chieken, attended and of course, true to his word, Sherman flew in from California. After dinner, each rose and spoke about how they felt. Some had tears in their eyes and their voices broke with emotion. Then we sang the old boy scout songs with nostalgia and pride. Before I knew it people were shaking hands, embracing, waving farewell. It was over. What remained, besides the photo album and the sweet recollections, was a renewed friendship with Sherman, Al Gennes and especially Herb Schneider.

There is something special about childhood friends. Childhood friends shape each others' personalities in a way friends in your adult life can never do. Childhood friends are with you in that formative and malleable time, when the days are long and the memories lasting.

Tom Strauss

In late 1985 I considered selling public stock in my company, FA Components. I made contacts in Wall Street and several investment banking firms came out to see my company. Lehman Brothers sent a young analyst named Tom Strauss. After the meeting was over, Tom and I discussed our vacation plans. By coincidence he and I were planning a ski trip to Aspen at exactly the same time. Thus began a close friendship. Tom is about fifteen years younger than I but one of his many charms is a disregard for the ages of his friends. Some people must live in their own age. Tom, on the other hand, relates well to Rachel, Patricia and me. He shows a genuine interest in our interests. Tom's disregard for selecting his friends by age extended to his choice of a wife. In his late thirties Tom at last made the big decision and chose Wendy, a woman twelve years younger. Wendy, in fact, is only a few years older than Rachel, which created a mild dilemma for Rachel. Rachel was confused as to her relationship to Wendy. Was Wendy a peer or the wife of her father's friend?

Tom is a wonderful friend. His good manners are equal to Patricia's and we can always count on Tom to be on time and true to his commitments. Tom came from a German Jewish background. He was raised in Westchester, surrounded by books and high culture. So assimilated are the German Jews that it was many months after our friendship began that I learned he was Jewish. I see much of my father's enthusiasm, talents and optimism in Tom and that is perhaps why I am so fond of him.

After Tom left Lehman Brothers he went to work for the investment banking division of Barclay's Bank. In 1994 he left Barclay's to work as an independent investment banker. I speak with Tom almost daily.

Park Avenue Friends

First, I should explain how we got to Park Avenue. For years Patricia had been traveling into Manhattan from Fresh Meadows to view performances at Lincoln Center or Carnegie Hall. And she was a regular visitor to the museums as well. So it was natural that as soon as we could afford it we moved to Manhattan. Real estate agents showed us cooperative apartments in the midtown area near the East River. They told us certain buildings would not admit Jews. It might be possible for Patricia to get into such a building and I could move in across the

Boy Scout twenty-five-year reunion, 1983, JFK Airport Hotel.

My mother with Steve Maybar and wife.

Steve Maybar speaks with Mike and Elisa at reunion.

Sherman Zell.

Herb Schneider speaks to Sherman Zell.

street, into a Jewish building, and we could wave at each other. Patricia refused the suggestion. We finally began to look at apartments on Park Avenue in the 70s. After looking at a few choices we settled on a bright two-bedroom cooperative unit on the 19th floor of a postwar white brick apartment house. The apartment had three exposures, faced Park Avenue looking west, with large rooms everywhere except the kitchen. It had a narrow, long terrace which had a commanding view of the penthouses across the street. And the building was a mixture of Jews and non-Jews. It was perfect. Cooperative boards interview prospective tenants. I felt a bit fraudulent as I dressed up in my best suit to leave a good impression. The examining committee gave us passing grades.

We settled into our new home in late 1983, somewhat intimidated by our new and formal surroundings. Just before moving in I asked my mother to spend a day to wait for the painter. There was nothing in the room but a small TV which I brought over so my mother would have something to watch during the day. When I switched it on nothing happened because Con Edison had not turned on the electric power yet. What I forgot to do was turn off the set. That night, at about 2:00 A.M., Con Edison turned on the power to our apartment and the TV began to blast away at full volume. In the apartment next door, the Larimers were awakened by the noise and thought someone must have died. Hector, the superintendent, was summoned and entered to find a lonely television broadcasting to an empty apartment. We had not even moved in and already our profile was higher than we wished. Within two weeks after moving in one of our two cats, Thistle, escaped through an open window. We feared she had plunged nineteen stories to her death. I scanned the roofs and streets below for evidence of a flattened cat. But there was no sign of Thistle. The next morning I stepped onto the terrace and heard a meow. Two stories below us on a narrow ledge was Thistle, looking up at me. She had somehow climbed down pipes and plants to this ledge, inches from a 170 foot straight drop onto Park Avenue. Quickly we knocked on the neighbor's door, nearest the ledge, and a frightened old woman let us in to rescue our pet.

We spent quite a few years at 799 Park Avenue before making any friends. I am normally quite a friendly person, but a twenty second elevator ride is, even for me, too short a time to establish rapport with a stranger. However, one summer day, I went up to the roof to sunbathe on deck chairs set up for that purpose. It was there I first met Perry Wolff and had a decent conversation of over twenty seconds. Perry was a raconteur of the first order. He had been a CBS producer specializing in news documentaries. He had met or worked with many of the makers and shakers of the early days of television. I was fascinated not only by these experiences but also his astute observations. Later Patricia and I met his wife, Tuulikki, who had a studio in the building where she painted. Tuulikki was very shy but also kind and warmhearted. It took a while to get to know her but it was worth the effort. We had many dinners with the Wolffs and, encouraged by the pleasure and convenience of our first 799 friends, we thought it might be fun to throw a house party for neighbors, which we did during one Christmas.

As a result of this gathering we got to know Dan and Sylvia Gersen. Dan is a successful attorney and a model of diplomacy and poise. Equally at home in a discussion of science or the arts, Dan was as close to a renaissance man as I have ever met. Sylvia's salient attributes were well-formed views and the courage to express them. Together they make a very engaging and elegant couple. With both the Wolffs and Gersens we go to films, restaurants and cultural events. I suppose we are all intrigued by each others' differences. And like my friend Tom, we are happy to associate with people outside our age group. Both the Gersens and the Wolffs are about fifteen years older than we are.

After the interview to get into 799 Park Avenue, I was rarely seen in jacket or tie. My standard outfit consisted of corduroy pants, suspenders and T-shirt. I was proud of my souvenir T shirts purchased in strange and far off lands. One day Perry said he would like to purchase my entire collection. For a moment I was highly flattered, until he announced his plan to burn them all. After that I began wearing shirts and even proper sports jackets. Compliments from other neighbors reinforced my new sartorial appearance.

Rodney Devine

We met Rodney and his wife Genie around 1984, while on a hiking weekend in the Adirondacks. We were by coincidence staying at Saranac Lodge, a rustic backwoods hotel. Subsequently, Rodney would remind us how impressed he was as we stomped into the lounge in our walking gear. It turned out that Rodney and Genie lived not far from us in Manhattan. They both had lengthy American pedigrees which was a novelty to a descendant of recent immigrants. Most of my New York friends were also one generation away from being immigrants. But Rodney and Genie's ancestors were actually in America before the Civil War. Rodney belonged to the Union Club, an elite "waspy" establishment. He invited me there for lunch and drinks and suddenly I saw a side of New York I never knew existed: dark wood panels, hushed reading rooms with vaulted ceilings, members quietly and slowly gliding through ample corridors. The honking taxis, littered streets and the homeless were left far behind. Rodney has a wonderful and earthy sense of humor and an eye for the women. I always enjoyed Rodney's company and our conversations could get quite hilarious. Rodney is politically very conservative but is saved by his sense of humor and Genie. She brings him down to earth in her charming way. Unfortunately, Rodney and Genie did not like living in New York and, in 1994, moved to Essex, CT, just too far to see each other regularly.

Vivien Ambler

Around 1973, while Patricia was working for a short period as an industrial nurse at Bear Stearns, the Wall Street investment bank, she met Vivien. Vivien, who was purchasing paper for Bear Stearns, originally came from Yorkshire, England. The two became good friends. Later, as I got to know Vivien, she became my friend too. Over the years Vivien, who never married, has been close to our family, including Rachel whom she saw grow from a six-year-old child to an adult. Vivien was like an aunt to Rachel. Later, working as a cabin attendant for TWA, Vivien was always in and out of town. She had a longstanding love/hate relationship with TWA but the nomadic life seemed to hold a fascination for her. During a lengthy airline strike she accepted a job at my company and worked in the sales department. Vivien is extremely bright and soon became one of the most knowledgeable sales people in the room. But when the strike ended Vivien returned to TWA.

Al Lipsky

I first met Al at Sperry Gyroscope where he was a senior engineer back in 1965. We lunched with a group of fellow engineers that included Leon Sternick and Sol Rubin. But it was only Al who remained friends with me. In 1975, when I was desperately seeking work after getting fired by Ideal Corporation, he offered to hire me as a consultant engineer while he was chief engineer at Hydrosystems. After a fruitless search outside engineering I relented. I was broke and had used up all my savings and Al's gesture came when I needed it most. It was a favor I will never forget. Over the years Al has kept in touch regularly and we have had many dinners together during which he would unload his work frustrations. These I listened to with great patience, always remembering how much I owed him. Al always had such a gentle personality and was completely without pretense; behind this modest demeanor was a fine mind and a very talented engineer.

Kent, CT

In April, 1989 we purchased a townhouse condominium in Kent, a small town eighty-five miles north of New York City. Our original plan was to make this our primary home, but as time went by it became more of a summer and winter retreat. Before selecting Kent we searched the northwest corner of Connecticut and even as far north as Vermont. While Vermont offered true rural living, being that far from my relatives and friends was a big negative factor. We compromised on a hilly and underdeveloped area just north of New Milford, CT. When Patricia asked a realtor for "a small town with character" she immediately told us to go to Kent. There a very low key sales agent by the name of Keith Krezan showed us a number of homes, but the maintenance-free feature of the condominium units on a hill overlooking the town proved irresistible. Next to us lived Bob and Connie Sanders, who were awaiting the completion of their permanent new home designed by their son Rob. The Sanderses were to became our very good friends in Kent. Our retreat has a commanding view of the Housatonic Valley with rolling hills on the other side of a river that flows past the town. From our front deck we can see the changing weather as it rises in the west and drifts towards us. Summer heat changes to thundershowers. Winter winds bring snow and gray clouds. I prefer the winter because we have a fireplace in the living room and a sauna in the basement. What a pleasure it is to hike on the nearby Appalachian Trail covered in a white frosty blanket, to feel the face and fingers go red from the cold brisk air. Then, after some miles of tramping, it is back to the warmth of the living room fire and the sauna. After a hearty meal what is left but to watch night fall and doze off in the light of glowing embers.

The town of Kent has one main street with numerous boutiques and art galleries catering to day-trippers from New York City or weekenders such as ourselves. For Kent is a town of many populations. In addition to weekenders, there are also retired urbanites such as the Sanderses and shopkeepers, representing the business community. They may have moved from the Big City or grown up in Kent. Then there are the locals who might be service contractors or employees of

Good Friends

My engineering buddy, Al Lipsky, 1997.

English hiking companion, Andrew Opie, 1997.

My young friend, Tom Strauss, 1997.

My childhood friend, Herb Schneider, 1997.

the shops. As a result, Kent has a split personality on issues such as zoning, taxes and conservation.

On each trip from New York to Kent I always have to readjust my city mentality. In Kent strangers say hello to each other on the street. Only the homeless in New York approach strangers. People in Kent have lots of time to stop for a lengthy chat. Even shopkeepers have long gaps in the day and are only too happy to converse during these periods. In New York, most have busy agendas. Stores are rarely quiet. If they were, the high rent would soon force bankruptcy. On the other hand, the low cost of doing business in Kent permitted the pace of life to slow down and the result is an almost anachronistic civility.

My parents, especially my father, loved Kent. They joined us frequently and my father began to fill the condo with handmade furniture. First he constructed a basement workshop in the garage. Then, over a period of two years, he built a dining room table, a Dutch cabinet, a dresser, at least five tables, a chair, a birdhouse, picture frames, deck furniture and a basement room to house the sauna. Eventually I asked him to stop or the condominium would look like a furniture store. He continued to build furniture for Elisa, my cousins Elaine and Darlene, and their parents. My father especially loved to work in the summer with the garage door open so that he could see the hills across the valley. He made a sign and posted it on the wall of the garage. It read "Welcome to Shangri-La." My mother remained upstairs in the living room, either reading or doing the *New York Times* crossword puzzles. As time went by my mother's arthritis made climbing the stairs to the guest bedroom too painful. She would sleep on the living room couch and my father would sleep upstairs.

We enjoyed furnishing the condo. Besides my father's creations, we purchased furniture on a trip through South Carolina. And many of our travel souvenirs were brought to Kent, particularly Indonesian batiks, African art, and a photo gallery from our animal safaris. It was easy entertaining in Kent and we invited other family members and friends. Elaine really got to like it and we gave her permission to use it any time. As a result, Elaine probably visited Kent more than we did. Elaine sometimes felt that she was imposing on us. We often reassured her by telling her that what is the point of owning an unused asset. We—Patricia and I—got pleasure out of seeing it put to use for the benefit of a family member or friend.

After Bob and Connie moved into their impressive home on Studio Hill, they would invite us over whenever we came into town. We spent many pleasant evenings with them, chatting or playing Hearts, a card game they taught us. One winter we joined them in Abaco, Bahamas for a week at a splendid house by the sea.

When we first moved into Kent, the real estate sales agent, Keith, was very welcoming and, in fact, became a friend. Each time we came up he would visit us and we would hike in the area. But our most memorable adventure together was canoeing and rafting down the Housatonic in the spring of 1990. Our first attempt, in a rented canoe, resulted in us capsizing on some rocks in the rapids south of Cornwall Bridge. Undaunted, we set out again a week later in a more stable rubber raft. This time a lightning storm passed over us. With bolts of lightning coming down all around us we beached the raft on the shore while the rain poured down. Eventually we completed the fifteen-mile trip to the Kent bridge and pulled out the raft by the Kent School. Wet, but elated by our achievement, we returned to our condo.

Patricia and I made friends with Bob and Alex who lived in a condo just down the hill from ours. They were retired antique dealers who had lived together for about fifty years. Their unit had been decorated in bold, dark colors with every square foot of wall covered by marvelous artwork. It was like walking into a nineteenth-century drawing room in a fine English home. Both Bob and Alex had engaging personalities. They were lively and amusing and we enjoyed many visits with them. Each winter they would close up and move to La Jolla, California, returning to Kent in the spring. Sadly, Alex was fighting cancer which, within three years from the time we met him, killed him. Toward the end we saw the devastating effects on his once massive physique and cheerful disposition. Alex quickly weakened. Aged and depressed, he died a painful death. Bob lived through those terrible days with courage, as his partner of decades faded.

Part III

Internal and External Adventures

9
My Human Body Adventure

Age is a very high price to pay for maturity.

—Tom Stoppard

Since I consider visits to the doctor an adventure, this seems to be an appropriate place to discuss medical experiences throughout my life. My first hospital visit took place when I was thirteen. Two congenital hernias needed correction. I received a spinal injection to paralyze me from the waist down. I remember that as I was being wheeled into the operating room my father arrived to give me a plate block of the new 80-cent airmail stamp. I was thrilled. The simple joys of childhood are filled with these moments of undiluted pleasure. After my recovery the doctor had to remove some fluid from below the incision. He inserted a large hypodermic needle into my groin area and withdrew black fluid, which I guess was old blood. My father was watching this and nearly fainted.

After these operations I enjoyed many years of perfect health. After I got married, Dr. W. T. of NYU Medical Center became my physician, my first line of defense against Mother Nature. I always came away from my annual checkup with some wry comment from Dr. T. Once I told him I had a problem with very cold hands: what should I do? Dr. T replied, "Buy some gloves." Once Dr. T asked my age. When I told him I was fifty, he said, "You don't look fifty." I thanked him and then he said, "You look older." On another occasion he asked where I had been during my recent travels. I told him we had just returned from India where we met Mother Teresa. Dr. T said, "You mean that fraud." I was surprised and asked him why he felt that way. "Nobody can be that good," said Dr. T.

After the age of forty I began to get cholesterol readings in the 240-280 range and Dr. T advised me to eat less saturated fats. By eliminating red meat and whole milk products, I brought the readings down to 210, but living in New York and surrounded by great restaurants proved too tempting. After several years my cholesterol readings rose again to 240. I told Dr. T I knew what I should not eat but it was just impossible to avoid all the wonderful desserts and sauces placed before me. In 1993 he prescribed Questran for me. This orange powder was to be taken twice a day with fruit juice, to disguise its taste. It worked in the bile and just flushed away the cholesterol before it got into my blood stream. Soon my cholesterol readings were in the 170-195 range, which was lower than ever. During this period Dr. T observed my blood pressure rising toward mild hypertension. I took a series of readings at home, using a monitor I purchased from a surgical supply house. My readings averaged 138/86, which was lower than Dr. T's readings. We met, compared results and concluded that his presence had the effect of raising my pressure.

At the age of thirty-nine I purchased a chinning bar and every morning I would try to do as many pull-ups as possible. I reasoned that since gravity is working to distribute weight around our middle section this exercise would develop the upper portion of the body as a counteraction. In the beginning all I could do was nine pull-ups, but as the weeks turned into months this number increased. At twenty-five pull-ups I reached a plateau. My arms were aching continuously. Then one day I squeezed out twenty-six pull-ups! From there the number rose to a high of forty-four pull-ups, which I achieved before my forty-fourth birthday. Even as I write, at age fifty-seven, I can still do thirty-eight pull-ups, though I only attack the chinning bar once a week now. This exercise developed my arms, chest and upper back. Predictably Patricia, the closet intellectual, was not very impressed.

In late 1994 I twisted my knee on a Wyoming ski slope near Jackson Hole. Some of the pain remained after a few weeks. My friend Tom recommended that I see Dr. Elliot Hershman at Lenox Hill Hospital. The knee had cartilage damage and required surgery. I asked if I could have a videotape of the operation since it would be performed arthroscopically. Dr. Hershman agreed as long as I brought in the blank tape. I also planned to watch the surgery on the TV monitor in the operating room, but the anesthesiologist had not only given me an epidural but also a tranquilizer. I was devoid of all willpower. Even turning my head to look at the monitor seemed hardly worth the effort. It was a lonely experience, though Patricia was outside waiting for me. I also felt helpless, surrounded by strangers now in control of my life. This minor knee surgery was forcing me to contemplate my own mortality. In twenty minutes it was over. They wheeled me out of the operating room leaving behind monitors, electronic boxes, blinking lights and stainless steel gear. In the recovery room my numb legs slowly regained sensation. My penis was also numb and lifeless. To my great relief it regained sensation along with my legs. I was led to a lounge chair by a nurse and told that I could leave as soon as I was able to urinate. I was having a nice chat with another patient when Patricia came in and asked what was taking me so long. "Think running water," she said. After a while I went to the bathroom and passed the test. It was a four-block walk back to the apartment, but even then I felt the crutches were unnecessary. Recovery was swift.

The video of the operation was fascinating. Dr. Hershman made two holes. One was for a tiny camera and the other was used for the tools. One tool was a whirling, grinding sphere and another tool was a small pair of scissors. With these tools Dr. Hershman cut away what looked like stringy bits of lobster meat. He turned rough edges into smooth ones. After viewing the video I wanted all my friends and family to see it, but to my chagrin only Herb Schneider showed any interest. Most politely refused. Some were revolted by the suggestion.

Earlier, I made reference to my lower back pain. I first experienced this problem in 1975. I discovered one day that I could not straighten up without severe pain. For two weeks I walked around like a monkey, not fully upright. Later these episodes became annual and then more frequent, eventually turning into an annoying ache rather than a distortion of my posture. One day, while at my health club, the East Side Fitness Center, I noticed something called a roman chair or hyperextension bench. Using it I was able to give my back a good stretch and exercise back and stomach muscles. To my surprise the next day my back felt better. After repeating the exercise a few more times my backache totally disappeared.

If I ever decide to write a second autobiography to deal with my older years, I expect this chapter will have more additions than any other. . . .

10
Vacations and Adventures

Man can learn nothing unless he proceeds from the known to the unknown.
—Claude Bernard, *Bulletin of New York Academy of Medicine*, 1928

I have traveled to over eighty countries in my life. Patricia and I both enjoy active holidays.

Here is a list of most of our wanderings since our marriage.

Summary of Our World Travels

Date	Where	Comments
June–September 1964	France, Spain, Morocco, Italy	Honeymoon
Winter 1966	Puerto Rico	
Summer 1968	Eastern Europe, USSR	My vacation from responsibility
1969 and 1977	Bermuda	
Summer 1978	Peru, Ecuador, Bolivia	
Winter 1981	Mexico	With Rachel; we toured by car
Summer 1983	USSR	Trans Siberian RR to Irkutsk, Samarkand, Tashkent
Summer 1984	China, Hong Kong and Japan	A group tour, the Great Wall, Beijing and Canton
Summer 1985	Baffin Island	Backpacking up North, Inuits and the Arctic

Date	Where	Comments
January 1986*	Antarctica, Chile, Brazil	Penguins, seals, scientific bases, icebergs
Summer 1986	Norway, Iceland, Greenland	Route of the Vikings by ship
November 1988*	Nepal, India	Trek in Himalayas; first trip to India
August 1989*	High Sierras, California	Backpacking at 12,000 ft., climb of Mt. Whitney
January–April 1990*	East Africa	Gorillas, pygmies, Mt. Kilimanjaro, truck safaris
September–November 1990	Hungary, Czechoslovakia, Turkey, Egypt and Israel	Mideast; just before the Gulf War
February 1992*	Quebec	Dog-sledding adventure
April–July 1992	Britain	Patricia's big walk end to end
June–November 1993*	Round the world	A six-month journey across Asia and Australia/New Zealand
Summer 1994*	Poland, Norway	The short painful journey of my kidney stone
April–June 1995*	Holland, Belgium, Luxembourg, France	Walk across Europe. Part I: Holland to Swiss border
January 1996	Cabo St. Luca, Mexico	Marlin fishing
February 1996*	Cuba	Sailing to Havana with Dave Brown
June–July 1996*	Switzerland, France	Walk across Europe; Part II: Swiss border to Tignee

*See descriptions of these trips in this chapter.

Some of these trips were especially memorable.

Trekking in Nepal, November 1988

High point of trek, 15,500 feet. I was sick on the food and the altitude.

Patricia joins hardy souls who climb to 16,000 feet.

Walking the Great Britain End to End—Kirk Yetholm, Scotland, May 1992. Left to right; author, Eric Fitzpatrick, Eric's friend, Moira, nephew James Staff, Patricia.

Author and Patricia at John O'Groats, trail's end, June 1992.

Pakistani women considered Patricia unusual. We had our pictures taken many times.

In search of the Hill Tribes of Northern Thailand.

My Uncle Louis Freeman drew this 1986 cartoon after our visit to Antarctica and backpack expedition to Baffin Island.

Baffin Island, August, 1985

Patricia and I read some interesting information about the Auyuittuq National Park, the most northern park in the world. By flying north from New York about 2,000 miles, we could do some great backpacking and maybe meet some Inuit. We invited Ahmed, one of our key FA employees, to join us. First we flew to Montreal, then Frobisher Bay and finally the remote Eskimo village of Pangnirtung on Baffin Island. On landing, we raced towards the small airport building to collect our knapsacks, only to be shouted back to the plane as all the luggage was being dumped on the dirt runway. We booked into the only hotel in "Pang," the Payton Lodge, and a more interesting place would be hard to find. In the rustic lounge we soon met a French fur trapper turned dog-sled guide, experts on Inuit stone carvings, two Soho painters plus other nondescript characters who found their way to the end of the earth. The bearded French fur trapper held us enthralled as he acted out the running of his dog team and the wonderful canine relationship he had developed. His arms clawed out in front of him as he demonstrated the pulling and straining his animals unleashed at his command, how they would look back to see if he was helping out on the uphill parts.

"Pang" consisted of a collection of modest shacks with tethered dogs howling away amid plastic and paper refuse, announcing the early and ugly arrival of the twentieth century. We soon arranged for a boat to take us the nineteen miles up the estuary to the trail head. The next few days we spent trekking deeper into the park, which was mainly a long valley leading fifty-five miles to Broughton Island on the other side of Baffin Island. On the crests of the peaks and plateaus on either side of us were glaciers and snow fields. The melting ice and snow formed fast-flowing streams which led to a river. Crossing these streams was no easy matter. In the beginning we removed our boots and socks. But the water was too cold and the stream bed too jagged with rocks. We tried leaping over narrow sections where the stream broke into delta-like multiple streamlets. But even this method left us stranded. Finally Ahmed took the plunge and with boots on just plowed into the stream getting thoroughly soaked. We followed and for the rest of the trip had cold wet feet.

Since we were walking in late summer there was continuous daylight. This made it convenient to start or stop whenever we wished. There is a phenomenon in the Arctic regions known as katabatic wind. It arises when cold air suddenly drops from a high plateau into a valley and races at high velocity down the valley. Early one morning we heard

Back in Delhi, the crowds pressed in on us from all directions. Wherever we walked Indians noticed us. Some changed course and came toward us to sell or beg. It was impossible to move unnoticed. The poverty was overwhelming. Beggars waved stumps of legs or arms at us to demonstrate their need for help. Bicycle rickshaw drivers rode alongside pleading for us to become passengers. Then came the chaos and madness of the Muslim section of Delhi where the crowds, begging and desperation reached a crescendo. Hands and faces were pressed against our half-curtained taxi. One desperate fellow was masturbating near the entrance to a mosque.

Our hotel was like a walled fortress, and we would prepare our emotions with each departure through its gates. However, one visit to a Hindu temple, the Lakshmi Norain, convinced us that India had a lot more to offer the visitor than sights of human misery and poverty. Here, among beautiful marble pools and vaulted ceilings, two musicians played, one on a harmonium and another on a tabla. This music of praise and peace resonated against the walls of the temple and transported us to another world, another time. After my return to New York I tried to get tapes of that music and those musicians, but was unsuccessful. For me it was like a musical Shangri-La, a lost kingdom of beautiful melody.

We flew to Katmandu, Nepal to begin our trek. Originally we were to trek to the Everest base camp, but bad weather forced our leader to take us instead to the Annapurna highlands. After a long bumpy bus ride we arrived at Pokhara and with our group of English and American walkers we set out climbing toward Thulobugin, at 15,500 feet. Our trek took about two weeks and included stops at villages such as Dhampas, Ghorapani and Tatapani. Unfortunately, the food made me sick and I did not sleep well. This made me very grumpy. Group members asked Patricia how she ended up marrying such a disagreeable fellow. In spite of my misery, I still remember marvelous views of the enormous Himalayas, interesting little villages perched on ridges and the bells announcing the approach of mule teams carrying supplies to communities along the trekking route. From the route's high point, we looked across the Kali Gandaki river valley to the Dhaulagiri mountains, with summits rising to 27,000 feet. From the valley below to the peaks above, we observed an altitude change of over 17,000 feet.

For two weeks after my return to New York I experienced a profound culture shock. Sitting in my favorite bistro, Mezzaluna, I overheard conversations about fashion, money and power. Images of poor Indians struggling for survival, and the truncated limbs of Delhi beggars kept intruding on the babble of East Side wealth. I was home physically and yet New York seemed far away. I was an observer of, rather than participant in, my surroundings. Gradually, the guilt and depression faded and I rejoined the present. I vowed never to return to India. But there was something haunting and mesmerizing about the place and five years later we would revisit India for a closer and deeper look.

Backpacking the High Sierras, August 1989

King Lee, a West Coast contact from the computer industry, responding to a discussion we'd had, sent us maps and a letter spelling out an exciting backpack trip in the Sierras. Soon Patricia and I had our expedition pack filled with dried food, canned food, tent, air mattress, boots, cooking gear, and an assortment of clothing for ten days in the wilderness. We flew to Reno, rented a car and drove south to the Shepherds Pass trail head. Starting at 6,000 feet this path wound its way up to 12,000 feet. We spent our first night just a mile into the trail. The next day we slogged up to about 10,000 feet and camped at the base of a steep ascent to a ridge. I was carrying about forty-five pounds and Patricia thirty-seven pounds, which was heavier for her, considering her body weight. The terrain changed as we ascended from a dusty, dry desert with minimal vegetation to pine woods. The next day we reached the crest and a wondrous vista opened up. Across the high plateau were open alpine meadows interspersed with dark green conifer forests and at the horizon an array of Rocky Mountain summits. We joined the John Muir trail and headed north. After a while we decided to go off trail and camp at a cirque lake. Wallace Lake was surrounded on all sides by steep walls that led up to towering peaks. The only access to this lake was via its outlet stream. While running around the campsite in my sandals, I caught my little toe on a rock and broke it. The pain and swelling prevented me from putting on boots. For a while we were wondering how I would be able to walk out of this remote area. For two days we camped by the lake. Not a soul appeared. We watched the sun rise over peaks in the east and set behind peaks in the west. We swam in the clear fresh lake in the nude and sunned ourselves on slabs of rock by the shore. At last we decided it was time to continue our hike and, using my open-toed river sandals, I was able to walk out. We continued north until finally reaching the trail up to Mt. Whitney, tallest mountain in the lower forty-eight states. From the high plateau it was an easy 2,000 feet up to the summit where we met a small army of climbers relaxing and having photos taken. From there we began the long descent to trail's end. This backpacking trip was one of our most enjoyable vacations. We worked harmoniously together to solve survival problems in the wilderness. We lived for ten days solely on what we carried into the mountains, and we experienced nature intensely in total immersion. Returning to the road with its traffic and busy fast food restaurant was a jarring experience after the pristine tranquility of the High Sierras.

East Africa, 1990

Our East Africa vacation was quite an adventure. We left on January 10, 1990 and returned April 3, 1990 after visiting Kenya, Rwanda, Zaire, Uganda and Tanzania. Most of our traveling was by overland truck, a rough mode of transportation in which one lives off an eleven-ton vehicle. We camped generally in small two-person tents and assisted with the cooking, dish washing and drying (flapping). Occasionally, we assisted in far more strenuous and unpleasant chores, of which more will be said later.

We arrived in Nairobi after a seemingly endless flight via Frankfurt. While in Frankfurt we picked up Larium, the new anti-malaria wonder drug that kills all strains, as well as your liver and kidneys. Our hotel, the Jacaranda, was a pleasant surprise with modern rooms, swimming pool and a great buffet breakfast. The Kenya safari was also the easiest of the four we planned to take. On the Kenya safari we traveled in mini-vans with pop-up roofs, and the tents were large four-person types that one could stand up in. Also, the Kenya staff cooked and washed the dishes. We first traveled to Amboseli Park in the south and saw many elephants and giraffes. We also saw a cheetah. The roads were potholed and later turned to dusty, dirt tracks. We thought these were pretty bad, but that was before we got to Zaire, where "bad road" takes on a new meaning. We started to learn Swahili. For example, the ever popular greeting in Africa is *Jambo*. Whenever I saw an elephant I would shout to him "Jambo Jumbo." Heading north we visited Samburu game reserve, where the guards watched over us at night with semi-automatic weapons to protect us from wild beasts and bandits. There we saw the unique reticulated giraffe. After a long dusty road we arrived at the Rift Valley and visited Lakes Baringo, Nakuru and Naivasha. We saw hippos, zillions of flamingos, plus the usual game park regulars which included topi, Thompson's and Grant's gazelles, lions, gerenuks, elands and my favorite, the busy warthog. Finally, in the Masai Mara, we saw two cheetah devouring the innards of a gazelle. This bloody sight turned Patricia into an instant vegetarian.

Leonard, our driver, and I had an argument. I wanted to stop and visit a Masai village and he didn't. After a few hours of tension all was resolved amicably. It is not wise to attempt to redesign group tours. One must go with the flow. Each of our four safaris had their share of wonderful, neutral and disagreeable people. However, let me say that, in the future, if possible, Patricia and I will travel without groups.

One evening we went to the famous tourist restaurant, The Carnivore. It's a huge place with an open roasting pit. Meat is served from a long skewer and carved at your table. This is the opportunity to eat what you have seen in the game parks: zebra, hartebeest, alligator and so forth. At first Patricia refused to even set foot in the place. Finally, after much pleading, she reluctantly came along. I suspended my low cholesterol diet and gorged myself. Patricia ordered the vegetarian platter. To tell the truth, I'd prefer a good roast chicken to any of those exotic meats.

Rwanda and Zaire

After the "Faces of Kenya" tour ended we flew to Kigali, capital of Rwanda. There we joined the "Gorillas, Volcanoes and Pygmies" tour, a three-week expedition. This trip was rougher. Every night the natives in Rwanda or Zaire would gather round our campsite to watch the strange behavior of the Mzungus or white people. We pitched our tents, opened the table, brought out cooking equipment and prepared and ate our food to the unblinking and astonished gaze of 50 to 100 Africans. On the road—if you can call a mud track a road—Africans waved and cheered as we passed. Entire school yards of children would stop whatever they were doing and run to the road to greet us in wild ecstasy. Often a wave would transform itself into the upturned palm of begging. "Give me a pen, a book, money, your hat." Whatever.

At one point in our trip through Zaire, I ran out of clean laundry and wore my red flannel pajamas in the evening around the camp. It caused some amusement among the group. A short while later nature called and I trotted into the nearby bushes to relieve myself. It was dark but I managed to find among the dense foliage a nice little depression in the ground and squatted down. Suddenly I felt a sharp sting at my ankle, then more stings up my legs. I turned on my flashlight to discover, to my horror, that I was squatting on top of an ant hill. Black African ants are about half an inch long and take little pieces of flesh out when they bite. Now an advance party of these nasty insects were methodically making their way up my legs, gorging themselves as they went. It couldn't have happened at a worse moment. Quickly assessing my miserable choices, I rose and took off in a panic, tearing my pajama pants to shreds. All this was going on within yards of the campsite. My fellow travelers seemed totally unaware of my predicament as they amiably chatted and joked. Somehow, half-undressed, I made my ignominious way back to our tent, hopefully removing all the ants before climbing inside.

A few days later I had the pajama pants repaired by one of the many tailors that work in the town markets. A crowd of Africans gathered round to watch and seemed very amused that the crotch area was completely torn apart.

After one long day's travel we arrived at a deserted Belgian Plantation located alongside Lake Kivu. Our leader, Jerry, offered to put together a dugout canoe trip onto the lake for a moonlight swim. There was reason to hesitate. First, guidebooks caution against going near East African lakes because of bilharzia. This insidious ailment starts if you step on the host snails in the reeds. A parasite in the snail bores into your foot, developing into worms which finally make their home in your organs. If left untreated, a lot of important body parts get destroyed. As if that isn't bad enough, Lake Kivu has volcanic activity beneath. Poisonous gases bubble up in places and hover about one foot above the lake. It's no problem if you can swim with your nose 18 inches above the surface. Swimmers unable to perform this feat have asphyxiated. Most of our group declined Jerry's offer. I asked Patricia if we should go for a swim. Without hesitation she said "Let's go." It was a delightful swim. We were able to scrub off the grime of our travels and the water temperature was just right. Returning, we assisted the natives by taking the oars and adding our voices to a primitive Swahili rowing chant. The following morning some more members of our group decided to go and Jerry put together another lake trip.

We arrived in Beni, the last major town on our trip north. Browsing about on the main street, I met a part-time store salesman/school teacher who spoke English. We invited him to join our group that evening for dinner in a nearby hotel. At dinner and while constantly looking over his shoulder, he spoke of the hatred and hopelessness that grips Zaire. Patricia asked how he would rectify the situation. He said he would like the Belgians to return and run the country. Patricia asked if he would prefer that the Belgians train his people to run Zaire themselves. "No," he said, "We are too corrupt."

The next day as we headed north toward Pygmyland, Zaire grew more primitive. Grass huts, coffee beans drying in front, topless black women, tropical forests, a roller coaster mud track and dugout canoe trip were our introduction to the little people. The pygmies greeted us with innocent eyes, did a dance in their bark underwear with leafy accessories and then they and we stood around just looking at each other. These forest people are surrounded and insulated by the regular Africans, themselves pretty poor and "traditional." It's amazing that today Pygmies still exist at all.

We passed potholes eight feet deep and fifteen feet long. You drive down into and out of these monsters. Our leader, Jerry, told me these are nothing. He has seen potholes in Zaire taller than our truck and four trucks long. Mind you, we are not talking about a side road, but the major north-south route in Eastern Zaire. President Mobutu lives in splendor while his country goes to pot. On our truck I invented a game. I called it "Name that Dictator." The questioner calls out an African state and the winner is the first to call out the dictator of that country.

On the other hand, we were impressed by the clean, neat grass huts, decorated with colorful flower arrangements. Often women could be seen sweeping around their huts. The front of the huts were working surfaces to dry coffee beans. I pronounced Zaire to be "the cleanest poor country I have ever seen."

Uganda

We only spent three days in Uganda. A few miles inside the border our driver, Jerry, mistakenly drove past a tire standing in the road, a sort of checkpoint. A young soldier began shouting and our truck screeched to a halt. The soldier began to wave his semiautomatic rifle at us, yelling at Jerry for not stopping. Patricia started to tell him off, calling him "rude" and other British pejoratives. Fortunately, he ignored her and concentrated on Jerry. Jerry was very cool, offered the soldier a cigarette and soon all was calm.

We camped near a lake and visited some terrific hippo colonies. It is hard to describe hippos in delicate terms. They wallow in mud and their own feces, belching and farting in a continuous revolting "harmony." It was easy to tell when a hippo discharged its waste. His small tail began to spin like a propeller, spreading the stuff in all directions.

After a late dinner in a nearby lodge, we walked to our tents. Suddenly in the darkness we saw the huge outline of a hippo between us and the tents. The lumbering, goofy-looking hippo kills more humans than any other African animal. These strange creatures slobber around in the mud during the day and walk the earth at night. To come between them and their watering hole sets off nasty instincts. We gave our hippo friend a wide berth and climbed into our tents. The angry grunting and honking noises soon began, followed by heavy footsteps, as the hippos munched grass outside our tents. "You know they could crush our heads very easily," said Patricia cheerfully. That night I didn't sleep well.

The gorillas were exciting. We visited two families in Zaire and one in Rwanda. One giant silver back male, called Maheshi, charged us. We were told to get down low and humble when this happens, since the gorilla is just showing you who is boss. Patricia got humble and I ran like hell, knocking over some fellow tourists and their cameras. Those gorillas were dangerous!

Back to Rwanda

After returning to Kigali we flew back to Nairobi to catch the night train to Mombasa, on the Kenya coast. Sleeper compartments are assigned and posted on a bulletin board on the train platform. We got our compartment number and settled in. After a few minutes a conductor came by and announced a change. We must move and take the same compartment in the next car up. We did so but noticed someone else's baggage was in our new location. Never mind, we thought, he will have to move up one car just as we did. After a while a large German, about twenty-five years old, arrived and, evidently unaware of the changes, announced firmly, "You will leave my compartment now." Patricia and I tried to explain the changes but this only altered his mood from aggressive to belligerent. Patricia did not care for his tone, pronounced him "rude" and said firmly she was not moving. I was also getting pretty annoyed. Finally, I said, "Look, neither of us knows who should stay and who should leave. Why don't we wait for the train conductors to sort it out?" This suggestion didn't work either. Fortunately, the changes in assignments reached his group leader, who called to him in German. In a huff, he grabbed his baggage and stormed off. At last, we had a compartment.

Our adjoining neighbors were two emancipated Nairobi ladies who spent a couple of hours explaining how women in Kenya were mistreated and demeaned. The conversation led us also into stories of local corruption, inefficiency and tribalism. At last we went to dinner, returned to our compartment and attempted to sleep as the train "clackety-clacked" down to Mombasa.

On the coast it was hot and humid and Patricia did not like this kind of weather. We took a bus ride to Malindi and stayed two days at a nice beach hotel called the Driftwood. We snorkeled in the Indian Ocean. The water was the temperature of a warm bath. Most people preferred the swimming pool. We then got a taxi to the airport to fly to Lamu, a Moslem, Arab town on the north Kenya coast. Unfortunately, the second engine on our six-seat aircraft wouldn't start. Another plane was wheeled out but had only four seats. So which of the six passengers should go and which should stay for a flight later in the day. We had befriended two of the passengers, a Belgian expatriate lady who had lived in Kenya for thirty years, and her husband. Additionally there were two Australian women who were going to Lamu for a few days. One of the Australian women said the Belgian couple ought to go because they were day-trippers and time was an important factor for them. I agreed and said, "Let's flip a coin to decide which of us will get the remaining two seats." "No," she said, "we got to the airport first so we should go." "But," I said, "we are going for only a day and a half, how long are you going for?" "That doesn't matter," she replied. "But it mattered for the Belgian couple," I said, now getting somewhat annoyed. Suddenly an official appeared and, pointing to the Belgian couple and us, announced that we were going. We scurried off towards the plane leaving the bewildered and fuming Australians behind. As we taxied to take off the Belgian lady leaned forward and said, "I've lived here for thirty years and I know how things are done. When no one was looking I told the official in Swahili that we four were going together, gave him 100 shillings [$5] and that's it."

Lamu reminded us of Arab towns in North Africa with narrow passageways, minarets, and the wailing call to the faithful to pray at the many mosques. We took a dhow and traveled up the coast to Pepponi's, a fancy hotel catering to the wealthy and pampered, definitely not for us down and dirty overlanders. We walked many of the alleys and had some nice seafood meals.

A fellow tourist told us an interesting story about the local hospital. The Saudis wanted to donate a complete hospital and equip it for the good health of their fellow Muslims. All went well, the hospital was built and the ship stood offshore ready to deliver the medical equipment. Then suddenly Kenyan officials said they wanted duty paid for import taxes. "But this equipment is a gift," said the Saudis. The Kenyan officials insisted (guess the destination of the import taxes). Offended, the Saudis ordered the ship with its equipment back home. We visited the hospital. It's a beautiful structure, all white with open hallways to catch the sea breeze but completely devoid of medical equipment. The next day we headed back to the Lamu airport and returned to Nairobi.

We spent a night at the Jacaranda Hotel and then took a taxi to the airport to fly to Arusha, Tanzania to start our trek up Mt. Kilimanjaro. As normal procedure the security guards frisked each passenger behind a curtain. The guard felt the wallet in my pants and asked what it was. I took it out and he very carefully opened it and examined the currency. On finding some Kenyan bills he asked if I planned to use this currency where I was going. Of course this currency cannot be exchanged or used outside of Kenya. It was a strong hint to give the money to him. I told him I needed the money for the waiting lounge where we planned to eat snacks and have some drinks. Evidently that answer was acceptable and he didn't press the point. Government employees are forced into fleecing tourists to make up for unrealistically low pay scales.

Mt. Kilimanjaro

Our climbing group met in Arusha, drove to the Mt. Kilimanjaro base and then ascended to Mandara Hut at 9,000 feet. The next day we climbed to Horumbo Hut at 12,000 feet and then Kibo Hut at 15,500 feet on the third night. Arising at midnight, we had some tea and by 1 A.M. we began plodding single file up the cinder cone to the 19,000 foot summit. Three group members soon turned and headed down with bad cases of altitude sickness. I was carrying only a day pack and camera bag, but pretty soon I was puffing away and then I suddenly collapsed. Our guide took my camera bag and my pack, while the group encouraged me to get up and continue. The guide told me to walk slowly behind him and after a few hundred feet, he turned to me and said I could make it to the top. By going very slowly I reached the crater rim in six hours. Near the summit, it was ten slow steps and rest, ten slow steps and rest, repeated many times. We had been advised before the climb to leave our wallets behind because the thrill of reaching the top was so great that climbers have been known to give their guides all the money they had with them. I can attest to that emotion as tears of joy welled up in my eyes upon reaching the crest. Patricia had far less difficulty and could have gone farther to the rim's highest point but stayed with me instead. We saw the sun rise and a magnificent view of clouds, and the plains of Tanzania below. Then we began a mad dash down 7,000 vertical feet to Horumbo Hut, with one stop at Kibo Hut for a brief nap. It was a long exhausting day. The next day we exited and had a celebration dinner at the hotel at the base.

Tanzania

We returned to Arusha and started our last and most chaotic safari, the "Tanzanian Explorer," or "How to dig an eleven-ton truck out of the mud in three difficult lessons." It started out fine with just a minor change. Mark, our leader, was about to be put in jail by the Tanzanian government on a visa problem. He later got a one-month reprieve with a $1,000 bribe (this is all normal). Anyway, he was replaced by John, an amiable and optimistic Englishman. John announced he would get us to Lake Natron even if it meant some pushing and digging. We got past the Serengeti, Ngorongoro Crater and Olduvai Gorge as planned, observing the usual animals plus the rare rhino. Then we reached a marshy plain where the truck promptly sank into axle-deep mud. The group dug throughout the night and into the next morning, a total of twenty-two hours. This included hauling gravel from a nearby quarry and making a bed for the steel sand mats under each wheel. It was back-breaking, mucky work, made more difficult in the hot sun. Finally the truck was freed only to sink again a mere thirty feet later. Demoralized, we dug and built gravel tracks again. This time it took only fourteen hours. The road-building team was improving.

Even the bemused Masai, standing around, were impressed. The next ten miles were a series of hair-raising near misses. Perhaps 20–30 times we almost sank again. Finally, we did. Let me add that the truck needed push-starting each morning from our first day on the road. The battery would mysteriously run down overnight. This meant that while we were stuck in the mud the engine could not be turned off. It also meant that for the past several days the engine had been running nonstop. This time John had to turn off the overheated engine. Now when you are up to the floorboards in mud, push-starting a truck is impossible. We needed a tractor. The cook was sent to hike out the remaining fifteen miles to Lake Natron. Meanwhile, we were left to get the truck ready for the tractor. This meant more digging and road-building. Instead of gravel we had rocks, half of which had scorpions under them. So care was indicated. The next day saw no cook and no tractor. Since we were out of water, we drank from a nearby stagnant pool with cows standing in the water doing their thing. Patricia and I decided to leave the group the following morning with our full packs and take our chances reaching Lake Natron. Besides, we found some members of the group cliquish and unpleasant which made leaving even more attractive. I told John about our intentions. That night John announced we would hike out together that very evening. We packed and at 9:30 P.M. set out down a steep, dark, rocky road. Patricia and I were carrying full packs while the others just carried sleeping bags, so we were losing our balance more easily. Some who had flashlights went ahead leaving the others to stumble about in the blackness.

Finally the moon came up and we could see better. Patricia decided suddenly that this was fun and could be made even more enjoyable by picking up the pace a bit. Suddenly she began to move at double time and coming up from the rear passed everyone. It was like some kind of heroic horse race film, the one with the bad start and the climactic ending.

By 2:30 A.M. most of the group was tired. We decided to camp in a dry river bed surrounded by desert and scrub brush. Our leader, John, didn't know where we were or how far we had to go. We knew from the arid surroundings that when the sun rose it was going to get very hot very quickly. We had no food and little water. I thought, as we tried to sleep, *is this going to be where we die?* At 6:30 A.M., we rose and resumed our march hoping to avoid the sun and heat. By 11 A.M., most of the group was out of water and dropping from exhaustion. Patricia was way out in front with Gage, a young lady struggling to keep up. Some soda ash workers miraculously appeared and were drafted by John as porters for our packs. At one point Patricia and Gage were followed by a group of Masai men who began to do a native song and dance routine to amuse them. For Patricia this was very memorable. The rest of the group, far behind, were too tired to think of anything but water. After more hiking in the midday sun we finally reached a river. As group members arrived they literally threw themselves into the water, drinking and soaking at once. Patricia filled a canteen and ran back about half a mile to get water to the exhausted stragglers. The tractor arrived and we were rescued. At the campsite we each had about five or six Cokes. John ordered that a goat be slaughtered to celebrate the end of our ordeal. But it was not quite over. Now behind schedule by three days, we began a mad dash across Tanzania with twelve- to fourteen-hour days of bumpy dusty roads, until we reached Dar es Salaam on the coast.

With great relief we left our group and flew to Zanzibar, the famous spice Island, for a couple of restful days on their eastern shore. The forty-mile trip took our taxi over two hours but the trip was worth it. The east coast town of Bwejou is built on sand and surrounded by unique white stone houses and palm trees. It is unspoiled, which is rare indeed. The local people actually went about their lives as if we weren't there. The town had not a single tourist shop. The Dere Guest house faced the warm Indian Ocean and featured no running water, no electricity and a built-in outhouse. It was delightful. For lunch and dinner we ate multi-colored psychedelic lobsters, giant crabs and fresh fish. Then who should arrive on our second day in Paradise, but The Clique from our Tanzanian Explorer. In a mini-van we traveled back together to Zanzibar Town the next day. It seemed as if we would never get away from them. But in town we went to a different hotel, The Spice Inn, and that was really the last time we saw our fellow travelers from the ill-fated Tanzanian Explorer.

Zanzibar Town is a very Muslim, busy, exotic place. After two days we became veritable alley rats scurrying up and down the narrow passages. We rented a taxi and got an excellent spice tour which included much tasting and nibbling. The plane back to Dar was six hours late. But that's normal for Tanzanian Airlines, where a reservation and even a boarding pass is no guarantee of a seat. They overbook without conscience and are probably the only airline with every flight 100 percent full. It just shows what can be achieved when an airline is free to treat people like cattle.

Back in Dar we ambled around the lobby of our hotel and met an American lady who had remained on in Tanzania after serving in the Peace Corps twenty-three years ago. She had given up her U.S. citizenship, married and divorced a Tanzanian. The stories she told about life in socialist East Africa were either pathetic or laughable. "Very little here works properly. In Dar, the electricity and the phones are cut off frequently," she said. "Sometimes the water is shut off for a week. People stop going to work because they have to find water which they carry home in buckets. I was evicted from my home to make room for some official with connections. Black political refugees, members of the African National Congress, who had fled from South Africa to Tanzania, were appalled by the living conditions in an independent Black state."

On and on went the tales, one more ridiculous than the next. Now she was ready to return home to the U.S. The following day Patricia and I went to the airport and flew back to Nairobi and the Jacaranda. Our credit cards had either expired or been terminated after eighty-five days of nonpayment. We were out of cash and travelers' checks. It was time for us to go home. I made some fast rearranging of flights. For the last time we went to the airport, got the obligatory frisking and bid farewell to Nairobi.

That, briefly, was how we spent our time in East Africa. We returned to New York with 300 photos, some souvenirs and a lot of memories. Would we go to East Africa again? No. Were we glad we went once? Definitely. Yes.

Dog Sledding in Quebec, 1992

Running a dog sled has for many years been our dream. After our recent trip to Alaska and our visit to Nome, and the termination of the famous Iditarod race, we decided to investigate the options. So in late February, 1992, we flew to Roberval, a town of 11,000 people on the shores of Lac St.-Jean, 300 miles north of Montreal. Our guide, Gerard Sawyer, was waiting for us at the Roberval airport as we stepped off the plane. Gerard normally took up to eight clients on his sledding expeditions but this time we were the only ones who signed up. He was about fifty-five years old, five feet, six inches tall, bald with gray hair on the side which he swept around his head. Gerard had a serious intense look and spoke English poorly. He was clearly much happier speaking French. We were taken to a motel in Roberval and the next morning after breakfast Gerard showed up with a small truck filled with supplies and fourteen Alaskan malamutes or huskies. We drove south for four hours and finally arrived at the entrance to the Reserve Fuanique de St. Maurice. This park was set aside specially for dog sledding and snowmobiling in the winter. With Gerard's terse instructions we managed to unload two sleds from the roof of the truck and take the fourteen yelping dogs from their little cubicles and leash them to little cyelets running around the sides of the truck. It was our first experience with huskies. They are born to pull and as soon as we took the leash from Gerard, who was inside the truck, these animals were off and running—or at least trying to. It was a struggle.

The sleds were then filled with ten 50-pound slabs of frozen meat, a lightweight stove, a twelve-foot-by-fourteen-foot prospector's tent, our personal gear, other food and supplies for a ten-day expedition into the bush. The tent and another large tarpaulin were put into the sled first and acted as a large container for everything else we placed in the sled. The sleds were then tied up under Gerard's instructions. Gerard's sled weighed about 800 pounds and ours about 1,000 pounds, including the passengers. We were each told to stand on one of the two runners which extended back two feet from the end of the sled. Between the runners was a rubber pad which had studs made of nuts and bolts. This pad swivelled and was suspended over the snow with two rubber shock cords. When the driver wanted to stop he stepped on the pad which forced the numerous bolts to drag in the snow. The driver also shouted "Whoa." Gerard said our first stop, Refuge Parkman, was about eight miles away. Gerard stepped onto his sled's runners, shouted "Attention" and "Au Canada" and, with a lurch, his sled began to move forward at a fast pace. And suddenly our sled lurched forward right behind him, without any commands from us. There was no stopping these huskies who had been patiently shelved in their little cubicles for the past six hours. Nor did stepping on the brake and shouting "Whoa" have much effect in slowing up their mad pace across the frozen river and onto a soft snowy trail on the other side. After a while Gerard's team and ours slowed to a normal trot as the first burst of canine energy had been spent. We were moving at about four miles per hour—faster downhill, and slower up. In fact, on the uphill sections, we had to get off our runners and walk behind and push the sled. Dog sleds are like underpowered automobiles running in third gear. In two hours we arrived at the refuge for our first night in the bush.

Of our nine days in the wild, we spent two in our own erected prospector's tent, two in park-installed tents and the other nights in refuges or small cabins. Except for the second night, the three of us slept in the same shelter. On the second night we were joined by three other dog mushers. It was a full house that night with every bunk occupied, and all snored, except for Patricia. In vain she tried to stop the noise.

We would start the day by feeding the dogs using stainless steel bowls filled with powdered milk, eggs, small biscuits and vegetable oil. Meanwhile, Gerard prepared our breakfast of dried cereal, powdered milk and coffee. After packing up and preparing the sleds we unleashed the dogs who were tethered to a steel wire. These mini locomotives would play and pull as we struggled to put them into their harnesses and clip them to the gang line on the sled.

Finally, after two hours, breaking camp was complete and we would mush to the next night's campsite. Usually we would arrive between 2 and 3 P.M. After unloading our gear we would cut frozen meat into cubes of three to four pounds each, using a bow saw. We then hurled these bricks of meat in the general direction of each dog, who in turn would snap them out of the air with their open jaws. The huskies would then ravenously and quickly devour the cubes. Gerard would get the stove going as soon as we arrived and in an hour the refuge or tent was warm. On a couple of nights the outside temperature fell to -30 degrees Fahrenheit.

The dogs weigh about sixty lbs. each and can pull double their weight. The front dog is called the leader and understands commands such as gee (right), haw (left), and whoa (stop). The dogs immediately in front of the sled are the wheel dogs. Strength is the primary requirement for wheel dogs.

The refuges have outhouses. While mushing, if nature called, we just went out on the snow. As for washing, we did not have a shower for ten days. We changed underwear once.

Gerard gave the dogs a rest day after six days out. Patricia and I went off on snowshoes to explore the surrounding area. The snow was six feet deep, and without the snowshoes you could sink up to your waist. With the snowshoes on we sank only about ten inches into the powder. The park had gentle rolling hills, wooded, with evergreens heavily laden with snow. In the bright sun the snow glistened like diamond chips on a white carpet. We hiked about three miles altogether to look for a waterfall which we never found. But the walk itself was worth it.

On the first night Gerard pointed out the aurora borealis. It was not particularly spectacular but it was the first we ever saw, so that in itself was exciting. Two or three times each night the dogs would begin to howl and yelp in a coordinated, almost orchestrated manner. The song would start with a lone howl from one particular animal and would soon be picked up by a second howler. Soon the remainder of the pack, mostly "yelpers," would join in. After about two minutes, the music would rise to a crescendo and suddenly stop as if a conductor had waved a baton.

The huskies had names such as Maxine, Bajaques, Biscuit, Casade, Lakshu and Palov. Gerard always called his dogs by their names, but us he referred to as "you, he, she, her or him."

After our hardship in the Canadian wilderness we felt that we had earned two nights of luxury in Montreal. This included a first-class hotel and some good French cooking. In spite of the discomfort, I am glad we dog sledded. We now understand why the Inuit were quick to switch from huskies to snowmobiles when the choice was offered.

Around the World in Six Months, 1993

Our journey took us through England, Scotland, Greece, Pakistan, India, Thailand, Malaysia, Singapore, Indonesia, Australia and New Zealand. We began travel on May 22, 1993 and returned to New York on November 16, 1993, flying from Auckland via Los Angeles.

We traveled by plane, bus, boat, automobile, rail and walking. What possessed us to undertake this trip? Well, Patricia is naturally adventurous and has a flexible working arrangement with St Luke's

Hospital. And I got bored wandering around the East Side of Manhattan. Plus, we would collect some interesting visa and border entry stamps in our passports.

The journey was filled with adventures and also days not worth recalling. Here are a few high and low points. Patricia left ten days early to visit her family in England. I joined her later and together we visited most of my English in-laws. We also had a rendezvous with my sister and her family in S. England at the Gables Thatch, Porlock Village. They had just finished walking part of the SW coastal path. Later we hiked 200 miles in two weeks on the coast to coast walk across N. England. During the walk we were joined by our daughter Rachel and our English friends Andrew, Moira and Eric. After completing the walk we took a train to Scotland and I had a thirty-five-year reunion in Glasgow with my Scottish opponent in that Brooklyn College debate held in 1958. The man was located with Rachel's help. Bernard Anderson turned out to be a successful attorney and he, with his family, took us out to a fine Scottish dinner at his country club.

We then flew to Athens and toured the Greek islands of Crete and Santorini for eight days. On Santorini, the beautiful people jammed the crowded narrow streets wearing the latest fashions. One hot sunny day we managed to win a race up the hillside, pitted against the mules that cart tourists from the boat to the top. However, in deference to the mules, they were carrying tourists and (the mules) did not know it was a race.

Pakistan was definitely off the beaten path. From Lahore we flew to Bombay. Our first visit to India, a few years back, prepared us for the onslaught of humanity on this second visit. We had a personal visit with Mother Teresa at her hospice headquarters in Calcutta. We also traveled to Bombay, Goa, Cochin, Mysore, Nilgiri hill station, Darjeeling and Bangalore. From Calcutta we flew to Bangkok, Thailand, called "the land of smiles" but more accurately "the land of smirks." Patricia and I trekked to the hill tribes of Chiang Mai and experienced the horrendous smog choking traffic of Bangkok. I learned, firsthand, what an oriental massage really means. We visited notorious Pat Pong Road. This is a street where you can buy Ralph Lauren or Gucci fakes and go next door to watch preteens engage in live sex. I purchased eight Rolex copies for $9 each. Finally we visited the "island paradises" of Phuket and Ko Samui.

From Thailand we flew to Malaysia and rented a car. Malaysia was great. We only got ripped off once in four weeks, as compared to every other day in Thailand. We found the people to be honest and genuinely friendly—no hustles and no aggressive hawking. From the mainland we flew across to Borneo. Malaysia owns the northern half. We climbed Mt. Kinabulu (13,500 feet) up a footpath that seemed like the world's longest staircase. Then it was on to shop-till-you-drop Singapore. Here you can see miles of high-rise shopping centers loaded with electronics, gadgets, clothing, beauty products in the zillions. Who buys all this stuff? After four days we flew to Bali, Indonesia. Indonesia is spread over many islands and is a geographically confusing, multicultural place, part Hindu, part Muslim. We also visited Java and the island of Lombok. Patricia and I saw Ramayana dance/drama three times. The best was in Yogyakarta. People applauded and cheered for ages. We rented a car on Bali and toured sites like Ubud and climbed the mini volcano Mt. Batur. And we both caught 30-day colds in Bali.

Coughing and snorting we took an early departure for Australia. We flew to Sydney, then Melbourne, Hobart (Tasmania), Adelaide, Alice Springs, Cairns, Darwin and finally Brisbane. Australia's a big, friendly place. Sydney went wild over the Olympic selection and we felt part of the enthusiasm. We booked for the year 2000 before we left our hotel.

Arriving in Auckland, New Zealand we stayed with Julie Petit, a friend of my cousin, Elaine Freeman. Julie was a great host. She took us to an island summer home of her friends and the farm of another. Later, on the South Island, Patricia had her feet tied to a rubber band and bungee jumped by leaping off a bridge 140 feet above a river. We took a video of the courageous event to prove it (Patricia preferred to describe it as fun and foolhardy rather than courageous). Feeling wimpish I felt compelled to hang glide the next day. Patricia participated also. We each had our own tandem instructor/pilots. Leaping off a mountaintop we suddenly discovered that there was nothing under our bellies but 3,000 feet of thin air. We traveled to Te Anau with our rental car and hiked the famous Milford Track, a four-day walk through magnificent scenery. Our tour of New Zealand ended in Christchurch. We flew back to Auckland, had a fine dinner with Julie and the following day prepared to return to the United States. The morning of the flight I threw my back out. This seemingly annual event forced us to cancel the stopover in L.A. and beeline home for R and R after the journey. We needed a rest after this vacation.

This was a brief outline of our journey. What follows is more detail.

England Coast to Coast

Britain's most famous walker, Wainwright, pioneered this hike across the Yorkshire moors and dales into the dramatic mountains of the Lake District. Add the hospitable and, at times, eccentric bed-and-breakfast establishments, and you have a delightful holiday. Rachel joined us for a piece and, later, our friend Andrew Opie did too. Eric and Moira Fitzpatrick, fellow walkers, joined near the end and we all celebrated at a restaurant in St. Bees Head. The early part of the walk was rainy and miserable, the kind of gray and dreary weather Patricia calls "delightful." In the Lake District it cleared and we had fine and sunny days to take in the vistas. We arranged to stay at our favorite guest house, the Sharrow Bay, which as ever lived up to its reputation. We arrived tired and dirty one afternoon and without missing a beat they seated us at an outside patio for a fine tea served with style and warmth. As they say, "expensive but worth it." The dinner was superb. All the staff seemed to know about our walk. It was as if the staff met each day to discuss and share the interests of each guest so they could say or ask something relevant.

Reunion in Glasgow

As mentioned in Chapter 4, during my Brooklyn College years I participated in a debate with a team from Scotland. The subject of the debate was "Resolved: That the sun has set on the British Empire." A partner and I represented Brooklyn College on the affirmative against two champion debaters from the University of Glasgow. Needless to say we were demolished by the wit and repartee of the visitors from Scotland. For thirty-five years a reel-to-reel audiotape recording of the event gathered dust on a shelf in our closet. One day, curiosity and nostalgia overcame me. I copied the tape to cassette, made duplicates, located the two Scotsmen with Rachel's help, and mailed one to each. While in England and before our coast-to-coast walk, I received an invitation to meet one of the gentlemen, Ronald Bernard Anderson, who debated us so many years before. After the walk we journeyed to Glasgow and finally met. We had a fine evening together but, like so many events in life, getting there was half the fun.

Greece

From Glasgow we returned to London and from there flew on to Athens. Athens is a busy, smoggy city. The Plaka was pleasant, with quiet sidestreets away from the hustle/bustle. We saw the sound and light show at the Parthenon one evening. I was certain it was the same score I heard thirty-three years ago. On a chilly hillside we listened to endless puffery about "glorious Athenians." A better script with more facts would have been appreciated.

We flew to Crete, rented a car and toured Minoan ruins, mountain scenery and quiet fishing villages. Quite by chance we stayed at a German nudist hotel where you were prohibited from using the beach or pool if you wore a bathing suit. We didn't want to swim anyway. Fortunately, the dining room had a dress code.

A long and delayed ferry boat took us to Santorini. This small, hilly island is crammed with hotels, restaurants, guest house and craft shops. It is geared for Euro-tourism, big time. At night, la dolce vita can be found down each steep cobblestone alley.

Pakistan

From Athens we flew to Karachi and caught a connecting flight to Rawalpindi, our first Asian stop. Pakistan is not a major tourist destination—and for good reason. The country is poor and the politics corrupt. Air travel was unpredictable and characterized by overbooking and frequent cancellations. By land the roads were miserable, with unbelievable dust and fumes, plus bone-jarring potholes. The local population was very friendly and curious as to why anyone would want to visit Pakistan. We had our picture taken many times by the locals in a curious reversal of behavior.

Rawalpindi was depressing. We stayed at the best hotel in town, because second best was awful. Once on the street, the heat and dust was relentless. Sidewalks were occasional. Businesses operated out of run-down, ugly buildings or stalls. We arranged to hire a car, which always came with a driver since visitors were not allowed to drive. Our plan was to head north to Gilgit and the Karakoram Mountains. We did not get there but the effort was interesting and exhausting. Landslides blocked the road at many places and almost continuous repair work was handled by the large and ubiquitous Pakistani army. As we headed north the road deteriorated until we finally commissioned a jeep and driver to take us along what was now a dirt track winding its way high above the terraced and precipitous terrain. We met four Pakistani men who asked to join our Jeep (it was more like a large Land Rover) and we agreed. So for a few days we had their company and a chance to exchange views. They disassociated themselves from extremism and felt such people are not true Muslims.

The last part of our northward trip took us up a side road to Lake Saiful Mulik near the Karakoram Mountains. This road was as bad as any we had seen. It can best be described as driving over a rock pile about two miles long. The rocks were loosely attached to the side of a large mountain. We were all bouncing around the inside of the Jeep so much we began to laugh. I mean, what kind of lake and scenery could justify this degree of discomfort? Well, it was a pretty sight once we arrived.

The trip back to Rawalpindi was everything in reverse. We staggered into our hotel exhausted and covered in a thick layer of grime.

By taxi we toured the nearby planned city of Islamabad. Like so many planned capitals, there was a cold, engineered quality to Islamabad. But even here the frenetic and chaotic character of Pakistan intruded the small shopping arcades. For example, a baker was observed spitting into the wall of his oven to test the temperature.

The mosques wherever we went were splendid structures. Islam is taken seriously in Pakistan. In Lahore, where we next stopped, we saw young men dressed in white beat themselves with spiked steel chains till the blood turned their white garments red. Drenched in their own blood they proudly walked the crowded streets. The occasion was a festival to honor the nephew of Muhammad who was martyred centuries ago. These young men were from the Shiite sect and revered this martyr.

India

We flew from Lahore to Bombay. Bombay is the commercial capital of India. Out of 900 million Indians, only one percent earn enough to be taxed and half of them live in Bombay. And yet even Bombay is poor by Western standards. We stayed at the Taj Mahal Hotel facing the Gate of India monument by the harbor. Inside the hotel all is opulence, outside, squalor. Beggars surround the hotel. Could this be New York's future?

While searching for India Airlines, an Indian approached and offered to help us. Sharm was an Associate Professor at an Indian university. We went to a nearby restaurant for drinks. Sharm turned out to be some kind of manic depressive in the manic state. He was an intense, nonstop talker and impatient with his country and countrymen. Sharm reminded me it was the Fourth of July, my national holiday. He then proceeded to turn the empty glasses on the table upside down and shake them furiously. We assumed this was to empty them of any insects that might be sleeping inside. Sharm vividly painted a picture describing the stupidity of his fellow countrymen. Meanwhile the waiter standing behind him was making signs and faces to indicate that our host was nuts. Sharm felt India, as a nation, was a mess, disorganized, incompetent and lazy. He wanted out but was trapped. It was a sad tale from an intelligent and frustrated man. We were to hear this story in different forms throughout our stay in India. It may explain the intense emotions we felt on both visits to India. Here we were confronted by people struggling against overwhelming obstacles. They were poor, but so far as we could tell there was no hatred, envy or dislike of us because of our comparative wealth. Perhaps it came from Hindu or Buddhist teachings.

One evening at our hotel we were treated to a cultural performance. A female Indian dancer performed a graceful interpretation of a "tik-tak" sounding music. Mesmerizing were her eyes as she would look left and right. First her head moved left and her eyes right, then vice versa. With each "tikky-tak" sound she moved her head and eyes. It was spell-binding.

From Bombay we headed south and flew to Goa, the former Portuguese colony, for rest and relaxation at a beach resort. We heard more sad stories from a masseur and a taxi driver. Actually, a few taxi drivers told us their sad stories during our four weeks in India. They were told without self pity and in a very matter-of-fact manner.

Finally we reached Cochin in South India. People here actually had a life that did not involve us. They went about their business of buying and selling commodities such as tea, coffee and spices. Twenty-five Jews still lived in the small "Jew Town" within Cochin. We visited the synagogue. The Cochin Jews arrived 1400 years ago, so they were not Sephardic. I spoke to one, Sam Cohen, and we had our photo taken by Patricia. His appearance was very Eastern European Jewish, with no sign of Indian genetics, which was really quite amazing considering they were a small population living among Indians for over sixty generations. Sam Cohen told us that most of the community had gone to Israel so that this generation was the last of the Cochin Jews.

In Cochin, Patricia wanted to see the Kathakali dancers. Kathakali is an ancient religious dance drama tradition performed in the state of Kerala. After a search we found a company of dancers on the second floor of a small building in town. With only one other couple present and total box office receipts of $2.00, two dancers and the teacher spent the next three hours applying elaborate face paint, donning impressive costumes and giving us a detailed description and performance of the Kathakali. During the performance the power failed and we had to watch mostly by candlelight. And then the monsoon rains came pouring down, causing water to drip on the stage and benches where we sat. It was, nevertheless, unforgettable.

We spent one day on a personal tour of Alleppy, the Venice of India. Here people live on small islands in a flooded plain and navigate down canals in canoes of various sizes. We drank the local brew called "tuok" at a tavern reached only by boat.

From Cochin we flew to Coimbatore and then traveled by bus and train to Nilgiri. This hill station, once popular during the British Raj, is a place to escape the coastal heat. Here, among the clouds and coolness, we walked to a coffee plantation and watched women harvest the beans for forty cents a day.

We moved about Nilgiri and many other towns in India using a three-wheeled mini taxi called a "tuk-tuk," probably named after the sound it makes. We even used man-powered tricycle rickshaws or "trishaws." Patricia and I debated the ethics of this. On one hand, we are exploiting a human being and making him work like an animal. On the other hand, we are providing income to a person who is self-employed and voluntarily so.

We traveled by bus to Mysore and there toured the ornate and glorious King's Palace. The architect of this great Hindu and Muslim-inspired edifice was an Englishman. And we visited more temples and memorials to the ancient and powerful sultans who once ruled this region.

From Mysore we drove by taxi to Bangalore, spent the night there and flew to Calcutta the next morning. We booked into the Grand Oberoi Hotel, the best in town. Once again we experienced the jarring difference between wealth and poverty, but even more so in Calcutta where poverty reaches even lower depths than in Bombay. It is quite normal on the streets of Calcutta to see men in loincloths, soaping up from head to toe, and rinsing off using water faucets provided on the sidewalk. It is normal to see an office worker in tie and suit, holding a briefcase in one hand and his shoes in another, stepping barefoot into the monsoon flooded street. It is normal to see a street barber giving a shave and haircut, he sitting on one wooden box and his customer on another. It is normal to see Bangladeshi refugees living in cardboard hovels, drinking and washing in the same stagnant pools of water that surround their squalid shanty towns. You must hold your nose or gag in the five-minute taxi ride past this part of town. And from all this "normality" we sought grateful refuge in the very "abnormal" air conditioned and tranquil, walled fortress called the Grand Oberoi Hotel.

On first arriving at the Grand I suggested to Patricia that we must try to meet Mother Teresa. It seemed unlikely that this famous Nobel Prize winner, a woman likely to be sainted in years hence by the Catholic church, would receive visiting tourists. But that is exactly what happened. Our concierge made a call to the Sisters of Charity and the next day we waited expectantly on a stone bench on the second floor of her mission. Suddenly down the hall she came in her blue and white habit, barefoot, with a deeply lined face and intense eyes. She sat next to Patricia on the bench and we chatted for five or ten minutes. Mother Teresa told Patricia to dress more warmly during the monsoon. Patricia asked about her health as we had been told she had just been released from hospital. Mother Teresa said she was too busy to worry about it. She asked if we could deliver some mail to the USA on our return. Patricia asked if Mother Teresa could write a note to the patients with AIDS at St Luke's Hospital where Patricia works. Mother Teresa went back to her office and returned a few moments later with a note. She wrote:

Dear Patients at St. Luke's Hospital,

May God's blessing be with you. Offer all your suffering for peace in the world.

God bless you,
Mother Teresa

We left the mission thrilled.

From Calcutta we traveled by plane and taxi to Darjeeling in the Himalayan foothills. We were advised to stay at the Windamere Hotel, famous during the British Raj and visited by the King of Sikkim and Hope Cook, the Aga Khan, Albert (King of Belgium) and Lowell Thomas. Presided over by the imposing Madam Tanduf-La, a grand old Tibetan woman of eighty-five, the hotel retained the faded charm of an English guest house. This being the off season it was easy to get a room; otherwise, one must book far ahead. Darjeeling was shrouded in mist every day. We rarely saw the adjacent hills and never the snow-capped Himalayas in the distance. Still, it was great walking the steep streets to Buddhist and Hindu temples and visiting the museum lionizing the Sherpa Tenzing along with other Everest memorabilia.

But the most memorable experience was Shri Ram, a man who, without schooling, acquired knowledge and, in spite of poverty, wrote, traveled and philosophized. He stopped us as we walked to the Japanese temple to ask if we could correct a letter he had written in English to a foreign friend. Since we were rushing to see the temple we reluctantly agreed. But soon we were caught up in the sentence structure and grammar, knowing what he wanted to say and trying to figure out the best way to say it. He in turn gave us helpful facts about the temple and the area. As we walked back toward our hotel he insisted that we see his home. It was meager indeed. The one room was shared by him and his wife. In the room was a small cooking stove, a rickety bed and a floor to ceiling bookcase. The books included the works of Shakespeare, Milton, Byron, Alexander Pope and many other classics, all well-thumbed. When the British pulled out of India, they left things behind. Somehow, Shri Ram had picked up this library and read the books after learning English by himself. Now Shri Ram, at fifty- seven, had a lifetime of stories to tell about his travels through India from top to bottom, accomplished without money. We invited him to come for tea to the Windamere so we could see what he had written. Sheepishly he showed up the following afternoon with his handwritten manuscripts, perhaps two inches of stacked lined writing paper. The writings contained numerous essays and a few were quite moving. We were fascinated by what he had achieved with so little support from anybody. How does one end such an encounter? He didn't ask but we gave him some money to help him out, and we said farewell. We hoped he would publish someday but doubted it would ever happen.

Thailand

From Calcutta we flew to Bangkok. First impressions were startling. Harsh, abrupt Thais rushing about at the airport made it seem like arrival at JFK in New York. Then began our introduction to the worst traffic problem we have seen anywhere. It took ninety minutes to get into the city center. Modern buildings, shopping malls, auto fumes and neon signs announced that we were out of India now and into one of the very fast-growing SE Asian economies.

Earlier, I spoke briefly about the tourist and sex trade in Thailand. I might add that Thailand is also filled with beautiful ornate temples; many of the most attractive ones are in Bangkok along the river. We traveled by train to Chiang Mei and joined a small group of trekkers. We climbed some hills into the isolated hill tribe region. Here we slept in straw huts on stilts. At night, below us, cows and pigs "mooed" and "oinked" as they wandered under and around our thatched house. It was like sleeping in the zoo. The hill tribe people were friendly but obviously we were far from the first outsiders to visit. As we entered each village, women would surround us hawking local craft. They still smoked opium up here, though this was coming to an end under government pressure. The colorful outfits differed from village to village and we took some great photos. Later we traveled north to the Golden Triangle, an area that looks across the border to Burma and Cambodia. We even entered Myanmar (Burma) for a few hours on a day tour, but this was not very memorable. Our guide was an intense young Burmese who crossed the border every day to work at the Burmese travel agency in Chiang Rai, Thailand.

To avoid the twelve-hour return train to Bangkok, we flew back and this time stayed on the river at the Shangri-La Hotel. It was far better than the first hotel which was right in the center of the traffic jams. We twice saw the Thai dance interpretations of the Ramayana. These performances were studied and graceful.

Next, we flew south to Phuket. This famous island resort is now overdeveloped with one beach hotel after another and more T-shirt shops than can be counted. We also saw quite a few male European tourists on the special Thai "rent-a-wife" program. The sexual services and companionship of young women could be purchased by the day, week or your entire stay in Phuket. We visited the so-called James Bond Island which was worthwhile. (One of the Bond 007 films was shot here). The steep domed mountains and huge vertical cylinders of rock rising hundreds of feet above the water were startling. From Phuket we flew to Ko Samui Island which was quieter, but by then we began to wonder what the purpose was in going to beach resorts in Asia when we have the same thing in Bermuda, Florida or the Caribbean. Shouldn't we be focusing on the particularly Asian experience?

Malaysia

With this attitude we flew to Penang Island off the coast of the north Malaysian mainland. Our entry into Malaysia was very pleasant. We were greeted by a genuine smile and welcome by the customs agent and that friendliness continued consistently during our five weeks in this country. Penang, too, had beach resorts which we now avoided on principle, but they clearly looked more luxurious and less tacky than the ones in Thailand. We toured the island for a few days, rented a car and drove across the peninsula to Terengganu, down the east coast to Kuantan and across to the capital Kuala Lumpur. En route we spent one night at Genting Highlands, which can best be described as a mini Las Vegas/Coney Island on top of a mountain.

After Kuala Lumpur we headed south to Malacca, the old Portuguese city on the west coast facing Sumatra. We visited the Chinese section and the fort, and saw the remnants of British rule. Our last stop on the Malaysian mainland was Johore Bahru (referred to as JB by the locals). Here we encountered the only unpleasant experience in Malaysia. We got taken in by a stranger offering to give us a free tour of the city. He made a deal with a taxi driver to share the booty after they overcharged us for the cab ride. Even after four to five months of travel we were still suckers for this, but at least we could see it coming and got off with a small loss of money but a big reminder about what some people will do to make a buck.

While traveling we discovered two ways to deal with strangers. We could walk along with blinders on, speaking to no one, in which case it was less likely that we would be cheated. Or we could speak with and engage strangers with a greater likelihood of being cheated. But if one was willing to take this risk, travel was more eventful, whether the stranger was honest or dishonest. Patricia and I chose to engage the locals as often as possible.

From JB we flew to Kota Kinabalu, the capital of Sabah on the island of Borneo. This northern half of Borneo was united with Malaysia in 1963. In Kota we arranged a wild life adventure and traveled across Sabah to the town of Sandakan to meet our guide, Sonny. This eccentric Malaysian had created his own unique tour. First we visited the orangutan sanctuary near Sandakan and had a close encounter of a strange kind with these human-like beasts. One stole my water bottle, drank from it and salivated all over it. Another shook hands with Patricia and gazed lovingly at her. We spent the night on Turtle Island and saw a giant tortoise lay about fifty eggs on the beach. These were harvested and artificially hatched in caged areas to increase the survival rate of this endangered species. We spent another night in the modest straw house of a rural villager and went up river to see the proboscis monkeys cavorting in trees by the shore. Later, Sonny took us to a cave with bats covering the ceiling and monstrous insects clinging to the walls. Bat guano dripped onto our heads in a steady and disgusting drizzle. In the darkness two glowing eyes peered at us. The flashlight illuminated a wild cat hunting for bats.

Back in town, after leaving Sonny, we decided to climb Mt. Kinabalu. At 13,500 feet, it is the highest in SE Asia. A seemingly endless staircase, cut from tree roots and rocks, led up to a refuge where we spent half a night sleeping. The final ascent required rising at about 2 A.M. and climbing up several thousand feet with the aid of a flashlight and steel cables staked into the rock face.

From Kota we flew to Miri and then to Mulu to see the great caves. We did some adventure caving which involved walking in dark small passageways with water up to your shoulders. Mulu has four major caves and we visited them all. Some reeked with the pungent smell of bat guano (referred to as Mulu perfume by a Malaysian tourist). Other caves had great stalactites and stalagmites rising in impressive, ornate and colorful columns. Some of these caves are time-shared by swiftlets during the night and bats during the day.

Back at Miri we drove by bus to see the Niah Cave, which is famous for three things: its enormous size, the archaeological site dating back 40,000 years and the very valuable birds' nests attached to the cave's ceiling. From the cleaned and boiled residue of the birds' nests, the Chinese make a soup that sells for $40 per bowl. This kind of financial incentive sent men shinnying up bamboo poles 100 to 150 feet high to poke and prod these nests till they fell to the cave floor where an assistant scurried about picking up the pieces. The cave extended kilometers into the mountain and through many large chambers, each with dozens of men and bamboo poles.

From Miri we flew to Kuching, where the thirtieth anniversary of Sarawak and Sabah joining with Malaysia was to be celebrated. They call it *Merdeka* (Independence). For three days we watched the locals practice the parade and then we saw the real thing, with dignitaries from all over Malaysia, including Dr. Mahthir, the revered Prime Minister. One could not help but notice the seriousness of purpose with which the marchers marched. There was a genuine pride in Malaysia, evidenced in their faces. And it was not the mindless patriotism that leads to xenophobia, but rather a goodnatured and positive feeling that seemed connected to their national goals of economic progress and respect for their multicultural harmony.

Borneo has many tribes, the largest being the Iban. Others include the Rejang, Melanau, Penan, Kenyah, Kayan, Bidayuh and the Ukit. We visited longhouses which were their traditional dwellings. They consisted of single-story attached apartments on stilts, which share a common porch. The longhouse can extend 300 or 400 feet.

From Kuching we flew to JB and then by taxi arrived in Singapore. Like Hong Kong, Singapore was a shoppers' paradise. Do not chew gum here! It is a punishable offense. The government now has a campaign to encourage the citizens to smile more. At the time of our visit, frowning was not a punishable offense. The shopping malls were vertical and built around enormous atriums. There must have been over 100 such malls running for miles down and across the main street. Since Singapore, the city state, was only twenty years old, the architecture was ultra modern and very western. Our entry visa was good for two weeks, as this was considered enough time for shoppers to do all their shopping. We ordered our obligatory Singapore Slings at Raffles, visited the botanical gardens and a great war museum, bought an electronic scheduler and flew out to Bali four days after arriving.

Indonesia

Bali was unique, being 90 percent Hindu while the rest of Indonesia was mainly Muslim. Denpasar is the capital of Bali and the name of the airport. Upon arrival we went to Sanur Beach which was not as overbuilt as Kota Beach. However, if one wished to see Balinese culture, the beach was not the place. We used Sanur Beach as a base, rented a Suzuki mini jeep and toured the island for four days. We climbed Mt. Batur, walking through the rice fields and along footpaths to see small villages. We spent two days in Ubud, an artist center. I nearly had my pants pulled down by extremely aggressive monkeys in the Monkey Forest. They saw me buy bananas and tuck them under my shirt to feed them at my pace. But these monkeys wanted to eat at their pace. I was so disgusted by their poor manners I threw the entire bunch of bananas at them, which was exactly what they wanted.

While in Bali we witnessed a major Hindu festival. All the roads were decorated with tall bamboo staffs, bowed with the weight of woven flowers and baskets made of bamboo reeds. The baskets were filled with food, an offering to the Hindu gods. Of course it was symbolic. The food was hung for one day, taken down and eaten by the worshipers as part of the festival.

In Bali, a taxi driver informed us that if we ran over a dog it was not necessary to stop. But a cat was a different matter since they are considered holy by the Hindus. If a cat was killed, one must stop, and a ceremony and an offering must be made for the animal.

We saw some dance/drama performances but none as memorable as the one we later saw in Yogyakarta. From Bali we flew north, backtracking a bit to take in this important Indonesian tourist and cultural center. In our hotel we saw the best performance ever of the Ramayana by a wonderful dance troupe. The audience gave the performers a long standing ovation. It was really unforgettable. I am grateful that Patricia persuaded me to watch.

One morning, at about 6 A.M., I looked out of our hotel room to see the traffic blocked on the main street of Yogyakarta. Down the entire length of the street hundreds of citizens had assembled to practice tai chi.

From Yogya we took a day tour up onto the Dieng Plateau to see the highlands of central Java. This included a stop at Borobadur, the famous gigantic Buddhist temple, and Pramanbanan, the Hindu temple dedicated to the god Siva.

The next day we left Yogya and headed south in a minibus and arrived in Malang where we spent two nights. From there we drove to the base of Mt. Bromo, a small volcano which we climbed, and looked down into the active caldera. You could hear the rumbling, see the smoke and bright yellow sulfur deposits near the vents hundreds of feet below.

From Surabaya, nearby, we flew past Bali to Lombok, the next island in the chain. Unlike Bali, Lombok is primarily Muslim. The island was less developed as a tourist center. We hired a taxi and toured the nearby countryside, including a visit to a rural village. People here lived in straw huts on raised mud floors. There was a windowless claustrophobic hut within the hut set aside for the women in the household. This secluded area prevented unwed daughters from being seen.

We stayed by the beach in Lombok at the Sheraton Hotel. One day I went scuba diving off a smaller island. We also had time to take a horse-drawn cart, bumping our way along small roads around the island.

During our stay in Bali, Patricia picked up laryngitis, which became very annoying and tiring. In Lombok I caught it from her. These colds lasted thirty days and had an enervating effect on each of us, which we felt both in Lombok and on our return to Bali. Also, we were tired of Asia after four months. We felt our recovery would be speeded by a return to the West. We had spent an extra week in Malaysia. Now, by leaving Indonesia a week earlier than planned, we would be back on schedule, so we headed for our next planned stop, Australia. Perhaps it was our colds, or travel fatigue, but Patricia and I had a terrible argument at the Bali airport. It was really over nothing important but it just got totally out-of-hand. We were fuming through most of the five-hour flight to Sydney but by the time we landed the fight was history.

Australia

On landing in Sydney, a friendly young lady working at the airport visitors' desk got us a great deal at the Sebel Town House where we stayed for ten days. What a liberation that first morning when we went out for a snack at a nearby coffee house. First there was the fluent exchange of English, without misunderstandings and with an easy humor and friendliness. For the first time since leaving Asia Patricia felt that she was being treated like a person, rather than as a female nonentity. Women addressed her directly rather than through me.

The Olympic Committee was about to decide the site for the year 2000. Most Australians felt Beijing would win. What a surprise when Sydney was chosen. There were huge crowds everywhere the next day in a festive, happy mood. Sydney is a great city. Set amidst several magnificent harbors, with spectacular views, a vital center, clean streets, beautiful and safe parks, it has much to teach Americans about the potential attractiveness of urban life. In fact, all the cities we saw in Australia were vital in their centers, not dead in the middle like so many of our cities. While many of our cities, like Detroit or Washington, are deserted and dangerous at night, Australian cities had wonderful arcades, restaurants and theaters in their centers.

One evening we attended the famous Sydney Opera House, where we saw a performance of *Tosca*. While in Sydney we did a lot of tourist things, such as visiting museums, taking harbor cruises and joining city bus tours. We went on a day trip to Canberra, the capital. Like many planned cities, such as Brasilia, it shut down at night and, on the weekends, people often went to a more interesting place, such as Sydney. They did have a fascinating war museum where we learned about the meaning of Gallipoli and Ansett Day, which is their Memorial Day.

We drove through the Blue Mountains and saw wild and unpopulated terrain. Australia is as big as the United States but has a population of only eighteen million people.

From Sydney we flew to Melbourne, where we spent one evening with Tony Beaconsfield, a travel companion from our Africa truck safari in 1989. Patricia liked Melbourne because it seemed to have character. She felt that a certain amount of chaos and dirt made it interesting.

From Melbourne we flew to Launceston, Tasmania. Tasmania is an island south of Australia. We rented a car and toured for five days. During our stay we took a boat trip up the Gordon River. The seaplane flight back was hair-raising. The river had steep cliffs on both sides and was serpentine, so the seaplane had to zigzag while accelerating down the river and then continue its steep turns as it ascended. This it continued doing until the plane's altitude exceeded the top of the cliffs.

The tourist authorities proudly advertised their convict history. Visiting a restored and preserved prison compound, we saw a vivid picture of prison exile. Our travels ended in Hobart, a small town with a big cultural life. From Hobart we flew to Adelaide where we spent three days. One day we toured the Barosa wine district which had a small German community.

The site for Adelaide was picked by Colonel Light, the town's founder and planner, though he faced much political opposition in his day. There was a wonderful memorial to him on a hill on the far side of the river that runs past the city. Light is shown standing and pointing toward the exciting skyline of Adelaide. On the pedestal are the words from his memoirs. While I cannot recall those words exactly, they said something like this: "I had much opposition in my site selection for Adelaide. Let posterity look and decide whether my decision was correct." Anyone now looking from that hill across the river to the dramatic skyline of Adelaide would have to conclude that Colonel Light had been correct in his judgment.

From Adelaide we flew to Alice Springs, the jumping off point for Ayers Rock, called "Uluru" by the Aborigines. This was an introduction to the ubiquitous and numerous flies that inhabit central Australia. Flies were everywhere. It took five hours to drive by bus from Alice Springs to Ayers Rock and during that time the driver gave us a continuous commentary about the history and wildlife of the region. His knowledge was extraordinary. In general, we found the guides in Australia to be knowledgeable and personable. At each rest stop the flies would almost immediately discover us and about fifty would perch on each tourist. The driver told us to brush them off the back of each tourist in front of us as we climbed back onto the bus. He advised us not to squash any flies that did get into the bus as it would attract 100 more to the funeral. Finally, we reached Ayers Rock, which is owned by the Aborigines, who consider the rock and the surrounding areas to be sacred. There was a cluster of hotels discreetly hidden over a small hill a few miles away. We visited the nearby Olgas, a group of interesting domed hills. The following morning Patricia and I climbed Ayers Rock. It took us thirty-six minutes to get to the top. The first part was steep but a chain on that section helped the walkers. At the top the wind must have been blowing at over sixty knots. It was hard to stand up at times. There were dozens of people milling about, taking photos of themselves and the flat brown sandy plains that spread to the horizon in all directions.

From Alice Springs we flew to Darwin in the north. Now we were back in hot weather. Darwin has a stronger Asian influence on the population and the food. With a tour group we drove by Jeep to Litchfield National Park and ate some "bush tucker." From here we flew to Kakadoo National Park for a boat cruise along the Yellow River. The park was teaming with thin-necked, elegant birds, sneaky alligators and noisy German tourists. Later we saw cave paintings made thousands of years ago by Aborigines.

Let me say a few words about Aborigines. There are only about 250,000 of them left, which is about one percent of the total Australian population. We saw some of them hanging around like homeless people in New York, but they weren't begging. The Aborigines are well-subsidized by the government but getting them to participate in or be accepted into the mainstream has been difficult. They appear gentle and passive but there is a new militancy among the Aborigines for regaining their land, similar to our Native Americans. We went to a cultural performance in Cairns and were fascinated whenever we heard the didgeridoo. The didgeridoo is a piece of log that has been hollowed out by termites. Into this tube the player must exhale through his mouth while inhaling through his nose. Vibrating lip and guttural throat sounds are amplified by the tube to create an eerie haunting buzz that seems to imitate the wild animals of the Australian outback.

Patricia had an especially close encounter with an Aborigine woman in Darwin. As we were leaving our hotel to go to dinner, a large dark woman dressed only in bra and panties came rushing over to Patricia. She had been yelling at another Aborigine woman and, upon seeing Patricia, she decided to gain her sympathy and support. The Aborigine hugged Patricia and sobbed that her clothes had been removed by the other woman. Patricia soothed her and was about to run upstairs to bring down some clothing, though it seemed unlikely to me that the Aborigine would fit into anything Patricia owned. Moments later a hotel doorman arrived and took charge. Relieved, we left for dinner.

From Darwin, we flew to Cairns. There we went snorkeling and scuba diving on the Great Barrier Reef. The coral was impressive but I think the Caribbean has more colorful fish. Cairns was a pleasant stop. One day a big parade came down the main street. Funny floats went by and people on them squirted water at the crowds from high-powered toy water guns. We ate in some good restaurants. One specialty, which I consumed in great quantity, was small lobster tails, which are called "bugs."

From Darwin we flew to Brisbane and spent just one day, walking about town. Brisbane was pleasant, situated on a river, with an impressive performing arts center and shopping arcade. From Brisbane we flew back to Melbourne for one night to join up with our international connection to Auckland, New Zealand.

New Zealand

My cousin Elaine had put us in touch with her friend, Julie Petit, in Auckland. Julie turned out to be a wonderful host. She put us up in her apartment, took us out to an island to spend a day and night with friends at their summer house and later we met more friends on their sheep farm. Julie stored most of our luggage while we headed out to tour the North Island and then the South Island. We spent over three weeks in New Zealand and we were on the move every day. First we went to Cape Reinga, the northern tip. We returned via the ninety-mile beach on special buses adapted for salt water and sand. At the Bay of Islands, it rained, but we were nevertheless able to see the beautiful scenery shrouded in mist and buffeted by waves. Heading south by plane we stopped at Rotorua, a thermal area, surrounded by steam, sulfur fumes and geysers. Our bus touring included a Maori cultural performance and "Hangi" feast. The food was cooked slowly underground in warm earth heated by hot rocks.

The Maori are very different from the Aborigines. The Aborigines came to Australia 50,000 years ago whereas the Maori arrived in New Zealand only 1,000 years ago, coming in ocean-going canoes. The Maori people are assertive and proud and are far more integrated into the Western culture of New Zealand. You see them working in shops and offices. As a minority of 14 percent, they have a significant political and cultural influence on New Zealand life, especially on the North Island, and appear to be respected by the white majority. Upon our return, a New Zealander told us there is greater tension between the Maori and Polynesian minority than with the white majority. This was surprising to us.

From Rotorua we flew to Wellington, the capital. It was a rainy Sunday evening and we were leaving the next morning by ferry for the South Island. A nice bed and breakfast, a good seafood dinner, a walk in the evening along the wet and empty downtown area, was all we had time for.

The ferry across the straits between the two islands of New Zealand took about three hours. On the other side we rented an Avis car and spent the last two weeks of our journey touring this way. We drove down the west coast. One of our stops was the Franz Joseph Glacier. We took a scenic flight over the glacier and around Mt. Cook. The area has many peaks and looks like the Swiss Alps. We got some excellent photos on a perfect day. The next morning we walked a few miles into the woods until we came to a high point and got an excellent view of the glacier from a different angle. There we met a Maori park ranger and discussed the recent plane crash on the Glacier.

From Franz Joseph we drove through mountainous terrain to Queenstown. Queenstown is the place for adventure. The first thing we saw was the bungee-jumping center founded by A.J. Hackett. Over this 140-foot gorge is where it all began. Patricia had already decided in Australia that she wanted to jump. After learning that they had no fatalities in 160,000 leaps and that her recent lunch would stay down, or up in this case, Patricia took the plunge. I couldn't bring myself to do it. However, the next day we learned that one could hang glide. This we both did on separate gliders and each with instructors. We drove to the top of a mountain called "The Remarkables." After a briefing we harnessed up, clipped on to this contraption of nylon and aluminum tubing, ran three steps in tandem with the instructor and jumped off the mountain. Soon we were soaring like birds with nothing between our bellies and the ground but 3,000 feet of thin air. The instructors showed us how to control diving, stalling and steering by moving a bar and soon we were controlling the thing. After about ten–fifteen minutes my instructor and I swooped down to a sheep meadow and bumped along the grass to a thankful end. Patricia and her instructor landed a few minutes later. She later told me she asked if they could do a loop but the instructor said that only high performance hang gliders can do that. "However, would she like to do acrobatics?" "Oh, yes, please!" she said. There followed a series of sharp dives, climbs and turns. There are many such activities in Queenstown.

From Queenstown we drove to Te Anau, the start of what is called "the most beautiful track (footpath) in the world." Of course such a statement is debatable but we only had time for one walk so this had to be it. We spent six hours sailing up the lake to the trail head with a fellow named Murray and eleven other walkers. Taking walkers up the lake was Murray's business and in the six hours we learned something about him. It took him ten years to build his sailboat, which was about forty feet long and had bunks and kitchen below. He started with trees, cut them down, hauled them to a sawmill and had them reduced to planks. That was the beginning. Ultimately he ran out of money, canceled his dream of sailing the Pacific and decided to start a business based on his boat and a bank loan.

The Milford Track is highly regulated. A maximum of forty people start each day and everyone must stop at each of four huts on the four days of the walk. Walkers must all go from south to north and not the other way. All these rules guarantee a bed each night. And even though 10,000 people hike this path each year, because they are all walking in the same direction and because walkers spread out as they move at their own pace, one is soon alone on the trail. The views were spectacular, no doubt about that. The path threaded its way up a valley to a pass and then down a valley on the other side. Most of the walk followed a river and, as we headed toward the pass, we saw more and more snow-capped peaks and cascading waterfalls. All this culminated at MacKinnon Pass in a 360-degree panorama of tall snowcovered peaks and low green valleys. We went to the pass twice; once after arriving at the hut just before the climb, and the second time the following morning when we had to move on to the next hut. It was good we made the extra effort because after the clear day of our first ascent the weather turned foul. The next day we went over in a snowstorm and could not see much through the wind and weather.

The huts were fun. They had communal bunks and a kitchen with gas rings. All we had to pack in was food, sleeping bags, kitchen pots and clothing. There were lots of people on the track who were clearly not used to walking. They came in with very heavy backpacks and new boots. At the end of the walk they had lots of blisters and sore limbs.

From the trail end we took a boat cruise on Milford Sound. Countless waterfalls cascaded off high cliff walls, dropping directly into the ocean sound. The tops of the cliffs were shrouded in a vaporous mist and the air was saturated with moisture. After the cruise we took a bus back to Te Anau and celebrated with fellow walkers at a nice Italian restaurant. The next day we drove to Dunedin on the East Coast. Dunedin once had a strong Scottish influence but now it was difficult to find. The accents are all various shades of New Zealand. There was a tartan shop, and some place names and architecture were Scottish in origin, but that was the extent of it. We drove out onto the nearby Otago Peninsula to see a colony of yellow-eyed penguins and seals. After a couple of days we drove north to Christchurch. There we stayed at Eliza's, a wonderful bed and breakfast and the closest we've seen to an English-style B&B. In the final days of our journey we were becoming lazy tourists. We aimlessly wandered around town paying little attention to the odd museum or church. Punting on the small river fit well into our slow pace. Christchurch had an interesting open market and we spent some hours poking among the stalls and watching the street entertainers.

Christchurch is a jumping-off point for the Antarctic. Many of the scientific vessels heading south fueled up here. In a renewed burst of tourist energy we went to two museums in Christchurch with big exhibits on the history, equipment and adventure of the southern continent. The second museum was near the airport, which was convenient for returning the car before flying back to Auckland. Julie greeted us warmly and we exchanged stories over a fine dinner at a nearby restaurant. The following morning, while packing for the flight home, I threw out my back. Because of my intense pain we decided to fly directly to New York instead of stopping in L.A. or San Francisco as originally planned. Julie met us that evening and took us to the airport where we said our farewells, boarded the plane and began the twenty-four-hour trip home.

Final Observations

This journey was the most eventful of any six-month period in our lives. Each day was different and many stand out as vivid and memorable. Entering each country was like starting a new vacation. In a sense this journey was a series of journeys strung one after another. The Asian experience lasted four months and, during this period, the cultural isolation was greatest. If it was the toughest region to travel through it also left the deepest emotional impact. We in the West know so little about Asia, therefore, the surprises were frequent and powerful. After our first visit I had vowed never to return but five years later, there we were, back in Asia. And I know that we will one day go again.

It was wonderful coming home and seeing my parents waiting for us at Newark Airport. We missed them and all our relatives and friends very much. That warm protective blanket surrounded us. The traffic, the highway to New York, the streets, the potholes, the overflowing litter bins—we were home. The familiar faces and places gave us comfort. Kaleidoscopic change, tiring challenges, were ended for now and, for a while at least, we welcomed the resumption of routine. And so preparations began for the homecoming of our daughter Rachel and the arrival of a large Thanksgiving turkey.

Great Britain, Poland and Norway Trip, 1994

May 3–4. After saying goodbye to my folks at Newark, we were packed into a crowded SAS flight to Copenhagen. We left at 7 P.M. and arrived at about 8 A.M. on a chilly morning. The taxi took us to the Hotel Imperial where we left our luggage and, though tired and sleepy, walked over to the Danish Resistance Museum. There we spent an interesting couple of hours looking at the courageous record of Danes conspiring against the brutal Nazi army of occupation. Especially moving was the display of plaques sent to the Danish people over the past fifty years from the US Jewish community, thanking and praising them for smuggling out 8,000 Jews to Sweden. Ninety-four percent of the Danish Jews survived the war because of the Danes' moral strength.

Returning to our hotel we hurriedly ate a lunch of smoked salmon, went up to our room and slept away the afternoon. At 5 P.M. we got up and went out.

Noisy football fans roamed about; a big match between England and Italy was about to begin. We escaped into the relative calm of Tivoli Gardens, a sort of nineteenth-century Disneyland. Begun 150 years ago, Tivoli is an odd mixture of high and low culture. It's probably where Walt Disney got his many ideas for a theme park. In a single evening one can listen to classical music performed in a fine concert hall, and then play carnival games or ride a roller coaster next door. Tired and with limited time, we wandered about, ate in one of the many restaurants and then ended the day early.

The next day we arose and took a walking tour led by an American who had married a Dane and really knew the city. After the tour we visited Rosenborg Castle and saw the crown jewels plus other treasures of gold and precious stones. We took a taxi to the Little Mermaid and walked back into town. We then took another taxi out to Bispipyer Tor, where I had rented a room thirty-five years ago as part of my six-week student exchange work program. The street and apartments were the same. Only the times and I had changed.

From there we took a bus back to the center of town and had an afternoon snooze. We were still feeling jet lag. In the evening we went out for a light dinner, walked around a busy mall filled with restaurants and movies. We got back early to prepare for our 9 A.M. flight to London the next day.

Getting up early, we took a taxi out to the Copenhagen airport. The plane was filled with football fans returning from a victory of their team, Arsenal, over the Italians. They were large, beefy fellows, loud and vulgar. Patricia did detect a kindness and good-natured attitude among them. Landing in Heathrow we got our Hertz rental car and drove down to Bexhill to meet my in-laws, Sheilah and Gerry, and their children, John and Sarah. Gerry had lost weight and was down to only ninety pounds as a result of his illness. But his sense of humor and intelligence were in full force. Gerry and I traded computer talk. He showed me his new color printer and I showed him 3D Body Adventure, a CD Rom tour of the human anatomy. We both put on 3D glasses to get the full effect. We spent one night in Bexhill and the following afternoon Patricia drove our little Fiat to Christchurch. The trip took two and a half hours, which is quite fast. At times our car was moving along at over ninety-five miles per hour. Wendy greeted us as we parked outside of Sidney's house. Sidney, Patricia's father, at ninety-three years old, was witty and sharp as ever.

We spent some evenings watching British TV and one evening we played Scrabble. During the day we visited neighbors and the nearby towns of Boscombe and Bournemouth. We also booked three grand lunches at the famous and great Chewton Glen Hotel. These meals were enjoyed by all. Typically, we had aperitifs in the lounge bar, relocated to a bright room for lunch and finally completed the feast with coffee in a large pleasant lounge. The grounds of Chewton Glen consist of sweeping lawns, forest and ponds. Footpaths wind through the forest and around the ponds. I videotaped the occasion for posterity.

After saying our farewells to the Staffs we drove to Gable Thatch, our favorite guest house in South England. It is an original thatched cottage set in the charming village of Porlock in Somerset. There, a fine young man, David McWilliam, warmly received, wined and dined visitors in the best English tradition. The next day we drove to Bristol, returned the rental car and, by a circuitous train trip, arrived at Chepstow—the start of our 180–mile walk from the south of Wales to the north. From our hotel dining room in Chepstow we saw the river change direction as we ate dinner. The famous Severn bore, downstream, with one of the world's highest tides, influenced the direction of the river even though we were two miles upstream. Not only did the flow change direction but the height of the river rose rapidly during our dinner.

The Offa's Dyke walk took us eleven days, seven of which were either cloudy or rainy. But we persisted through the cow and sheep manure, the mud and muck. At the end of the day I was so dirty I didn't want to take a bath with myself. Patricia, as usual, enjoyed it a great deal more as she likes the capricious weather.

We did have some high points. Our English friends, Andrew Opie and Eric Fitzpatrick, joined us at various prearranged points and we all marched together through fields of goo. We were disappointed that Patricia's brother Peter could not join us in the mud bath. The best days were the last two when the sun came out as we walked the Clywyddian hills. The views were grand on these open grass slopes that rose high above green valleys and farmlands. Unfortunately, the Black Hills, which should have had the best views, were shrouded in a heavy mist and the most we could see was about 200 feet ahead, which offered us an early warning of bogs.

We arrived at Hay-on-Wye in the midst of their annual book fair. In this small town thirty antiquarian bookstores offered hard-to-get, out-of-print rarities. Speakers at the fair have included such personalities as Salman Rushdie. This year Betty Friedan was speaking along with other authors and poets.

At one point, as we walked a wooded section of the path, two angry looking boxer dogs suddenly came rushing and barking at us. As I tentatively moved forward, Patricia reassured me they were harmless and sure enough they turned and ran behind a fence. In a moment they reappeared, one carrying a rubber ball in his mouth and the other a Frisbee. These ferocious guard dogs just wanted to play. I tossed the Frisbee and they were off searching for the thing in another field. Once again Patricia's uncanny interpretation of canine body language proved accurate.

Further north we reached the 200-year-old Telford Bridge. It is really an aqueduct for narrow barges and is part of the canal network that threads its way around the British countryside. We walked across this huge steel structure in parallel with a 6-foot-wide barge filled with vacationing sailors.

At last we reached the seaside town of Prestatyn on the North Wales coast. Since the Sharrow Bay Guest House requires a jacket for dinner and since I did not haul one across Wales, we figured the best thing was to pick up a used one at Dr. Bernardo's, the local equivalent of our thrift shop. For $15 I was outfitted respectfully and a nice tie was thrown in for free. We then got on the train for Penrith in the Lake District. Our stay at the Sharrow Bay was much appreciated luxury. For two days we stuffed ourselves on the gourmet food and relaxed and conversed with guests in a lounge with a wonderful picture window overlooking Lake Ullswater. One day was spent walking to the far end of the lake and taking a steamer boat back. On June 1 we headed to London by train. We had one full day in London with glorious weather. We walked through St. James Park and over to Buckingham Palace. In the evening Andrew joined us for dinner at the Connaught Hotel Restaurant where we discussed the rest of our walk and the possibility of walking the South Downs Way in Sussex.

On June 3 we flew from London to Warsaw. Arriving in a state of confusion as to how to get to Lodz, we decided to rent a taxi and drive

100 miles. The flat green fields and farms flew by and we soon arrived at this city of textile factories and road works. The next few days were devoted to meeting Rachel and her colleagues at the folklore and ecology conference on the edge of town. We videotaped Rachel at every opportunity in spite of her occasional embarrassment. The attendees, numbering about twenty, came from Greece, Serbia, Croatia, Canada and Poland. Violetta, who is a professor at the University, was the organizer. She invited us all to her home for a party. Most of the attendees were full professors and much Rachel's senior, which was daunting for her but I think, in the end, added to her self-confidence. Patricia and I had some time in Lodz to visit three museums. One had a section devoted to native son, Arthur Rubenstein. In the same museum was a section devoted to the war years and the history and fate of the Jews of Lodz.

We rented a car from Hertz and drove south, stopping at Auschwitz en route to Krakow. We hired a guide and passed under the sign ARBEIT MACHT FREI and entered Auschwitz ONE. The camp was established in 1941 and was originally intended for political prisoners. Himmler visited the camp, put Rudolph Hess in charge and ordered him to expand the camp to accommodate Jews and others. Here the first exterminations by gas and ovens took place. However, the big mass killings took place at Auschwitz TWO about three kilometers away. Auschwitz TWO was also called Birkenau. Auschwitz ONE is now a museum, but Auschwitz TWO has been left untouched as a memorial. We visited both. Each leaves a very different impression. Auschwitz ONE, with its large museum rooms filled with mountains of shoes, eyeglasses, neatly labeled leather luggage and human hair all testify to the enormous horror which took place here over fifty years ago. Large groups of schoolchildren noisily rushed past. I doubt they were really taking this in. Photos of victims were on display. Under each was the date of arrival and the date of death. The men lived about ten–twelve months, women for only three–four months. Auschwitz ONE was a holding area where a variety of Jews, political prisoners and others worked as slave laborers or were used by doctors for experiments. Our guide said that at least 1.3 million Jews were exterminated at Auschwitz. This was a minimum provable number. Possibly many more died here.

Our guide took us to an underground prison. In a small dark cell we saw a flame burning. It was a memorial to a priest. The Pope had recently journeyed here to pay homage. Why? Here is the story. The Nazis selected three Jews for extermination. One burst into tears, saying he had a family that needed him. A priest, who was also a prisoner in the same cell, stepped forward and offered his life in exchange. The Nazis accepted the offer and the priest was killed along with the two remaining Jews. The man he saved was still alive and visited this memorial yearly.

In a sad and quiet mood we drove the short distance to Auschwitz TWO. Here there was no museum and no noisy crowds. The Nazis tried to blow it all up before the Russians arrived. What was left was enough to piece together the evil. Before us stood the guard towers, the barbed wire, the wood and brick barracks, the partially destroyed gas chambers and ovens. Plaques briefly explained the purpose of each building. We stood by the railroad platform, with the pathways covered in white gravel and pondered what terror and horror took place on this very spot so many years ago.

It was difficult shaking the gloomy mood as we drove into Krakow. Krakow is a picturesque city and well-preserved in the central area. It reminded us of Prague with its ornate towers, clocks and heavy stonework. The next day we decided to drive south to Zakopane, the Tatra mountain resort on the southern border of Poland. The drive took about two hours. As we approached the town we could see the snow-capped 8,000-foot peaks on the horizon. After some driving in circles we arrived at the edge of a park which had roads and trails leading into the mountains. We enjoyed a picnic lunch and started to walk along a riverside road.

Suddenly I felt a sharp pain in the lower rear of my back. Having had this once before I knew I was in for a treat. Another kidney stone had decided it was time to make its move. With help from Patricia and Rachel, I made it back to the car. Now the pain was agonizing and we sped to the Zakopane hospital. The place looked deserted and dreary. Soon a nurse appeared. I was placed on a stretcher and wheeled down long corridors to a large room. There, a woman doctor who knew a few English words administered a painkiller, muscle relaxant and IV drip. The view of the mountains from the hospital room was terrific but I was in no mood to appreciate it. I slept and after a while I felt better. Upon awaking, and over the doctor's objections, I checked out and we began the two-hour drive back to Krakow. Almost from the start of this hellish trip the pain returned. Seated on the passenger side it was hard to sit or lie flat. I was trembling and nauseous. At one point we had to stop along the road so that I could vomit onto the verge. I would definitely call this the low point of our visit to Europe. Back in Krakow in our nice hotel room I was in no mood for another depressing Polish hospital. Patricia called their equivalent of EMS who soon came to the hotel and gave me more painkillers and muscle relaxants. Rachel brought up pizza so she and Patricia could get some food into themselves. This was tough on them also. The pain came in waves but after a while my stone calmed down and I slept. In the morning I felt better, but Patricia and I decided it was best to take it easy and sit in the central plaza. My ten hours of pain had at last ended. Rachel took a city tour and returned to tell us that she had seen an interesting synagogue among several sights.

The next day we drove five hours to Warsaw and spent one night there. Warsaw rebuilt its ancient center after the war with good results. We sought out the memorial to the Warsaw ghetto, behind which stands a park surrounded by middle income apartments. It was a powerful reminder of great courage in the face of certain death.

On June 10 we flew from Warsaw to Oslo. Going from Eastern Europe to Western Europe was an upbeat experience. The shabby and run-down was suddenly replaced by the modern efficiency of wealthy Norway. We arrived at the Hotel Bondenheim with time to walk around town and get oriented. I noticed that I still had a slight residual pain in my kidney and the next night it was time for more agony. After about five hours, the pain ended and I felt that the stone had finally passed.

Patricia and I hadn't slept much that night but the next day we managed to go to Bigdoy, a suburb reached by boat where they have some great museums. We visited an outdoor folk museum full of old houses, a stave church and song and dance events. Then we went to the Fram Museum which houses the original vessel used by Amundsen and Nansen in their polar explorations. We visited the Viking Museum filled with original Viking ships and a Polar Museum which detailed Norway's impressive contributions to discovery and science in both the North and South.

The next day we visited Vigeland park, named after the famous sculptor who designed the park and filled it with powerful stone figures of men, women and children. Oslo is a real party town. The streets were jammed with people and every block had a pub. At night we could hear the youth of Norway carrying on in the street below as we tried to get some sleep. At 4 A.M., when the pubs close, the noise peaked again as the crowd poured onto the streets fully tanked up with beer. Norway has a long dark winter and with almost twenty-four hours of summer daylight it was time to really tear loose.

We rented a car and visited two towns south of Oslo, called Sandefjord and Tønsberg. The weather was sunny and warm, making for a pleasant day.

We spent another day visiting Lillehammer by train. We hiked up the steps of the ski jump and walked along the forest trails used by the cross country ski contestants. Lillehammer was crowded with visitors. It must have been tremendously exciting to be there in person as compared to watching the Olympics on TV.

From Oslo we flew to the far north and spent nine hours between flights at Alta. We rented a car and drove to Kautokeino to look for the Sami and their reindeer. The Sami or Lapps, are an indigenous people who live in the north of Norway, Finland, Sweden and Russia. They tend to be shorter and darker than other Scandinavians. However, it was the wrong time to look for Sami as they were all down by the shore with their reindeer in the summer. We did see the museum in Alta, which had interesting outdoor stone etchings of human figures, animals and boats that dated back 6,000 years. These may have been the earliest recordings of Sami culture since no one knows when they first came to this region.

From Alta we flew to Honningsvag which is only twenty-one miles from North Cape, the most northerly point in Europe. We were now far above the Arctic circle at latitude 71 degrees. The sun did not set but moved 360 degrees around us, rising to a peak in the south and dipping low in the north. We spent four days in this small town and our visit culminated with our participating in the annual North Cape march. We, along with over 100 Norwegians, walked to the Cape. It took us six hours and fifteen minutes. A few did the round trip of forty-two miles in nine to ten hours.

A large tourist center was built at the Cape, complete with a movie theater, a large beer hall, a museum and a restaurant. The place was jammed with busloads of Germans. Tour organizers put together these mad dash tours to North Cape and retired Germans made the exhausting road trip up through Sweden and Finland to finally arrive here. They checked into their hotel late, drove up to the Cape, returned to sleep at 2 A.M. and rose at 5 A.M. to start the bus journey home.

In Honningsvag we visited yet another Resistance museum. As the Russians advanced against the Germans in World War II, the Germans decided to burn everything as they retreated. That included towns and farm animals. The museum contained many examples of resistance from underground newspapers to clandestine radio equipment. Britain played a major role in helping the Norwegian resistance, providing equipment and intelligence information.

This was the third or fourth Resistance museum we saw on this trip, not counting memorials and Auschwitz in Poland. It left a permanent record of shame for the elderly Germans who were now visitors to the places they once assaulted. And what must younger Germans think as they saw what havoc the previous generation rained on their neighbors?

From Honningsvag we took the coastal steamer to Tromso. We had to rise early and, after coming in late from our trek, we were bleary-eyed as we boarded the ship. The first few hours were spent dozing in our cabin. Later we watched as the steamer made its way through mist and mountains to our destination. Arriving at midnight—yet in daylight—we checked into our hotel. In Tromso the next day we rented a car and drove out of town to see more fjords and snowcapped peaks. Tromso was celebrating its 200th anniversary and we saw the king and queen twice that day at various ceremonies. The night before, Norway had beaten Italy in soccer and the Norwegians went absolutely wild. So, all in all, the town was in a festive mood.

From Tromso we flew to Bodø and there spent one night. We had time to take a bus to Saltstraumen, where flows the world's second fastest tidal maelstrom, at 33 knots. We arrived just past the peak flow to see great whirlpools and eddies forming and disappearing as the tide came racing through a narrow passage into the fjord; strong enough to sink large boats, we were told.

It was a dreary day in Bodø even as we boarded the night train to Trondheim. We had a couchette for three, which was a cozy triple decker. But the constant rocking and rolling at night made sleep difficult.

From Trondheim we flew to Bergen, a beautiful town where we spent two nights. In Bergen we took a city tour which included a visit to Edvard Grieg's home and a Williamsburg-type of museum made up of relocated old homes. Bergen has a great downtown area full of quaint wooden homes and cobbled streets. The fish market was also terrific and I gorged myself on lox, gravlax, cold poached salmon and shrimp.

We left Bergen by catamaran on a cloudy day. Nevertheless, the fjords were splendid, towering into the mist on both shores. At times the boat passed through narrow passages only 200 feet across. In about five hours we arrived at Flam and checked into our hotel. Flam is surrounded by steep mountains and we walked up to a waterfall using a footpath. The next day we took the 8:30 A.M. train to Oslo. The first part of this trip took us on one of the great train journeys, the Flam–Myrdal line. It passes through thirty tunnels in forty minutes and rises from sea level to about 6,000 feet. The views from the train were spectacular, complete with cascading waterfalls, snow fields, sheer rock faces and deep valleys. At Myrdal we changed to the Oslo–Bergen line and began the gradual descent to Oslo. We started in snow and clouds and ended in sunny, green farm fields. Oslo was still bustling with tourists and street entertainers. Our last meal in Norway was in a highly-recommended Chinese restaurant. Sam and Becky joined us for dinner. We had met them first in Bergen and by coincidence again in Oslo. Sam was a minister in Atlanta, jolly and rotund. They both took a great interest in Rachel and her activities.

At last we returned to our hotel and, early the next morning, Rachel left for the airport to fly to Newcastle and the train back to Edinburgh. Patricia and I got the 2 P.M. flight to New York, which included a 3-hour stop in Copenhagen.

I remember when Europe was poor and we Americans were rich. Europe on $5 a day was possible. On this trip a pizza cost us $20. The Scandinavian boutiques, the merchandise, the sparkle, all send the message that in the past thirty years much has changed. But now Europeans were getting some of our problems. Locals told us of drugs and spoilt teenagers with too much money.

Our visit to Poland was an entirely different experience. Here was a much lower standard of living. Services were poor, the streets and shops were shabby. The only unifying experience we found between Poland and Norway was World War II. The Resistance, the brutality, the destruction were shared experiences and the museums in both countries left the same sober effect.

A Long Walk across Europe—Part I: April–June 1995

The swiftest traveler is he that goes afoot.
—Henry David Thoreau

Patricia got a notion in 1994 to walk from North Cape, Norway to Calabria, Italy, a distance of 4,000 miles. As a compromise, and to put off further discussion, I suggested in late 1994 that we instead walk the shorter 1,300 miles from Hook of Holland on the North Sea to Nice, France on the GR5 (Grand Randonée), a marked route over dikes, bike paths, country and forest roads and connecting wilderness trails. The route traverses Holland, Belgium, Luxembourg, Switzerland and France, crossing three mountain ranges, the Vosges, the Jura and the Alps, before descending into the balmy Mediterranean lowlands. A big part of the pleasure in such an undertaking is the planning.

Planning

Calls to consulates, the Sierra Club, the Federation Francaise de la Randonée Pedestre in Paris and the Grote Routepaden in Antwerp soon yielded a collection of topographic guide books and Michelin road maps. A book, *Europe Top to Bottom*, written by two American women in 1984, plus a few articles written by other end-to-end walkers, completed the collection of published material. I divided the walk into twelve sections, each about 100–250 miles in length. I allocated a certain number of days to complete each section, depending on hilliness of the terrain and our fitness at the start. If we could maintain an average of sixteen miles per day with one rest day for every ten walking days, we could complete the journey in ninety days.

Equipment

Both Patricia and I carried Dana Design backpacks but each had different features. My pack weighed about twenty-six pounds and Patricia's weighed about thirty pounds. By loading up the wife, I hoped to slow her down so we could walk at the same pace. (This only seemed to work uphill.) Our packs contained first aid kit, toilet kit, rain pants, Goretex anorak, fleece sweater, sneakers, two or three pairs of wool socks, shirt, short and long pants, two sets of underwear, 1.5-liter plastic water bottle, guidebooks and maps. Patricia carried in addition a neatly rolled-up long skirt for a celebration dinner in Nice plus a camera and binoculars. We arranged with my father-in-law, Sidney Staff, and sister-in-law, Wendy, to ship parcels ahead to us. These parcels included guidebooks and maps for the next section of the walk and Questran powder, which I take daily to lower cholesterol.

Boots

My boots were made by Vasque. They had a leather exterior with a Goretex liner for waterproofing and breathability. They had Vibram cleated soles which wore out in about 650 miles.

Patricia's choice was the British walker's favorite, the Chris Brasher boot, also leather with a Goretex liner. Patricia tended to quickly wear away the outer side of her heels so, by the time we reached Luxembourg, the boots needed heel replacements. I purchased new German-made boots in France, made of artificial exterior and Goretex-lined.

Typical Day

The alarm was set for 7 A.M. We would get moving around 7:30 A.M., brushing teeth, washing up, getting dressed and packing our packs; breakfast at 8:30 A.M. and checkout of the hotel at 9 A.M. to start our day's walk. We might stop to buy food for a picnic lunch if no town was available at midday. We would walk until somewhere between 3 and 7 P.M., stopping for drinks at cafes if we were lucky or turning to our water bottle if not. On average we walked sixteen miles per day. Our longest distance in one day was twenty-seven miles and our shortest was ten miles. Arriving at our hotel we would check in, unpack the backpacks, wash dirty clothes in the sink if the weather was dry or if the room radiators were working. A hot soak in the tub was my goal but not always available. We'd eat around 7:30 P.M. after relaxing and perhaps walking around the town or village if it looked interesting. We'd turn off the lights at around 10 P.M.

Accommodations

We rarely booked ahead. We just walked into town sometime in the afternoon and started to look for the best available. At best it was a Michelin three-star hotel, with a bath, firm flat bed, and good food and service. At worst it was a Gîte d'Étape (hostel), with sagging dirty beds in a grim room. The toilet and shower would be down a dreary hallway. In one Gîte, there were six beds in a dormitory all facing a toilet with no door. Needless to say we were relieved that no one else showed up that night to share our room.

Foot Care

Our medical kit emphasized foot care. It contained moleskin, a soft pad, sticky on one side, which we would cut to size and apply to sore, red areas on our feet. Should our feet get blisters or skin breaks we applied "Second Skin," a British favorite. This gooey, slimy pad instantly relieved painful blisters. However, within twenty days of pounding, our feet had toughened up so that they could stand eight hours of daily walking without pain. My feet developed thick pads at the ball and heel and hard calluses on toes and along the sides of the feet.

In the past, my left knee would hurt after about 100 miles of hill walking. Anticipating this I brought a knee brace. However, two months earlier Dr. Hershman had operated to correct cartilage damage in that knee from a recent skiing injury. He evidently corrected prior damage as well since my left knee gave me no problems throughout the walk.

The Route and Some Observations

Holland

We began our walk April 22, 1995 on a cold cloudy day on the North Sea coast of Holland after flying into Amsterdam from London. We found the first trail markers, or balisage, red and white bars painted on trees and posts and set off with great enthusiasm. Netherlands and Belgium are not big walking regions and often the markers were confusing or nonexistent. Good maps and a compass proved invaluable.

The walk through Netherlands was largely on hard concrete and extremely flat. Bike paths led to dikes and sidewalks. Sometimes we would hear someone yell a warning to us from the rear and as we turned we saw fifteen to twenty cyclists in a tight group quickly approaching. It was a cycle club out for a fast-paced run. All the members had colorful matching outfits. A quick sidestep off the path was important to prevent the lead cyclist from having to swerve and produce a possibly disastrous pile-up.

An interesting stop for us was at Haringsvliet to see the Delta Expo project. A guide explained the system of dams and sluice gates that was built some years ago to keep sea water out of Holland. The gates open at low tide and allow accumulated river water to exit. The gates then close to keep high tides out. A number of these massive dams were built at key points along the Dutch coast and all work in coordination. They were built to last 100 years, after which this aging structure and a rising ocean will require a new design.

As we headed east towards the Belgium border the land became rural. At one point there were no accommodations for twenty-seven miles and we simply had to walk the distance. We arrived in

Kalmthout, Belgium with very sore feet, and a bath and bed never felt better.

Belgium

Belgium, too, was flat until we reached Liège. In the north they speak Flemish, which is similar to Dutch, and in the South the language of choice switches abruptly to French. We took some shortcuts by walking along the Albert Canal instead of the rather ordinary forests the GR5 winds through. The Canal runs for hundreds of miles from Liège to Antwerp. Narrow barges pass through locks carrying produce to the ports. They appeared to be family-run barges with a small home perched on the rear, with laundry flapping on clotheslines strung across the deck.

Maastricht was an interesting stop. It was a very brief re-entry into Holland and, a few miles into our walk south the next day, brought us back into Belgium and the French-speaking Flanders. Maastricht has a picturesque center with very old houses and cobbled streets. Shops have been attractively installed in these old buildings in a way that only big money can do. Our fancy overpriced hotel had a breakfast room in the basement which was also a Roman museum.

In the forests we saw a great deal of logging activity. Trees were felled and left lying across our footpath. These were annoying man-made obstacles we had to climb over and we wondered how long the forests of Europe would survive this aggressive harvesting of timber. Before arriving in Liège we called Phillippe. I met him via the Internet where I had posted a message asking for advice. Phillippe had replied with useful information and generously offered to put us up in his home. We accepted and, as we approached the university laboratory where he worked, he came out and warmly greeted us. After a brisk five-mile walk with Phillippe we arrived at his home, met his family and had a delightful one-night visit. The next day Phillippe walked with us until we linked up again with the GR5 markers. Soon after saying goodbye though, we got lost in a maze of confusing markers. Finally, we reached the Ourthe River but at Tilff, the wrong town. It was getting late and we should have pressed on, but just to gather up our thoughts we sat down by a river restaurant in Tilff and by good fortune had our best meal of the entire walk. What a treat. Eventually we arrived at Banneaux, one of the miracle towns, something like a mini Lourdes. It was touching to see believers arriving by the busload to get the cure and fill up bottles with holy water at the shrine.

Further on we reached Vielsalm, a small town with only one hotel. A rather stern-looking landlady greeted us and ordered us to remove our boots (which we do anyway) and brought us to her worst room, on the noisy top floor. It of course came with the mandatory sagging bed. She then asked suspiciously if we were married. Then she said that the police would come and lock us up if we were not married. How were Patricia and I to prove to her that we were married, and for 31 years to boot? Having separate British and American passports did not help. She carefully scrutinized each page and stamp. Patricia asked her if there was a problem with foreign spies in Vielsalm. I asked her if she had a room with better beds since my back was bothering me. "No," she said, "You can sleep on the floor." She then asserted that we two only slept in tents and were not accustomed to fine hotels like hers. I was beginning to actually feel guilty. She asked if we wanted coffee or tea for breakfast. I said coffee and Patricia said tea. "No," she said, "I can make coffee or tea, not both." "OK," we said, "We'll both have coffee." Having no choice we suffered these humiliations in silence. Actually in the morning she was quite nice asking about us and showing some curiosity about our walk. I am glad we did not leave the invective-filled note which I was planning to write, on the bed.

We passed through the Ardennes Forest and near Bastogne. With the fiftieth anniversary of VE Day we saw many American flags flying in the towns we walked through. The most moving was a lonely farm with two flags flying near the farmhouse, one Belgian and the other American. An elderly farmer worked the fields nearby. What memories he must have had of those terrible war years, and an enduring gratitude to the American and British liberators! In Luxembourg we walked to an American cemetery where General George Patton is buried with 5,000 of the men who fought with him. (One woman, an army nurse, was also buried there, along with 118 Jewish soldiers.) Reminders of World Wars I and II were everpresent in our walk across Europe, with many memorials placed by American towns or veterans' associations.

Luxembourg

They say Luxembourg is small, but if you walk the length it seems pretty big. We entered at the northern rural end and exited from the commercial southern end. Most of the walk was along the eastern edge bounded by three rivers, the Ourthe, Sauer, and Moselle. Although river walks are often flat, this one rose high up on the steep hilly slopes and we had a few long and tiring days. One stop was especially interesting. It was a small bar/hotel in a small town run by a Dutch expatriate and his friend, also from Holland. They were both intelligent, amusing guys who were quite happy to share their life stories with two walkers. Our breakfast came with piano music played by one of them.

In Vianden, we met Ed and Helen, a retired couple who planned to walk a part of the GR5 before renting a barge and navigating the French canals with friends. We had a fine dinner together discussing walking and more restful alternatives.

It occurred to me that what people do in their leisure time is a statement about what they value. Most work out of necessity, but leisure activities are *chosen*. How do we spend that most precious of assets, our leisure time? During this journey we met many who shared their choices with us.

On reaching the Moselle we began to see vineyards. Soon the slopes on both sides of the river were covered by vineyards. We decided to visit Luxembourg Ville though it meant a few days of road walking off the GR5. "Lux City" turned out to be an unexpected three-day stopover. First, let me say that the town is dramatic. It is situated on a fortified hill, since it was once a great fortress. Homes are built at different levels, some at the base of the great walls and others on top.

My lower back had been bothering me throughout the walk, but I was managing—until our first rest day in Lux City when I sneezed while strolling. I felt a sharp pain which remained, making walking and sitting painful. In the morning I got out of bed with difficulty. We considered giving up the walk. Finally, I decided to rest one more day and see how I felt. The next morning I was a bit better. So we decided to resume walking the following day at a reduced pace. The next morning we set out tentatively in the rain and after a short ten miles I felt no worse. With each subsequent day I improved, and eventually walked out the back problem.

France

South of Lux City we reached the French border. Patricia's French skills were coming back and she was eager to continue practicing. The fact that the French prefer to speak only French we viewed positively, as a discipline that would help her, and even me, gain more use of the language. Our first *post restante* mail drop, Escherange, had one problem. Escherange has a postal code but no post office. We pressed on across rolling hills towards the Vosges, our first mountainous region.

The weather was turning cloudy and rainy. It was a nuisance putting on and removing rain gear, sometimes four to five times per day. And you were never kept dry during a lengthy rain. The perspiration built up under the warmth of the anorak and rain pants. In fact, I preferred just walking in nylon shorts and just letting my legs get wet.

After miles of rolling farmland, we entered a forest. On exiting a few miles further, the Vosges suddenly appeared, wonderful mountains rising 4–5,000 feet. The best of these were the Grand Ballon and Ballon d'Alsace. At the summit of the Grand Ballon, the highest mountain in the Vosges, an American woman recognized me from an AMC (Appalachian Mountain Club) walk I was on five years ago. Since then, Gene had moved to Switzerland and begun a new life working for an ad agency in Basel. She was with a Swiss walking club and she joined us for lunch with her Swiss boyfriend. There was a nice restaurant about ten minutes off the summit. So here was a single woman, about our age, who just picked up her life and started over, learning German and making completely new friends.

The Vosges region is in Alsace which traded hands between Germany and France a number of times. People are bilingual and the food is heavier than the normal French cooking. One local specialty Patricia and I will remember with revulsion. There was no choice. The hotel had one set menu. The main course, a casserole, consisted of cut-up potatoes, a foul-smelling melted cheese all cooked in bacon fat. Fellow diners were shoveling this stuff down with gallons of beer. I asked Patricia if she noticed any men over fifty-five eating this food. To me it was an invitation to a heart attack. Plus it tasted awful. We had a few bites and then made do with the salad.

Ballon d'Alsace was described in our guidebook as difficult. However, the difficult bit was just a short scramble and very familiar to anyone walking up an Adirondack or White Mountain peak. This was our last big Vosges summit. From here we descended towards Belfort where we took a rest day. I bought new boots. We sat through a four-hour dinner at a restaurant celebrating its fiftieth anniversary, something I hope never to do again. Patricia heretically ordered "a la carte" instead of the highly touted Anniversary Menu. This brought out the chef and owner in a futile attempt to get her to change her mind. But there was no way that Patricia was going to eat those cute little veals. The next day we had a wonderful meal at a lower rated Michelin restaurant. I had the best grilled salmon ever and the service was prompt.

We were now walking through flat and commercial areas between the Vosge and Jura mountains. But in two days the Jura mountains appeared and we were ascending to 4,000 feet again. The Jura terrain is characterized by high plateaus with steep, deep valleys and river gorges. We started to see more local walkers and the balisage markers improved.

Most of the long distance walkers we met were Dutch. We encountered a single Dutch woman from Holland on her way to the Pilgrims Walk in SW France and Spain. We kept meeting two Dutchmen over a period of a few days and had some pleasant conversations and meals together.

The Dogs of France

Along our route we passed many homes with notices posted such as CHIEN MÉCHANT (guard dog) or the more ominous JE MONTE LA GARDE. Next to this warning was a picture of a fierce-looking German shepherd. Sure enough, as we passed a dog would appear. Often it was a French poodle doing his best to justify all the free room and board he was receiving. Barking at one end, tailing wagging at the other, these "vicious" dogs put on a great show but fooled no one.

What Did We Talk About

About 70 percent of the time we talked about nothing. On narrow paths, Patricia walked behind me so as not to race ahead, which I would find demoralizing. Up steep hills we were puffing too much, eliminating all desire to talk. When we did talk it was often about route finding. The conversation could become quite animated if we were lost. We generally blamed each other. The regions and people we encountered were another subject for discussion. There were frequent small surprises on the walk worthy of comment. Patricia would frequently stop to take photos of tiny flowers. I would strongly advise during these periods to stop wasting film. Considering that we were together twenty-four hours a day and sometimes tired, we were quite harmonious during the walk.

Why Walk

With all the work, the sweat and pain, why walk? There are many reasons. There is the pleasure of the outdoors, the forests, the rivers, the vistas, all that nature offers. There is the adventure of discovery, new towns, new people, the unexpected— all unfolding at a walker's pace. There is the exercise that builds strength, stamina and appetite, the pleasure of sitting down for a meal with the hunger of youth—of reversing, for a while at least, the diminished vigor of age and, at the end, there is the achievement, both physical and mental, but especially mental. For the walk is first conceived and completed in the mind, and its realization is a triumph of will over the body's desire for rest.

Surely it is more than a coincidence that Jesus, Muhammad, Moses and Buddha all took the long solitary journey into the wilderness to find religious inspiration and transformation. Before he began to teach, Jesus went into spiritual retreat at the age of thirty, after his cousin John baptized him. Muhammad had his vision in the Cave of Mt. Hira in 610 A.D. Moses climbed Mt. Sinai to return with the ten commandments in the 13th century B.C. Before beginning his teachings, Buddha wandered and meditated for six years in the Himalayan foothills. And in secular history, many poets, philosophers and thinkers returned from long walks with new perspectives.

Perhaps an agnostic such as myself will one day find some small measure of faith or inspiration in the course of our wanderings.

An Abrupt End

On June 11, 1995, we made a routine phone call to my in-laws, the Staffs, to see if anyone was trying to reach us. We then learned that my father had suffered a serious stroke and was fighting for his life in Overlook Hospital near his New Jersey home. We were all geared up for the next day's walk into the exciting Daub River gorge and the heart of the Jura mountains. In a matter of moments this focus was drained away and we did what had to be done. The race home began the next morning. A Swiss postal bus took us to a mountain railroad, which carried us to a larger train and then to Geneva. From there we got a flight to London and a connecting flight home to New York. The following morning we rented a car and drove to New Jersey and joined my distraught mother and sister.

My father, though eighty-three, was a vigorous, active member of the Westfield community. Now, with the help of his family, friends and the medical profession, he began a valiant effort to survive and overcome this paralyzing illness.

We had walked about 700 miles and about 600 miles remained. The mountains will wait for us. I vowed that one day Patricia and I would complete the journey. The credit for that achievement will, in no small part, go to my father, who taught me what the optimistic spirit can accomplish.

Sailing to Havana, February 1996

I resolved to resume our travels in 1996 after putting all this on hold during my father's illness. We would stay in close touch with my mother by phone so that, should an emergency arise, we could rush home. So with some guilt and uncertainty, I planned a sailing boat trip with my friend Dave Brown. We would leave his home port in Sarasota and sail to Marina Hemingway near Havana, Cuba. Patricia meanwhile would join Rachel in Switzerland for a skiing holiday and later visit her father, sisters Wendy and Sheilah, and brother Peter and their families. Patricia felt I needed a separate adventure to fulfill some inner desire I occasionally developed. I cannot express how much I admired her understanding and confidence to agree and even urge me to set off on these solitary journeys.

Dave Brown at fifty-two was an easy-going and eccentric fellow. With a gray beard, lined reddish face and a pleasant smile he proved a perfect companion for this arduous and at times terrifying trip. Back in December, Dave had telephoned me after a six-year gap and invited me to go with him on his boat to Havana. The timing was perfect. Two months later we busily raced around a Sarasota supermarket buying food and supplies in preparation for our departure. Dave has lived on his boat for the past seventeen years and has thirty years of sailing experience under his belt. For this I would soon be grateful. We set off south for Naples on a windy day. Soon the seas rose up with angry eight-foot waves and twenty-knot winds. The boat tossed about wildly. I got seasick with dry retching and was soon flat out on the bunk below. Even Dave threw up over the side. We . . . well, Dave mostly, sailed through the night and the following morning he managed to maneuver his craft past rocky obstacles and crashing waves into the quiet inlet of Naples harbor. His engine had died and so we needed towing. I decided to drive to Key West, rendezvous with Dave after the engine repair, and so minimize my time at sea, which I felt was not really my favorite pastime.

This worked out fine. We met in Key West and had a quiet crossing to Havana, motoring most of the way. The U.S. government had a policy at the time permitting travel to Cuba but not permitting trade. In other words we could go but not spend a cent while there. In spite of this we found quite a few American, and many European, tourists in

Havana. On arrival at Marina Hemingway, I told Dave I really preferred staying at a hotel in town rather than the cramped quarters of his small boat. Dave took no offense and we easily linked up each day to tour about.

Our first impression was that Cuba was in desperate need of plaster and paint after thirty years of neglect. Of the many Cubans we met, none were happy about the system or the American trade blockade. We met a taxi driver who was a surgeon during the day but found that $20 a month was not enough to live on. We met a belly dancer who made more in one evening than the $6 a month she could make as a nurse. A bus tour took us to Viñales, a mountainous area where tobacco is grown and made into cigars. After a fruitless search for a car rental we hired a taxi driver who took us to Veradero beach, a long uneventful ride past oil rigs and flat featureless terrain. The beach area was lined with luxury hotels filled with the European tourists who take pleasure in vegetative winter grilling under a Caribbean sun.

Back in Havana we strolled the Malecon, the oceanfront promenade, crowded with Cubans enjoying their unemployment. Large numbers of young women made themselves available on the Malecon and near the hotels for visiting tourists seeking female companionship. Prostitution had reached mythic proportions and compared favorably with Thailand as a good destination for a sex holiday.

After a phone call home to my mother, I grew concerned over my father's declining health and asked Dave if we could sail home a week early. Other sailors in the marina expressed concern as a weather front was approaching with gale force winds. Dave said "fear not" and so on a sunny calm day we sailed north into the Gulf of Mexico. Within a few hours the sky clouded over and the wind picked up. By night the storm hit with thirty-five-knot winds and nine-foot waves. Bonine seasick pills helped by keeping me drowsy and strange rather than miserable. Dave just threw up all over again. In spite of this he reefed the main and frequently adjusted the jib and autopilot as our boat tossed and bumped its way towards Florida. By the wee hours he parked the boat into the wind off the shallow reefs that surround Key West and waited till light to look for the critical markers that would guide us into port. Using his Global Positioning Satellite equipment, Dave was able to steer to within 100 feet of any point on the planet. But there is no substitute for a clear sighting of a buoy marker when surrounded by coral that could easily tear open the hull of our boat. Within three hours after sighting the first marker we sailed into the Key West marina. Soon I felt the reassuring wooden dock beneath my feet. A taxi ride to the airport and some quick bookings got me home in one day.

There are many experiences in life worth doing once and not worth repeating. For myself I would put ocean sailing in that category. I found the six-knot speed painfully slow, the cramped and humid sleeping arrangements uncomfortable and the seasickness unpleasant in the extreme. However, I learned something about navigation, the power of the ocean, the weather, and the endurance and attention to detail that is required to negotiate our watery world.

A Long Walk across Europe–Part II: June 11–July 20, 1996

Between February and June I traveled twice a week to Westfield to visit my parents. With each visit my dad appeared weaker, yet there was no telling how much time he had left. I felt eager to complete the walk across Europe and yet guilty about leaving my parents at this difficult time. Finally, with mixed emotions, I spoke with my dad, who by now was difficult to communicate with. I told him how much he meant to me, all the close and personal emotions which I held in my heart but could never articulate when he was well. I told him about the walk I was resuming and that when I dipped my feet in the Mediterranean I would dedicate the success to him. In a weak hoarse voice he whispered, "Thank you, thank you." Tears filled my eyes. It was the last time I really communicated with him.

We resumed our walk from the same hotel on the Swiss border, exactly one year after stopping, June 11. Patricia and I walked through the Daub River gorge along the Swiss frontier until finally entering Switzerland and descending to Lake Geneva. We took a ferry across to St. Gingolph on the southern side. There, our friend Andrew Opie joined us and we ascended into the Alps. Each day we would climb 3–5,000 feet, cross a pass and then drop into a village in a valley to spend the night. I estimated we must have climbed over 100,000 feet during our Alps crossing, or the equivalent of going up and down the Empire State building eighty times.

Andrew stayed with us for about ten days and was a most enjoyable companion. Every few days I telephoned Westfield to speak with my mother. My Dad's condition was deteriorating. After Andrew left us, we approached the highest point on the walk, the Col du Chavière at 9,100 feet. On July 7, the day we were to go over the pass, a blinding snowstorm hit. Halfway up from the mountain refuge we had to turn back. Our group of walkers was frozen and disoriented. The blizzard conditions were so bad one could not see from one cairn to the next and we soon were off the footpath, stumbling through boulder fields and icy streams. Using compass and altimeter we made it back to the refuge. The next day the snow stopped; the weather cleared and, in the company of a very pleasant Dutch couple, we made it over the pass. After Chavière, we entered the Mediterranean Alps, which meant less snow and a hot dry climate. Soon we were in torrid weather, with hundreds of flies buzzing around each of us. The temperature change in one week was tremendous.

By now my mother's reports were becoming ominous. My father had developed jaundice. Additionally, Patricia's father had a mild stroke. We were now only eighty miles from Nice, but once again we had to fly home. Patricia went to Bournemouth and I rushed back to New York. It was July 20th.

Part IV

Half Time Review

11
Eulogy

He who learns must suffer. And even in our sleep, pain that cannot forget, falls drop by drop upon the heart, and in our own despair, against our will, comes wisdom to us by the awful grace of God.
　　　　　—Aeschylus, from *Agamemnon*, 5th century BC

For fourteen months my father suffered the effects of a massive stroke. Mother bravely organized his twenty-four-hour home nursing and witnessed daily his steady decline. With the help of Martha, a wonderful live-in nurse from Slovakia, my father received the best of home care. After the first stroke my dad suffered a series of mini-strokes and each one left him less aware mentally and more physically dependent. His left side was totally paralyzed and the slightest attempt to move him brought excruciating pain. Martha learned how to minimize his discomfort, but his agony was obvious and difficult to watch. For months the family stood helpless as this great and generous man declined. The strokes gradually robbed him of all his physical strength and personality. Then, on the morning of July twenty-fifth, jaundiced and gasping for air, he died in Martha's arms as I was en route from Manhattan to visit him. My sister and mother greeted me in tears and sorrow with the sad news. At the funeral I tried to express my profound grief with a eulogy.

Eulogy for Samuel Freeman

Read on July 29, 1996 by his son

We live our lives as if in a dream. Then a nightmare shocks us into reality. A moment of reality. The illusion of an eternal friendship—a father's love, a brilliant vitality that was always there—is suddenly there no more. Surely what had no beginning for me cannot be ended. My dad was there as partner in my hobbies, partner in my school work, partner in my business, partner in all my endeavors. He called me Jim because he liked that better than my given name. It only sounded right coming from him. No else could call me Jim. We were so tuned to each other's thoughts I could finish his sentences and he mine. Often I knew his thoughts before the words were out.

My father was fascinated by people and ideas. Their concerns became opportunities to help. His love of life was boundless, his enthusiasm childlike. He had no time for pettiness and small-minded thoughts. There were so many productive projects to begin and complete.

His bright spirit was contagious and people were quickly drawn to it.

Incredibly, that is now gone. The long farewell has ended. Into the cold earth go his mortal remains and with his burial goes a part of me. Gone forever is Jim, gone is the mind whose thoughts tracked mine. With his passing I feel just a bit closer to my own death.

My father leaves behind a wonderful legacy of memories. His creations in wood, furniture widely distributed to many family members, were expressions of love. These will be treasured. His positive and rational philosophy lives on in his descendants and all those he influenced. I am reminded of him wherever I turn—his workshop in Kent, a construction site in New York, a photograph, a quiet moment alone. A wonderful thing, memories: they are so portable, so lightweight. They can be taken anywhere and brought forward at will. I desperately wish my father was with me now. But, sadly, I must settle for my memories of him. These will be treasured.

It also gives me pleasure to know that the next generation, his grandchildren, realize what an extraordinary grandfather they had. How easily he moved into their young world and shared their interests! They will carry his memories well into the next century and I hope they will one day tell their children that once upon a time there lived a wonderful man who happened to have been their very own great-grandfather . . . and his name was Samuel Freeman.

NICHOLAS NAQUAN HEYWARD, JR.

4TH ANNUAL DAY OF REMEMBRANCE

CELEBRATION OF LIFE

PROGRAM–1998

SCHEDULE OF EVENTS

WELCOMING ....THE NICHOLAS HEYWARD JR. FAMILY

PRAYER..........(AUNT) BLANCHE MANCE

CANDLE LIGHTING......(BROTHER) QUINTAN HEYWARD

BALLOON CEREMONY....HEYWARD FAMILY AND FRIENDS

GOSPEL SELECTION......HOUSE OF GOD YOUTH CHOIR

COMMUNITY MESSAGE...FORMER MAYOR DAVID DINKINS

BASKETBALL GAME # 1... SILVER BULLETS vs NAQUAN'S ALLSTARS

HALFTIME EVENTS..SCHOLARSHIP PRESENTATION

POETRY READING...NORMAN BLACKSHEAR

BETWEEN GAME EVENTS

MURAL COLLABORATION....AMY AND FREINDS

DANCE SELECTION...DANGEROUS ERUPTION

BASKETBALL # 2..SILVER BULLETTES vs NAQUAN'S ALLSTARS

HALFTIME EVENTS

GOWANUS DRILL TEAM..." THE WILDCATS"

GOSPEL SELECTION...PROFESSOR BUTCH HEYWARD
AND THE GOSPEL EXPEDITION

BETWEEN GAME EVENTS

RAP ARTIST...13YR OLD DERRICK MERRI

GOSPEL SELECTION.. REV.HERNANDEZ VICTORY OUTREACH CH

STREET SIGN MESSAGE..ARTIST JENNY POAK

BASKETBALL GAME #3..SURPRISE TEAM vs NAQUAN'S ALLST

HALFTIME EVENT...RAPPER DAVID VEG

SINGER.... INDIO THE MYSTIQUE

EVENTS THROUGHOUT THE DAY

HANDBALL & PADDLEBALL

ARTS AND CRAFTS OF ALL KIND

FACE PAINTING AND FINGERPAINTING

BALLOON CREATIONS

FOLLOWING CONTESTS
3 POINT SHOOTING
SPOT UP SHOOTING
HALF COURT SHOT
FREE THROW
BACKBOARD SHOOTING
SLAM DUNK
30 SECOND SHOOTOUT
3 ON 3 BASKETBALL CHALLENGE
VS
POWER RANGERS AND NINJA
TURTLE

GIGGLES THE CLOWN PHOTO SHOOT
MUSIC PROVIDED BY DJ SKILLS

REFRESHMENTS WILL BE SERVED

IN MEMORY OF NAQUAN

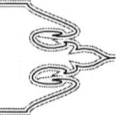

AS WE COME TOGETHER ON THIS SPECIAL DAY TO REMEMBER NAQUAN AND OTHER CHILDREN THAT WERE TAKEN AWAY. IT WASN'T THEIR TIME TO DIE, THEY WERE VERY YOUNG WHEN THEY SAID GOODBYE . NYPD, TA, AND HPD, HAVE CAUSED MANY FAMILIES TO CRY AND EVERY DAY THEY CONTINUE TO LIE ABOUT EXCESSIVE FORCE AND UNJUSTIFIED HOMICIDE.
GROWING UP IN NEW YORK IS ROUGH, GETTING THE PROPER EDUCATION IS TOUGH AND THE NYC POLICE OFFICERS ARE NOT SENSITIVE ENOUGH.
HOW DO PEOPLE OF THE WORLD BEGIN TO VISUALIZE AND UNDERSTAND THIS STUFF?
PRISONS ARE BEING BUILT, THE BLACK AND LATINO CHILDREN ARE BEING KILLED, MOTHERS AND FATHERS ARE CONSTANTLY CHANGING THEIR WILLS. I FAST AND PRAY THAT POLICE OFFICER KILLINGS, WILL COME TO A STANDSTILL, I AM TIRED OF SEEING YOUNG DREAMS BEING KILLED
AND NOT FULFILLED. THE PROFOUND MEMORIES WILL LIVE FOREVER AND ALWAYS SEEN THROUGH FAMILY, FRIENDS AND LOVED ONES IF YOU KNOW AND UNDERSTAND WHAT I MEAN.
SO CONTINUE TO KEEP THE FAITH BECAUSE IN GODS UNIVERSE THE DEVIL DOESN'T HAVE A PLACE. ITS GOING TO TAKE THE HARMONY AND UNITY OF EVERYONE TO KEEP OUR MOST PRECIOUS JEWEL SAFE........

IN PEACE FOR THE DECEASED
NORMAN BLACKSHEAR
POET

THE NICHOLAS NAQUAN HEYWARD JR. FOUNDATION WISHES TO THANK THE FOLLOWING:
ALL THOSE SPECIAL PEOPLE WHO CONTRIBUTED THEIR TIME AND EFFORTS TO MAKE THIS EVENT A SUCCESS. WE ALSO WOULD LIKE TO THANK ALL THE PARTICIPANTS WHO DISPLAYED ENORMOUS TALENTS
AS WELL AS THE WILLINGNESS TO MAKE THIS DAY A MEMORABLE ONE.
LASTLY, WE WOULD LIKE TO THANK YOU, THE COMMUNITY, FOR BEING THERE FOR US IN OUR TIME OF NEED.

LASTING LOVE TO YOU ALL,
THE FOUNDATION

My dad.

12
Endings and Beginnings

Life can only be understood backwards but it must be lived forwards.
—Søren Kierkegaard, *Life*, 19th Century

Endings

I complete this book at the age of fifty-nine. It is hard to believe I am well past middle age and at the threshold of old age. I still look out at the world with youthful eyes full of wonder and awe. I still say and do foolish things, learn things that amaze me. I love life as much as in my youth and if I had the choice I would want to live forever. I am not religious and I fear death which I believe is the end, a total black void, a dreamless sleep. I suppose my scientific education has led me to this conclusion. At times when I ponder the limitless universe, time without beginning or end, my agnostic soul hopes that perhaps there is a God. However, even if a God created this universe, I do not believe He personally watches over mankind or me. Science has for centuries studied the origin of the universe. One by one the miracles and creation fantasies of the literal Bible have been revealed as metaphors at best. So now we have a theory that explains the universe to within a moment after the "Big Bang." But are we really any closer to answering the ultimate questions? What came before the Big Bang? What lies beyond the limits of the exploding universe? The logic put forth by Thomas Aquinas in the 13th century still has validity. I doubt that mankind will ever find the answers.

Beginnings

They say that today is the beginning of the rest of your life. Or, more tersely, "the past is prologue." I like the philosophy implied in these statements. They express the importance of the present and the possibilities that lie in the future. My uncle, Big Sam, once told me an old Russian saying: "beginnings are always difficult." Perhaps that is why we so often turn our lives into routines, becoming "prisoners of our past." As we age it seems more difficult to break away from the well-worn path and blaze new trails across uncharted land. But with this awareness comes the answer. The task is to resist the routine, to seek out or, if necessary, create the challenge. I enjoy the easy patterns of my retired life, lunch at an Italian bistro or a sushi bar, playing with my computer, taking in a film and dinner with Patricia. But it is the adventure that is the passion. While fate can create adventure, so can design.

Just as life is a series of endings, we are also granted many beginnings. Patricia and I have exciting plans for the future. We have gotten to this point in our lives after some personal struggle, some disappointments and setbacks. But we consider ourselves fortunate. We face the future with anticipation and optimism. There are worlds to be explored, lands we have never visited, knowledge yet to acquire. We are secure financially and could surround ourselves with many more material possessions if we wished. But these we find far less rewarding than experiences.

I face my sixties with a sense of urgency. The physically-taxing adventures, the treks and long walks must be undertaken now before the aches and pains of age make such endeavors impossible. Later there will be time for the ocean voyage and quiet contemplative days. We must make plans to finish the walk across Europe. It will be the beginning of a new adventure. The effort and its completion will be dedicated to my father.

We celebrated the beginning of the year on January 1st but for me the real start to the year is the springtime. January 1st is an arbitrary date. The springtime is nature's beginning, a time of birth and renewal. The Adirondack mountain snows melt, the streams run faster and green colors appear in the low valleys. Those summits continue to call out their challenge across almost fifty years with the same clarity as in my youth.

My father, near the end of his life, lying in a hospital bed after a second stroke, said to Elisa, "Now it is your time to suck life dry," to get all that you can out of life. To the end he still pointed the way for his children. I carry that message with me into the future and pass it on to our daughter Rachel and the next generation.

Postscript-Spring, 1997

On May 14, 1997, Patricia and I began the final five days of our 1,300 mile walk across Europe, and on May 19 we dipped our feet into the Mediterranean Sea. Those last few days included some thirteen harrowing hours up in deep snow and rugged terrain before the descent to Nice. As the waters lapped onto the beach I read some words of remembrance about my father. I knew he would have been pleased.

Postscript
A Young Traveler Writes Home

Excerpts of Letters to my Parents, 1959, First Trip to Europe

June 23, 1959 Copenhagen

"Here I am, safe and sound in Denmark feeling very helpless and very foreign. But this is my first day here so it is understandable. This trip across the Atlantic had the usual excitements associated with flying; air pockets, bumps and delayed refueling at an unscheduled stop. The group was very friendly and I spoke with many of the students. I played five chess games and won them all, due more to their poor playing than my skill. This flight was long (16 hours) and sleeping was impossible. In Amsterdam, somewhat dazed from my half sleep state, I saw my first scene of Europe. Cyclists by the dozens riding the beautiful paths and roadways intersected and diverged, whizzing by in all directions. There were women with straight blond hair and blowing full skirts, cycling, some with one or two children in special carriers. There were young children and old men, laborers and dignified suit-clad businessmen. The more extravagant bought motor bikes, motor scooters and motor cycles. Though riding in a bus, from the airport to Amsterdam, these cyclists would assert themselves as if they were equal in tonnage. The City of Amsterdam though a busy industrial center, still has preserved the charm and picturesqueness of generations past. The typical Dutch architecture, the canals and the people present a most alluring introduction to Europe. I strolled around the area for about five hours waiting for the 8:04 to leave for Copenhagen. At last I boarded but I decided not to ride with the group taking the train. I explained to them that I wanted to sit in a compartment with Europeans so that perhaps I might know them better. I was glad I did for though the compartment I picked soon lost all its Europeans to early stops, one passenger remained. Malcolm was sort of an American expatriate by choice. A professional writer and loafer, he has been traveling through Europe for four years settling where he wishes as long as he wishes. It's all done on $10,000 he saved and some income from writing. Articulate, intelligent and interesting describe this man in his middle thirties. From 8 P.M. we talked till 12:30 A.M. about Europe, Europeans, their politics, customs, literature and art. Then we pulled out the seats to make beds. These are not sleepers but if you can sleep on a train you can sleep on this. Every time we stopped inspectors would come in and check our passports. Germany with its industrial machine once more rolling is an impressive pillar of progress to which the Germans look with pride. The German conductor spoke English well and nearing the ferry to Denmark, he told of Germany's rebirth and its desire for unity. He inferred that the Germans are superior to other Europeans because of this tremendous growth. 'The Danes are poor' he said, 'all they export is food.... We have two ferries in this line. The Danes have one.' The night was short and I slept very little if at all. The sun set as we sped through German steel districts, at about 10 P.M. and rose at 3:50 A.M. I know this last time because I waited for it as the sky grew bright over Chlesweg- Holstein. The ferry ride took 3 hours. Malcolm and I met two young women teachers and they continued with us to Copenhagen after we docked. We had a most interesting chat about segregation and later, women's right to the vote. Malcolm and I took the negative in a spirit of good humor. The ferry served breakfast. It was expensive ($1.10). At Copenhagen we said our good-byes. I took a taxi to Mrs. Christianson. She is a fine jolly elderly woman with a ready laugh. She speaks little English and we have set about teaching each other. I start work Tuesday, five and half days each week but less than 40 hours per week."

June 27, 1959 Copenhagen

"I received your letter Daddy. I am managing fine. I am digesting the food with little difficulty. It is a great deal like American food. A cow is a cow, milk is milk and fish are fish wherever you go. I had a small illness yesterday (101.6) but it's almost over today thanks to Terramycin which brought the temperature down to 99. I stayed home today and my wonderful landlady is taking care of me. She is only supposed to give me a room yet she often leaves milk for me when I come home. Whatever I mention she tries like hell to fulfill. I mentioned that it would be good to have a radio. I thought she had one. She didn't but somehow she got one. The next day there was a mirror and flowers in my room. I asked how I could get my wash done. She offered to do it, saying it was too expensive. I refused indicating she was doing too much. So she helped me with it and taught me how. Now she is making eggs, bread and butter and tea for me. She is the most cheerful, happiest woman I have ever seen. Daddy asked if I could write every day. This is a great deal to ask for. My days are so full. Letters are time consuming, expensive and don't really do justice to the experiences. It is better for us all to wait till I come home and with the aid of my pictures and a running dialogue you shall learn of my summer. Socially; I have dated a Swedish girl and got the address of an intelligent, attractive New York girl whom I met in Tivoli. She is traveling alone through Europe, the Mediterranean to Israel and Turkey. Needless to say she has spirit. This is her first time alone. She speaks French. She must be about 20 or 21. So it can be done, Elisa! I have noticed in a train timetable that there is a connection to Berlin. The wheels are turning in my head. My job is teaching me much. They use American equipment and especially a most important one, the Tectronix oscilloscope. It would be very valuable if I could learn how to use it. The workers are very friendly. My supervisor gives me the run of the lab. . . . "

July 2, 1959 Copenhagen

" . . . We just came back from a little office party given in the conference room. It was for a secretary who had been with the company 40 years. Wine was served and we downed it with a hearty 'yo yo yo.' Then our boss made a speech to us all about her service. He quoted King Christian X, saying 'What is a home without a woman' and adding 'what is a laboratory without Mrs.—'

"It was very personable and a touching thing to see such emotion in so large a company as the Danish Post and Telegraph. Last night I saw 'Twelfth Night' at Tivoli produced by no less than the Oxford Players. There I met a Dane and together we went into a beer hall in Tivoli. Smoked-filled, crowded to the gills, song after song, with steins held high and swaying along the tables it was the friendliest joint I have yet seen on both sides of the Atlantic. . . . We left just in time to see the dazzling Wednesday night fireworks show on Tivoli Lake. Last Saturday was a fine evening too. On that night Tivoli is packed with people. The guards are out. The bands and shows are everywhere. I saw a good concert of pop classical music for free. I was with some of my friends that evening; Abbu Khan, Khanna, Ellen and an Austrian. . . . We walked, talked and sang away the evening in Tivoli.

"Student transportation and accommodations all through Europe can be 50 percent of normal prices. A plane flight to Berlin costs $9.50. I have an itinerary which I worked out. It will take me to what I believe to be the most concentrated areas of European culture. If it works I shall see, in order:

"Berlin, Munich, Salzburg, Venice, Milan, Bern, Geneva, Lyon, Paris, London, Rotterdam, Amsterdam and New York. When I can, I will use student flights and trains, otherwise second-class non-student trains and buses. . . . I will have to leave Copenhagen on July 25 . . . which is a week earlier than anticipated because the student flight to Berlin is on that date. Oh, yes, I am healthy and all right Ma and thank you for asking. Please *read* this letter to Elisa. It seems she is most interested in finding English mistakes and less in what I have to say. We must all correct this sad state she is in, don't you think? I met another student at the Foreign Students Center. He is an Englishman. This is the second one I have met and spoken to since I started coming down there. I find them both conservative in manner and speech yet very witty, articulate and well educated. Although their technical schools are more specialized and narrowed than our own still these students have attained a liberal education and attitude as high as the best American arts and science student. Their humor is not dry and stodgy as some would think but clever, sarcastic and subtle stemming from tone and novel play on words. While speaking to one of them I said 'I can live here on 100 Krone but this is for the bare essentials. Of course I couldn't buy clothes.' At this point the British student said that if I were speaking before an English audience I would have been drowned in peals of laughter for I had unwittingly cracked a good English pun.

"My landlady is a woman well into her sixties yet she cycles to town and back every day, a distance of 3 miles each way and coming home it is up a long gradual hill. For a Dane, this is more typical than unusual. Grundtvigs Church is around the corner from my room. I climbed the circular staircase to the high tower the other day. From there I got some good shots of Copenhagen. The church itself is a marvelous and beautiful structure standing strong and apart from the red-tiled-roofed apartment houses around it. Inside the lines are tall, straight and simple. But from the high unbroken columns of Grundtvigs Church springs a majesty and power surpassing the encrusted and gargoyled churches of the past. Each morning at 8 A.M. when I leave my room and walk the block to the trolley I pass the street leading to the church. It is a broad clean cobblestoned street and very quiet. Then the eight loud gongs reverberate. It starts another day for both the church and me, in Copenhagen. I could not ask for a more dramatic beginning to a day. Now it has begun to rain. It is long overdue in Copenhagen and Denmark in general. The rain will drench a soil parched for more than a month and many a Danish farmer depends on and is very aware of the rain. Even in the city I have heard this mentioned. In New York we forget the plight of our farmers hundreds of miles away. But in Denmark farming begins where Copenhagen ends.

"I have just eaten lunch. It cost me only 45 cents and this is more than usual. Breakfast costs me about 15 cents. A glass of milk comes to about 1.5 cents. I usually buy half a liter or quarter of a liter. I saw women smoking little cigars. It is really very feminine. There are many parks in Copenhagen and I remarked to a Danish friend that we in New York are trying to do what Copenhagen did centuries ago. He said that the kings of Denmark owned huge tracts of land which they would make into game preserves or parks. Even during its early development towards democracy the Danish kings still had the power to obtain state funds for establishing these beautiful parks. For this reason and the fact that the Danes seem to love greenery and flowers, nature penetrates deep and often into the center and business areas of the city making what would normally be drab and dismal concrete-ism an area spiced with light and happy scenes.

"Tonight I go to the Students Club for a dance and social gathering. It should be enjoyable. Since I arrived the attendance at the club restaurant has increased greatly. I believe in that week many foreign students arrived and I was probably leading the crest. But now in this truly international city I will have no shortage of friends from all directions and distances. In a large sense one can do a great deal of traveling right in Copenhagen merely by association. Well as I said to my English friend when we parted one evening, 'cheerio.' "

July 15, 1959 Copenhagen

" . . . My flight to Berlin is confirmed and I shall leave Copenhagen in 10 days. Already, with more than half my stay here now history, I begin to feel that future date when I must sever the contacts, the friends and the familiarity of Copenhagen. It will be both sad and exciting. I shall look forward to those remaining six weeks. Perhaps I have been too ambitious in my itinerary but since I have no reservations or commitments I can change plans as I chose. This is the advantage to traveling alone . . . versatility.

"Last Friday morning I left at 7:30 A.M. for Göteberg, Sweden. For six hours I road [sic] the green flat farm land of Denmark and Sweden.

This countryside is clean, pure and tidy from its climate to its quaint country roads. Yet Sweden is industrial as I saw in Göteberg. A large ship building harbor, and a population of 500,000 make this city second only to Stockholm. But unlike the horrid industrial, smoke and dirt of cities in parts of the United States, Göteberg has retained its small town charm. Half of the city area is composed of beautiful parks. The air is as clean and fresh as the farm land about. Fortunately this city is not on most tourist maps and so unlike Copenhagen this was sort of trail blazing. As soon as I arrived I went to their tourist center which was quite deserted. I got information about accommodations from here and later at the Student Center. In one hour after arriving I had a nice hostel and was on my way down to the harbor to take a canal boat ride. I was the only one in the boat who spoke English. All the others were Swedes. That evening I went to a soiree at a student club and met a wonderful Swedish girl of 19 who spoke excellent English. She could write and speak four languages. She was intelligent and yet not prudish which I find a rare combination in the States. After the party we walked to her home which must have been about one and a half miles away. She took me up a quiet park high above the city and suddenly we came to a clearing and there I saw a most beautiful and romantic sight. Göteberg was spread before us. Countless diamonds of white, green and red sparkled against the dark velvet carpet of the land. And on the horizon silhouetting the low hills and trees in the distance, was a reddish glow from the sun. Such was the sight at 2 A.M. in the morning in Göteberg. The following evening we went out again to Liseberg, a modern Tivoli with somewhat less of an atmosphere . . . first to a night spot and then to some dance. It started to rain and then it poured. We were caught with no cabs, no buses and no shelter so we ran uphill in that downpour to her house. She took off her heels and ran barefoot on the pavement. . . . On Sunday I said good-bye to her and some British friends I had made. I boarded an 11 P.M. train and rested a restless night on a second-class seat. Arriving in Copenhagen at 9 A.M. I went straight to work and from there I went straight to a Danish home to spend an evening on the 'Meet the Danes' program. It was an uneventful chat with a high school student whose parents were away. Then home for a shower and a much needed rest.

"Tuesday night we had our regular dance at the student club in Copenhagen. There I met Kirsten, the girl I had dinner with weeks back. We meet often at these dances. She speaks English very well, is intelligent with a warm personality. It would be perfect . . . if she were just a little prettier. But now we are great friends and at ease with each other. At this party the boys and girls were just doing nothing while the music played. So I took Kirsten on the floor and danced on, right in the middle, alone, with the whole group just staring. She turned all red and said laughing this 'is the first and last time.' But soon someone else got up and started to dance and in a few minutes the whole place was dancing and she felt much better.

"You know, Europe is so enjoyable I believe I should like to work here. The best deal is to work for an American engineering firm and receive an American salary. They are certainly not crawling in poverty in Denmark. In Sweden they live at least as well as in the States and many things are within the reach of people which money cannot buy in the States. The chance to meet an active flux of people speaking many languages and carrying many customs, the healthy and clean climate and the temperament of the people, are priceless commodities.

"My boss is a man in his fifties. He is head of Post and Telegraph, so he is what we would call a top executive. Yet everyday for years and years, he has cycled to work. Can you imagine our own Cadillac prestige-filled 'captains of industry' doing this?

"I hope you are not moving at too fast a pace yourself, as you warned me not to do. As you know I am basically easy going and lazy and the opposite case is most likely for me. But Daddy is a fiend at cramming five days of action into one. I think travel should be not only enjoyable in retrospect but while one is actually doing the touring. So I urge you Daddy, to slow down as you urged me and I know that my plea has greater justification."

July 20, 1959 Copenhagen

"I just received your letter which you sent just before you left for Rome. I am happy to hear that you are enjoying yourselves and I hope that Ma is taking the whole thing in stride. I think that leading a group of adults, for Daddy, is a busman's holiday. Daddy seems to be making a running analysis of group action. I hope that I will like my work half as much.

"This I think will be my last letter from Copenhagen with barely 5 days remaining. Since my last letter I went to the beach at Klampenborg and to some student parties. I saw two more wonderful concerts in Tivoli and I went to a dance there. Yesterday my Indian friend Khanna invited me to use tickets he had for the Copenhagen–Halsingborg ferry. It is a two and a half hour ride up the sound to Sweden. Few tourists find out about such things and so the boat was just jammed with Scandinavians. After returning home I knew why it was so popular.

For the equivalent of little more than one dollar you are presented with the most fantastic pile of meats, fish, delicacies and sauces I have ever seen. We did not eat lunch going to Sweden but returning home we joined the people in the lower deck. We had not been seated more than five minutes when each Dane around us gave us a friendly smile and a good-natured nod. Then the food came. Spirits were high as we all dined. I was about to fork an egg into my mouth when a big red-faced, tattooed Dane leaned over and with a broad smile salted and peppered my egg. A happy Danish woman, elderly, offered me a sip of her aquavit, their national liquor. I took a sip and tried to say 'Tak' but nothing came out. Just to show them I really liked the drink I then ordered some. During the meal all eyes were on us and as soon as we reached for some food a Dane would point out the correct sauce to use. We Skoaled each other many times and when we got up to leave we said good-bye to a dozen good friends though we hardly exchanged any words. Nods and smiles, gestures and actions can communicate very often as well as language. On the boat liquor, beer, chocolate and cigarettes are sold cheaply since the boat goes in international water and is not subject to tax. This factor adds to the trip's great popularity. We spent some time in Halsingborg, saw a castle, walked the picturesque and clean cobbled streets before returning on the 5 P.M. boat. The sun was strong and I got a good suntan. I thanked Khanna for I had really enjoyed myself. He may come to the States someday and then we must try and put him up. His uncle is Under Secretary of State for India. He offered me lodging and food if I should ever come to India. He studies at Manchester University in England and he will be there for four years but will travel during the summer. We must have talked for 5 hours on the ferry and I learned a great deal about India and this Indian. He can speak and write fluently five languages, Hindustani, Urdu, Persian, English and German.

"Soon I shall say good-bye to my close friends: to Ian and Bob from England, to Terry from Ireland, to Abul from Pakistan and Khanna from India; then my fellow workers, and Kirsten and another Kirsten . . . and my wonderful land lady Fru Christiansen and the many acquaintances met once or twice. Oh yes there is Peter. He is the Austrian. His father was a general on the wrong side in World War II. He was shot and killed by soldiers without a trial. No comment. It is too mixed up to moralize either way. We are friends on simple, individual grounds and I cannot heap the misery and horrors of the world on this student.

"We, Abul and Peter were in Bakken, a modern Coney Island near Klampenborg on Friday night. We rode the roller coaster, walked, looked for girls, danced and talked. Peter rode from Vienna to Copenhagen in 3 days on his motor scooter. Abul became occupied with a blond so Peter and I rode home on the motor scooter. Wow was that great. We went 60 MPH through the streets right into Copenhagen. He is a madman. . . . I have let my hair grow and now it is quite long. I want to escape the stereotype of the crew-cut American. Now I look Italian. Saturday I had a date with a Danish girl from the office. She is not bad looking. . . . I think I like European girls. When you leave them you feel like a man and not a beggar.

"England, Ireland, U.S., India; we all eat supper together, We laugh and joke and kid each other about our countries. . . . The last time we ate together the boys regretted my leaving and said they now have to search for another American with a sense of humor. Bob said this was impossible. Abul was going to throw a party Saturday but since I am leaving then he is going to try and move it to Friday so I can come. I have never met a group of students who give of themselves, who contain such a large quantity of collective wit and happiness as this group. If I get to England in early September I have three offers to take me around."

July 27, 1959 Berlin

" . . . I left Copenhagen with nothing more than a pile of photographs, memories and an emblem. The only present I bought was for my landlady, a stainless steel soup ladle. The plane was an old prewar German army aircraft, rattling at the seams with loose windows and battered interior. Still it managed the hour and a half flight over the Baltic to Berlin. The city is a combination of ruins, scarred and bullet-riddled buildings and the modern postwar structures. Goods and merchandise, materialism, window shopping and buying typify the Berliner. There are busy streets like 5th Avenue or Broadway. I saw the Eastern Sector, the more extensive ruins, Stalin Allee, a new Communist business center, the Brandenburg Gate . . . There are 6,000 Jews now in Berlin, unorganized, intermarrying and evidently trying to hide their religion . . . I went to a Jazz joint . . . met some Germans there . . . We talked all evening . . . yet they lacked the . . . friendliness of the Danes . . . At the pension the owners do not try to converse with me as did my landlady nor do they offer me the little kindnesses that make one feel really at home. In the center of town is the Kaiser Wilhelm Church, a giant ghastly hulk . . . They are disputing how it should be repaired and so there it sits, a piece of history amid the modern present, black, scaffolded and ugly. Today I went to their famous beach at Lake Wannasee. It is warm in Berlin and I enjoyed the beach. People here like dogs, big ones and I often see them walking these monsters on the street. They also have hot dog stands where they serve for 25 cents shashlik on a stick. Their weiners and brockwurst are tasty but they do not drown you in piles of potatoes as the Danes do, so I often must spend more money for some filler. My suitcase weighs 30 lbs. and is too heavy. I shipped the other one to Amsterdam. So I may ship this one back also and buy a cloth satchel. I can probably manage on 15 lbs. There is a student bus leaving Wednesday from Berlin to Munich at a cost of $5.00. I should like to leave sooner though.

"At the Brandenburg Gate I got to talking with the people in the information center on the Eastern side. They were friendly and gave me reams of propaganda leaflets. One was called 'A List of 800 Blood-Drenched Nazi Leaders Working for the Adenauer Regime.' I asked the man why the East had not rebuilt as much as the West. He said the destruction on their side was greater in the war, the Americans were pouring money into the Western sector, and the rebuilding done in the East was largely industrial rather than housing and office building. How much of this is true remains to be proven by some neutral source, however a West German also told me that there [sic] progress was due to the tremendous influx of American aid. . . . The Germans are Europe's largest travelers. Just as Denmark has flower stores on every street, Berlin has travel bureaus. In Denmark the Germans are hated deeply and try to hide their identity by speaking English or French. The Danes can usually speak German but much prefer English. In the north of Europe it is one happy family where the Danes and Swedes hate the Germans, and the Danes hate the Swedes as well. This goes back to their history and is kept alive by sports competitions and the fact that the Swedes come across the sound to drink in Nyhavn where they get drunk, carry on and continue the ill will."

August 4, 1959 Vienna, Austria

"I am typing from the grounds of the Vienna Youth Festival. The past two days in this city have been full ones and perhaps I should first relate the series of events leading to them. I left Munich sooner than expected (by train) . . . We rode south through Bavaria and at last the German Alps appeared. Jagged and steep, rising from the rolling plains they presented a most impressive panorama . . . Then the blue lakes and at last the most picturesque sight, Salzburg set in a valley with 6.000 foot peaks towering high above. Quaintness, old world architecture, tourists and souvenirs dominate this pleasant city. I lived here for two days at one dollar per day. I could write reams about the buildings, the cafés, the beer gardens, the mountain topped castle and the magnificent scene from the ramparts . . . (I joined friends on a train to Vienna for the Communist-sponsored youth festival). The Alps grew smaller . . . and then Vienna. We found rooms in a plush dormitory-style hotel for 68 cents. This is expensive for Austria but it was crowded in cheaper hotels. That night we saw a most colorful spectacle, the Peiping Ballet. We got in for free because some people who had bought tickets did not show up. After the show I met some people in the audience I knew. One was a girl, vaguely familiar. It was the tall dark-haired girl from Camp Kinderland who went with Alice Kagan through Europe some time ago. She was cold and abrupt as I found many Americans were at the festival. The next day I went to the Austrian Youth Center. They are very anti festival and anti Communist. I took their free trip to the Hungarian border where I saw the watch towers and barbed wire. Across the field I saw Hungarian farmers. We waved to each other. We had lunch in a small village. The people dress as they did hundreds of years ago and still use ox and carts. Later (that evening) I went to the Russian farewell festival. I had no ticket and the black market outside was negotiated in rapid German so I was helpless . . . I went near the entrance and waited for a group to come and then I just walked in with them. The show was grand; a revue of Russian ballet, folk dancing, acrobatics, opera and other art forms. Five thousand people crammed the arena and jammed the aisles. The Americans have nothing to compare with this. The famous Leningrad Ballet took part in this as well as the Moiseyev group. Later I went to the fair grounds and listened to singing and dancing by students from Asia and Africa. The next day I moved into the American bunks. In the morning I went with some of the delegates to the Cuban and Spanish delegation and it was most shameful. I will tell you about it when I come home. [I recollect extraordinary verbal abuse heaped upon the American government and its 'lying controlled press.' "]

Excerpts from Letters to my Parents, 1961: Second Trip— Europe/North Africa

March 10, 1961, Hillel Center, London, England

"After one week in London I have decided to go to Paris and then south to Spain. Write to American Express, Madrid, which I must get to sooner or later . . . Here in London I heard the many voices of a society which prides itself on free speech and the English language. From Hyde Park to Parliament, from fanatic little old ladies to the polished wit of Gaitskell and Macmillan I have heard the issues foremost in the minds of Englishmen. The visit of Vorwoerd (South Africa's prime minister), the nuclear submarines, the National Health Service bill and disarmament . . . I was most impressed by the informality and ever-present wit of the members. They fearlessly attack the Prime Minister, their opponents and speak with disarming bluntness. I have heard one member tell another to 'shut up' and 'you're a paid political propagandist. . . . ' I looked in the papers for jobs but nothing looked interesting enough. . . . I am writing from jolly old Hillel. This place is simply overrun with Jews and kosher food."

March 14, 1961 Paris, France

" . . . There was this Englishman I met in Hillel, about 30 years old. He joined the Israeli army at 19, fought the Arabs in many campaigns including Sinai, stole tanks from the British to arm the Israelis, was thrown into British prison for a year when caught . . . and his parents won't speak to him . . . He came from a family . . . (of) notable military officers. Oh yes, he is not Jewish . . . a living example of . . . daring and idealism. He admired my own actions in sacrificing security and money to do what I wanted."

March 16, 1961 Marseilles, France

(After unsuccessfully waiting all night in Les Halles, the old Paris market, for a hitch on a truck) . . . "I boarded a train and left Paris at 9:15 A.M. Down the Loire and Rhone valley we sped, down 600 miles of steel ribbon. The rolling hills, the flat green and fertile bottom land, the quaint French villages, the homes, the rich fields drenched in sun all moved by: first Dijon and then Lyon and finally Marseilles and the Mediterranean. The clackety-clack of the train, the warm wind whipping by the open windows of the car, the half-dazed stupor of an unslept night now will be pushed into the past as I anxiously look for a room, a bath, a meal and sleep."

March 22, 1961 Barcelona, Spain

(In Marseilles) . . . "I asked a guide near the harbor what it would cost to go to Chateau D'f [sic]. I asked in Spanish. The answer, 500 francs. He even showed me the tickets with the price. Another guide rushed over and I answered him in English. They both started to pressure me to come into their boats, in English, but this time the price had changed to 2,000 Francs, and so did the tickets. After similar incidents it became my belief that these people have some sort of union which fixes the prices of goods and services for each nationality.

"I headed south by train after failing to hitch a ride. Along the coast we sped. This part of southern France is barren and marshy. At Port Bau we changed trains and languages. Spain at last . . . Just before the crossing I made friends with a Spanish boy, Vicente from Valencia and two other Spaniards . . . Vicente and I found a room in Barcelona . . . Before he left he invited me to his home. . . .

"Barcelona is famous for its seafood. A plate of shrimp costs about 20 cents. Barcelona like most of Europe has clean streets, broad boulevards and beautiful parks and fountains. Franco is God and cannot be publicly criticized. If there were an election he would lose but most people don't care or think about politics here. The police and military forces are everywhere on the streets, walking or speeding by on high-powered cycles with brown leather jackets."

March 24, 1961 Barcelona, Spain

"I am writing from a very nice hotel in a very quaint courtyard, with a time weary church, pigeons and narrow winding streets leading in all directions . . . Here in Barcelona there is the old and the new. The old could be typified by the four gigantic spires of the standing remains of an ancient crumbling church I saw in a plaza the other day. The front facade still inspired the feeling of spirituality and humbleness with its towering height, its rich gargoyled walls and its angels eternally blowing long horns. This is Spain's past, crumbling yes, but still calling its people back to historic Catholicism. And the new Spain whirls around the broad boulevards on cycles and scooter, with jazz and neon signs and straight lined buildings . . . There are televisions, transistor radios and other luxuries in the windows of the many fine stores but all are far beyond the means of the vast majority. A walk through Barrio Chino, the old city, reveals extensive squalor and poverty. . . .

"Tomorrow is El Dia Del Santo which begins the week-long holiday, Semana Santo. From long straw-like material the people weave colorful structures . . . The seafood here is ubiquitous. I go to these seedy-looking dives and gobble up delicious shrimps, snails, octopuses, lobsters, squids and other indescribable vermin of the deep."

April 1, 1961 Madrid, Spain

"In Barcelona the festival was all it promised to be. The streets were filled with people hurrying to church. Outside my hotel the priests of the church paraded in ornate splendor around the plaza as hundreds gazed in awe with their gaily decorated straw 'constructions.' Then off I went to the great cathedral of Barcelona where thousands had gathered to pray inside and dance the Sardana, a local folk dance, on the street, in white dress with pastel colored sashes . . . I left for Valencia . . . got on a bus the following day and went to Benifayo, a small quiet farm town situated on flat plains with dirt streets, a church and two ancient Moorish towers. This was the town of Vicente my amigo from Barcelona. Vicente was a wonderful host. He stopped his work, changed into his good clothes and took me all around town to introduce me to his friends which seemed to be just about everyone. I spoke only Spanish for that was the only spoken language. I learned a great deal about the life of people in a small poor and typical Spanish town that day. I met his fiancé, or *prometida*, of three years and his sister's *prometido*, engaged for ten years. Vicente explained that here one must save many years to first get a home, furnishings, fields and animals before one can marry. The father of his fiancé spoke intently of politics, troubles and dictatorship. I said I enjoyed talking with him because *'Usted piensa.'* Overjoyed by this compliment he took me to his ice making plant and offered me beer and spoke with great delight and length about his business. By now the whole town knew that an American an *'estranjero'* had arrived. I was the tallest person in the town, Vicente informed me. His home was typical of the rest, with no running water, dirt floors, animals walking everywhere. The horse was brought through the house itself to the small barn in the back each day. Vicente took me out to the fields that he and his father worked ... As in feudal times the fields were separated by large distances and every day a different field is worked. We rode old rickety bicycles along narrow paths between plowed fields and deep waterways to get out to his *campos*. His animals in the back of the house supply milk, eggs, meat and power to work the land and travel the countryside. Their fields supplied other foods making them almost completely self-sufficient in a subsistence economy. I ate their food, drank their fresh milk from the cow and shared half of Vicente's bed since there was very little room ... With the little they had these people were so generous. His sister wanted to wash my clothes, they wanted me to stay longer. His friends wanted me to return and all were intently curious as to my opinions and ideas. On returning to Valencia I sent Vicente a ... (present), a multipurpose pen knife. I wrote a note *Aquí esta un regalo para un buen amigo. Gracias y hasta luego, Jay*.

"Madrid is one of the beautiful cities of the world ... rich with historic relics. The Prado Museum, the Oriente Palace, Murillo, Joya, Cervantes and El Greco are but a few of the reminders of its historic wealth. Yesterday, as part of Semana Santa there was a great religious parade. For miles the streets were lined 7–8 deep to witness a pageant of religious symbols. The climax of the procession, which included purple hooded Klan type marchers, was a gigantic embellished gold coffin surrounded by half-sized statues of Christ. As it passed people knelt, crossed themselves and some wailed ... soldiers saluted. Christ was almost the end. For behind marched an impressive array of helmeted and armed soldiers ... But with all of Franco's exhibition of strength I would still put my faith in Vicente, his family, his town, his people. The simple peasant produces Franco's soldiers as well as his farmers. The deep resentment and dissatisfaction, the poverty and misery of Spain will rear itself and rebel."

April 13, 1961 Martello, Spain

"I am typing this from a hostel along the Costa Del Sol ... The town below is called Martello and is situated on the very blue and sunny Mediterranean coast. Behind us rest the steep and rocky mountains of this warm and scented paradise ... (Earlier, in Madrid I joined Charlie, a Dane, traveling south in his Volkswagen. We headed to Granada and I urged him to drive to the nearby Sierra Nevada Mountain) ... on the highest road in Europe. It wound around and around in an endless twisted ribbon until we reached 8,000 feet where the snow blocked our passage. Charlie was hesitant but I was full of enthusiasm to try to get to the top. So in only light jackets and walking shoes we set out across rocks and snow fields. At 10,500 feet we reached the rim near the top and could go no further because of the depth and steepness of the snow. The view from the rim was the most fantastic I have ever seen. Just over the edge was a straight drop downward of perhaps 3,000 feet. Before us spread a snow-filled mountain valley and on the side the ridge arced upward to a wind-swept craggy peak. The air was so clear I could see mountain peaks miles away with unusual clarity. But now clouds were moving in below us and should they block the sun and our path back down we might be in danger. Also the temperature was so low and wind so biting we could not stay long. Going down we ran like madmen leaping heedlessly through foot-deep fields of snow, disregarding our shoes, now filled with . . . ice cold water.

"The next day still exhausted we walked through the Alhambra and the gardens of the Generalize, the summer home of the Moorish kings. Then we rode to Malaga . . . Soon we head for Gibraltar. Afterwards we go to Sevilla for the great week-long festival 'La Feira.' . . . Now I have settled down to the idea of traveling and I feel quite satisfied with my position at present. I hope to make the Eichmann trial."

April 16, 1996 Sevilla, Spain

(We traveled to Gibraltar and then for 70 cents crossed by boat to Morocco stopping overnight in the town of Tauten) . . . "I can say that of all my travels through Guatemala, Mexico and Western Europe I have never seen anything so foreign, so primitive, so mysterious and timeless as this sprawling Arab community. The dress, the customs and the sounds and smells were breathtaking . . . We were not allowed into their mosques but through the windows and doors we could see the devout praying and washing themselves in the foot baths. The markets were divided into trade guilds. Charlie smelled some marijuana in the air. So we asked about . . . and . . . bought some. It's really against the law here but they all do it. We brought some back to the hotel and lit up the stuff but it must have been very (weak) because it just smelled like marijuana without any effects. Anyway we soon heard screams down the hallway and a German girl pounded on our door. The Moroccan bus guide had attacked her in her room. He came over to our room, staggering drunk . . . He didn't like Charlie and me. We had a six-inch switch blade knife concealed just in case he tried something but soon he left after we refused to give him the marijuana he smelled in the room. (Later returning to our room) . . . we looked under our beds, pushed a table against the door and went to sleep . . . (We returned to Gibraltar the following day by bus and boat). In the morning we headed north for Sevilla . . . I write from the City itself as it prepares for the great festival . . . Bazaars . . . vendors and stalls of all types run through the large fairgrounds which are streets themselves. At night fireworks, flamenco dancing and singing will dot the city streets. There will be bullfights every day. This is the promise of the festival."

April 23, 1961 Sevilla, Spain

"Now in Sevilla the final day of the Feria draws to a close. I write from a shabby room in a cheap pension. The sounds of a Catholic choir with a resounding organ filter up from a nearby church. Soon the final night of celebration will be over and I will leave Sevilla and Spain for good. The last week has been a week of exciting bullfights, flamenco dancing, a week of crowds, color and confusion, a week to remember.

"After my Danish friend left . . . I was fortunate enough to find this very inexpensive room, an amazing feat during the Feria week. Each day I would walk the streets of Sevilla towards the fairgrounds. The area is brightly lit at night and has countless *casettas*, little rooms with one side open to the street. Inside, groups which have rented the casettas dance and sing. These casettas are called 'particulars' because one needs a ticket or invitation to enter . . . There are two American casettas run by the Air force for their men and visitors but admission is high especially into the officers' casetta. I could not crash the non-officers' party but I did manage to get into the officers' casetta in an interesting manner. At my pension the other night I met a fine Australian fellow who is living here solely to learn Spanish flamenco guitar. We went out to one of the many bars in town and met an English friend of his who is a dancer and entertainer, very glib and a polished conversationalist. We all walked toward the fairgrounds and as we entered a well-dressed man in his fifties or sixties greeted Renny, the dancer. Renny introduced Mr. Michener and said he was some sort of writer. We talked for a while. Then I asked Mr. Michener what he wrote. Modestly and calmly he said 'South Pacific.' It took a moment to sink in and then boy I flipped. Here was James Michener. Well Jimmy was a 'real swell guy.' He took us to the officers' casetta and bought us all meals and drinks. I found him rather quiet and detached, pensive and concerned. His new book is coming out soon and this may be why. It's about the last election. Jimmy left early and we stayed and used up his credit stubs on hamburgers and drinks. We had a big laugh all evening over Renny's ignorance of Mr. Michener's stature because up till then he had been treating Jimmy as an unknown hack. . . .

"Down here in Spain social life is very difficult. It is almost impossible to meet a Spanish girl . . . They have duennas, escorts . . . To a Spaniard any girl out alone with a boy after 10:30 P.M. is a whore. This is also true of any girl who marries more than once. . . . "

April 28, 1961 Fez, Morocco

" . . . This is Fez, a city of two worlds, one Western European with palm-lined boulevards and the other enclosed in crumbling alleys, smoke and busy artisans and vendors. It is this Old Medina, the Arab Quarter that I reside in. Here iron workers, shoemakers, carpenters and weavers work much the same as their ancestors of 3,000 years ago. The clay kiln, a crude hammer or blade, these are the most advanced tools to be seen . . . The people dressed in the robes, veils and sashes of the ageless Arab world move through the dark, sheltered byways on foot or donkey. The women carry children on their backs wrapped completely in sashes . . . I wandered through the Jewish Quarter. As in Tangiers here too the Jews live well . . . In one of their homes this Jew wanted me to marry his daughter just like that.

"When one lives at home routine is commonplace. But for me adjustment to change is becoming commonplace. I have adjusted myself to this life of readjustment. So after three days in Morocco I feel more at ease in the midst of the Arab market, alone, with 50 peering eyes from every shadow and veil in sight. I have adjusted to 'footprints and hole' toilets and 'bring your own newspaper toilet paper' and 'take your life in your hands' food . . . How can I describe the music, the sounds, the sights, the smells . . . It's all around me, right here but the essence of it must remain locked in my heart and mind untransferable."

May 5, 1961 Touring Hotel, Casablanca, Morocco

"After remaining two days in Fez . . . I left for Rabat . . . I went to the bus station but they were sold out so I went to the highway to hitchhike. I met some Jewish students also hitchhiking from their home in Fez to Casablanca. We were about to give up when a car stopped. The driver had room for only one. The boys just wouldn't take no for an answer and literally pushed me into the car.

"Rabat is a small city with broad green boulevards, ultra modern white edifices everywhere and an Old City, typically Arab but less extensive than . . . Fez. Here I waited over the May Day weekend for the consulates to open. Then I got a visa for Libya after telling them on the form I was Unitarian. I got the train for Casablanca.

(I visited a Russian exhibition at the Casablanca fairgrounds). "I went to the Russian exhibitor and asked to see the director. I told him I was an engineer and couldn't read the French or Arabic description of the equipment. He then took me on a personal guided tour lasting one and a half hours. I saw their electrical, mechanical equipment and folk crafts from various regions. He introduced a young engineer to me with these words 'Here is engineer, please.' The engineer gave a short bow and proceeded to explain some equipment. When we passed by the book exhibition I asked if they still published Trotsky. It fell like a bomb. With slight displeasure he asked me 'What for? Why? We have not published him for many years.' To ease the tension I told him I was from New York City and Trotsky spent some time in exile here . . . It is evident that in Russia people not only do not have a free press but do not even recognize the intellectual or moral need for one. . . .

"I went to Marrakech for one day . . . The folklore festival was on (I sneaked in) . . . to a packed audience including the king, Hassan II. He passed by me twice, once inside and once earlier, before a riotous and cheering crowd of thousands as he entered the courtyard to see the performance. I must say it was dazzling as the mountain people from the Atlas Range danced and sang from a culture quite apart from the Arabs. . . .

"Now back in Casablanca . . . I finally selected the boat I will take tomorrow . . . for Marseilles or Genoa."

May 22, 1961 Rome, Italy

"For $30 I found an Italian freighter to Marseilles, which creeping at 10 mph, took six days. After two days of rough seasick weather I adjusted and spent four days sunning myself, eating sumptuous Italian meals with the captain and engineer, standing on the bridge or in the plotting room and learning about navigation . . . The crew were happy Italian seamen, who joked and winked their way around the boat. In Marseilles the younger fellows and I went out on the town. We came back late around 2 A.M. At 6 A.M. I got up, packed and left the boat at the dock. Through the night workers had moved out the cargo of tomatoes in the hold and replaced them with large mysterious gray crates. So they go back to Casablanca and I go to the station to get a train, which takes a Riviera run to St. Raphael and then a bus to St. Tropez. . . .

"The beach at St. Tropez is interesting at one end where they wear bikinis but at the other end it is fascinating where the [sic] wear nothing . . . a great nudist beach that I strolled down with men and women playing volleyball and splashing water at each other as natural as Adam and Eve before the apple. I felt out of place with my bathing suit.

(Traveling by train via Genoa I reach Florence and react to its great art). "The masterpieces overwhelm the casual museum-goer such as myself. There is a Bellini, then Raphael, then Titian and on and on until they become meaningless repetitions of color and form. But somehow towering above them, always arresting in his unique genius was Leonardo of the canvas and Michelangelo of the stone. These two, along with Giotto's architecture are the most dominant personalities of this city where Renaissance art dominated the world.

"Here in Florence I met Eliah, the Stuyvesant colleague from Paris and a group of girls from all parts. We hung around together, ate in the Mensa, a student dining room and used our student status to get into all the museums and galleries free. After supper one night we bought a huge flask of wine, passed it around and drank bottoms up. Latter [sic] some singing Italians came down the street, a birthday party . . . so off we went to a restaurant. I drink more, the world swims and my head becomes very heavy, down on the table top . . . I am really drunk. The party breaks up and I stagger out. My friends help me as I throw up. I dunk my face in a 500-year-old fountain, with Neptune and five orange peels for company. With my arms around an Italian and Eliah I stagger back to the pension. But you know helplessly drunk as I was, unable to walk, I could remember everything, every word and action. . . .

"After three days off to Rome . . . Florence may be princely but Rome is king . . . from the immense grandeur of St. Peter's to the stately classical tranquillity of the Forum. Here Charlemagne knelt in 800 A.D., here Paul built upon a rock, Christianity. Here Julius Caesar watched the Roman legions pass through those arches and here he was cremated. Upon these stones Roman orators spoke 2,000 years ago . . . As I walked and saw those ruins, those churches and temples I could imagine what emperors and Popes and the forgotten had seen across 20 centuries and in so doing I expanded my own brief life . . . placed it in some small way into the . . . fabric of man's existence."

May 30, 1961 Pensione Zara, Rome, Italy

"After eight days I have decided to leave for Naples. I have seen much in this great city: the Capitoline Museum, the Vatican Museum, the Borghese Galleries, numerous churches and cathedrals, the Catacombs, the Appian Way, Roman ruins, the Synagogue. . . . In addition to these studies of the past I have also seen *The Glass Menagerie* and *The Skin of our Teeth*, two excellent plays with Helen Hayes and June Havoc and two fine operas, *La Traviata* and *Madame Butterfly*. I have met people also; an elderly gentleman who treated me to dinner and talked about the select tours he leads for rich young Americans; a war-scarred Rumanian professor with a brilliant mind who speaks eight languages fluently. We discussed politics and people on two occasions. (The professor) . . . lost all his sight during the war. Plastic surgery replaced his nose and he regained thirty percent vision in one eye. I had to lead him around when we walked. Now he is a displaced person working as a language teacher in Spain. I found Dr. Popovich fascinating to listen to as he spoke about Iron Curtain life and the trials and tribulations of D.P.s. He told me that when he visited the Catacombs at Callisto, they had signs over the benches marking the various languages. He was standing apart from the benches so the guide asked him which language he spoke. Dr. Popovich said it really didn't matter and modestly demonstrated his ability to converse in all the languages marked over the benches. . . .

"I met an Italian girl here. She asked for directions on a street in Rome and we have been seeing each other since. She only speaks Italian yet we have remarkable understanding and really enjoy each other . . . I think I may try to head north from Israel through the Iron Curtain countries to Scandinavia. The world is just too god-damned big to see all at once. Asia and Africa and South America will simply have to wait . . . Bit by bit I shall see them all. This is not my last trip by any means . . . I am fascinated and pleased by every moment of this trip and it beats sweltering on Coney Island listening to . . . contemporaries talk as if the world revolved about their own . . . sphere of interest.

"Of course there is no sense blinding myself to a counter feeling. With all the news of a space project and young people in general doing constructive things in the world I feel my own talents and abilities going unused, getting rusty. I feel a desire to gain responsibility, to create technically and yes, to earn a great pile of money also. So all these flux of ideas, some contradicting others, are at play. In physics it is an easy matter to add up all the forces to find the resultant. Unfortunately it is very difficult in the human mind to add up the magnitude of one's various desires to find the resultant direction to take."

June 5, 1961 Tunis, Tunisia

"After a sad fair well [sic] to my Italian girl friend I set off the following morning, by train to Naples. The trip south passed through picturesque farm land with the Mediterranean almost always in sight. I found Naples a large busy seaport city set between the shadow of Vesuvius and a harbor framed by the rocky island Capri... I thought I would climb that ever-present mountain. That very afternoon I took the local bus half-way up to the top. From 2,000 ft. high I hiked the remaining 2,000 ft. It was a cold cloud-enshrouded climb, through cutting wind and a heavy spray of moisture. The path zigzagged steeply and footing was difficult on the finely powdered volcanic ash. I could not see more than 10 ft. ahead of me and so when the climb seemed an endless hopeless frustration, suddenly I was at the top. I heard tour groups coming along the crater's edge from buses nearby. I joined an Italian group who were amazed because I was carrying my jacket and still felt warm.... The crater was filled with mist from clouds and hot gases fissuring through rocks... That evening I boarded the ship for Palermo and bought a fourth-class ticket... I slept well and in the morning awoke to the shouts of Sicilian dockhands. In the terminal ear the dock a young monk offered to help me find a room which he did ... It was good luck for me because three students had rooms in the same pension and they showed me around Palermo that day and we discussed politics and world affairs of [sic] which they were very interested... I got on a standby list for a flight to Tunis. The flight was over the landscape of Sicily and towards a magnificent sunset... Tunis is unspoiled with less than 3,000 American tourists a year and 50,000 altogether. Yet it offers the ruins of Carthage to equal those of Pompeii, a fine beach and a peaceful Arab town in the suburb... set in blue and white colors. Tunis is more Westernized than Morocco with most women showing their faces or uncertainly holding part of their 'sari' over their mouths with their hands or teeth... The Medina is more enclosed by arched roofs... than those of Morocco and the shops are filled with beautiful and colorful shawls, blankets, and rugs of Mid Eastern design. But because of Western influence this Medina lacks some of the primitive charm of the laden donkeys, hand-fashioned tools and goods of the Moroccan markets... Tomorrow my plans are to head south by bus to Djerba, an island off the coast of Tunisia...."

June 9, 1961 The frontier between Libya and Tunisia

"Well here I am stranded in the middle of the desert at an isolated outpost with two sentries, hot sand, flies, no food and no bed, just waiting for a car to hitch back into Tunisia. How I got into this sticky mess is a story.

"After meeting this officer in Tunis I learned many things ... The people here are solidly behind Bourguiba who remains quite independent from Nasser. Of course the universal Arab dream of eliminating Israel, burns bright in his heart and those of his countrymen but on other matters Tunisia wants a free hand. Nasser was so upset at a recent rejection he sent an agent into Tunisia to assassinate obstinate Bourguiba. He was caught and confessed all ... (I traveled south from Tunis) ... across the land dotted by miles of olive trees planted in neat rows ... to Sfax by train ... then by 3rd Class bus to Gabes. The land evolves into the familiar sand dunes and drifts which sweep across the road in irregular patterns. At times the dry wind catches a spiral column of sand and swirls it across the desert. At Gabes in the midday sun I wait for a hitch to Djerba, the oasis island ... At last after 15 hours of grueling travel I reach Houmt Souk the largest village on the island. Here amid palm trees, beaches and sun I rest. The town is quiet in the morning. Camels and donkeys laden with bulky burdens trod slowly along hot flat roads ... I can rent a bicycle and ride to Hara Kigira an 'Izrealite' settlement with Stars of David on the doors ... Then I ride to the famous La Gherba Synagogue where Jews from all parts of the North Africa journey to, 33 days after Passover ... As I left an old Jew entered the Moorish looking synagogue. He was as I should imagine Moses to have looked garbed in ancient robes with a stately beard and a face that bore great strength and suffering ... I rode back to Houmt Souk and then took a turn off in the other direction as the sun set. The sky was reddish orange in the west illuminating shallow clouds and silhouetting the sharp features of the palm trees. After 5 km of riding I heard music off to the left over the sand. So I turned and rode over packed paths until I came to a small village festival. A wedding it was, with local dancers and singers using native flutes and drums to beat out a typical Tunisian rhythm. The groom was only sixteen. The Negro performers moved along the squatting Arabs and held out their palms as they sang, for a collection for themselves. I was invited onto a concrete platform used to collect rainwater. Here I had a spiced meat stew with some reticence because it was prepared in an unclean manner ... The next morning, to the sounds of a busy and colorful market day, I took a small bus out of Djerba to Zanzes. In Zanzes I waited for 3 hours for a bus which on arrival needed pushing to get started. I lent a hand but in the end the archaic rattle box couldn't do it so we changed buses and we were off for Ben-Gardane . . . the border post. There would be no bus for three days on the only road to Libya so I waited for a lift. A Libyan coming out stopped at the crossing and spoke to me in a deep Texas drawl which he learned from oil riggers in the desert. He treated me to an all-American canned food meal with American coffee. The American influence must be very strong in Libya ith its Wheeler Air Force base, its oil companies and its canned food. .

. . Well I waited all day at Ben Gardane and then got a hotel. This was the worst hotel I ever stayed in. The room I found out later was shared by an Arab fellow who stank. This bed stank. The single sheet stank. The pillow, black from greasy heads stank. And all these odors pervaded the room to such an extent that I am sure the one and half inch cockroaches that dashed about must have been affected . . . the bedbugs too. So through that hellish night we all, the Arab, the cockroaches, the begbugs and I tried to get some sleep in that God-damned hole. At 5 A.M. I had enough. The sickening thoughts, as I squirmed around in the fetid bed prevented me from sleeping well. I kept wondering what it would feel like if a bedbug bit me. Then I began to imagine I was being bitten, or was it real? Then I thought of the countless Arabs like the one next to me adding his revolting unwashed odor to this bed. Ugh! I gratefully got up to see the sun rise and the ever slowly plodding camels with their Arabs along the road. At 8:45 A.M. a Volkswagen arrived heading for Libya, the first in the 18 hours I had been there. After 32 km we reached the Libyan frontier. Then to my disappointment, my visa had expired! I called the American consulate. I told them I had no car, no bed and no food. I was helplessly stranded here. The American Consul . . . began to reprimand me and tell me the limitations of his power, of his inability to interfere with the local government procedures and the resentment I might cause. I said I'll worry about the broad philosophical concepts later. Right now I need help out here in the desert . . . I asked if he could speak to the sentry here but he did not speak Arabic. Well that's America, even the high foreign officials can't speak the language. He said he would do what he could to get me in which . . . implied nothing. Well I swam off the coast this morning and wandered across the desert sand looking for a miracle but none came . . . I planned to hit Cairo but now it seems hopeless. I must return 600 km to Tunis."

June 10, 1961 Djerba, Tunisia

"After waiting some time at the Libyan frontier . . . I hopped on a French touring bus back to Djerba. Today I rode to the airport . . . The plane is a DC-3 used because of the short runway. Reassuring isn't it? Then I cycled back through palm trees, olive trees, desert shrubs and sand dunes. In Houmt Souk after my 15-mile expedition I found another wedding getting started. The drums and oriental flutes beat an exotic melody in front of the grooms [sic] house. The puffed cheek muscles of the Arab flutist flowed like waves down the side of his face as he forced air through his reed pipe . . . we walked 3 km to the brides [sic] home. She would arrive later in shrouds on a camel. The women peeked out of white shrouds at the musicians . . . Then we set up two groups in a line and Arab horsemen charged between us and fired shotguns as they passed. One horseman shot my leg but since there was only paper stuffing in the gun it just felt hot . . . it was colorful, wild and biblical [sic] with goats, donkeys, horses and camels grazing amid palm and olive trees under a sunny clear blue sky. . . . "

June 14, 1961 Brindisi, Italy

" . . . The two-engine DC-3 rose quickly off the runway and felt every gust of wind as we headed northward. Below for miles I could see the perfect rows of green clumps of olive trees on the desert plains of Tunisia. We landed in Sfax and in the evening arrived in Tunis . . . I met a Swedish couple who I encountered at Ben Gardane on the Tunisian frontier. They were surprised to see me because they thought I would be in Tripoli by now. They were friendly and attentive people. There is something very attractive about Scandinavian girls. They seem to be so intelligent and interested in what you have to say . . . The Swedish girl helped me pick out novel number four, *1919* by John Dos Pasos . . . The ride through Sicily became a panorama of beautiful landscape, valleys, picturesque fishing villages finally culminating in 10,000 foot Etna with wisps of smoke above its top. Then on to a ferry and across to Reggio Calabria. I had two hours between trains to eat supper and look around. The town is noted for its unique production of special citrus fruit. In the central plaza, clean and quiet stands a proud status of Garibaldi with sword in hand. The departing train had two second classes, one with padded seats which was all filled up with people and luggage and meals on laps and floors. The other cars had wooden benches. I found an empty compartment, shut the door and curtains and tried to get some sleep. I remember getting up half asleep to show my ticket to a conductor and then saying 'Buona notte.' I bought some sweet Muscatel . . . wine at supper and brought most of the bottle on to the train. It made me a little high and left a bad taste in my mouth all that sleepless night. At 5 A.M. I awoke with the sun, had some cheese, bread and wine mainly to wash down the taste. At Taranto I changed trains and by 8:30 A.M. after 24 hours of traveling I arrived at Brindisi. At 10 P.M. tonight I will be on a boat leaving for a Grecian port some 200 km from Athens . . . Now I sit at a side walk [sic] cafe with a beautiful sunny and warm day with a gentle breeze blowing. The streets are filled with casual people leaving their work to begin the long Italian lunch hour. Motor scooters and bikes roar and purr by, pedestrians dodge the traffic as they fearlessly cross the white zebra lines. It is very pleasant to sit here but somewhat lonely. I look forward to Israel and Scandinavia . . . Here in Southern Italy the Italians look quite pale next to my dark brown skin. It's almost embarrassing. They probably think I am an Arab. Speaking of the Arabs we should not judge them too harshly. I am glad I have seen them live and listened to them speak. As a whole they are gracious, friendly and almost childish. They like guns and fireworks as toys. Some will cheat you but if you understand their ways and bargaining is part of them, then this too is a game. And when the price bickering is over you smile, shake hands and give each other a knowing eye, as if to say 'I know you are a cheap crook but I like you anyway.' Invariably when I talked with them they would order tea or coffee for me as an accepted gesture. They invited me to their homes, treated me to meals and gave me lifts or apologized if full or unable to . . . The individual Arab has developed these traits of generosity and friendliness perhaps because in this land of hellish climate, of parched desert, of barren wasteland, one's life may depend on a passerby's generosity . . . When I return I fear I shall be irrepressibly excited about the world around me, [sic] that if the sparks do not catch fire in my friends I will be very disappointed. For just a $100 you're in Panama and then south to the Amazon. It's the world just waiting. They can't ignore it!"

June 17, 1961 Sounion, Greece

"The boat trip from Brindisi took one night and the following day. The ship was a luxury liner complete with swimming pool and outdoor televisions. Since the meals were so expensive I brought food on board and ate out of cans during the crossing using my knife as a spoon. The

Adriatic was blue and calm and during the day we passed . . . jagged islands and mountainous coastline, much like fjords.

(In Athens) . . . "I visited the Archaeological Museum and saw statues and pottery of classical Greece. The historical roots of Athens and its remains form a continuous path leading from the Bronze Age at 5,000 B.C. to the rise of its great empire around 500 B.C. to the present . . . In the afternoon I went to the Acropolis. From that rocky hill surrounded by the marble ruins of the Parthenon, I could see . . . where Peter spoke, to first set forth Christianity and . . . where Socrates was tried and the prison where he spent his last month before he drank the hemlock.

"I took a bus here to Sounion to see the white marble Temple of Poseidon set on the most beautiful Mediterranean landscape I have yet seen with rock hills, green slopes and a bluish and greenish sea dotted with numerous rough cut islands. Here etched on one of the many vandalized stones of the temple is the name Byron, the great poet who loved the beauty of this land so he found it necessary to deface it. This was pointed out to me by a distinguished deep voiced confident elderly gentleman who turned out to be the U.S. representative to the Olympic Committee, meeting in Athens. . . . "

June 30, 1961 Sodom, Israel

"I write this letter from Sodom as I sit in a straw-roofed open restaurant, with fans overhead and the thick dry air of the Dead Sea Valley . . . After leaving Athens on an old scow I met Francis, from Bordeaux, age 20, intelligent and fine company. We both knew very little about Israel and seemed to have the same immediate plan. So we teamed up and decided to look up a contact he had in Ein-Hahoresh. The two day crossing to Haifa was uneventful. The sea was rough the first few hours out and I became a little sick but soon the Mediterranean took on a blue placid form and the remainder of the crossing was pleasant . . . After getting through customs at Haifa we spent two hours in town getting our bearings, changing money and getting tourist information. We then took a bus to a point just south of Hadera and then taking another bus west 5 km we arrived at Ein-Hahoresh. For one week we worked, relaxed and ate with these people. Up at 5 A.M. we left our small room and trudged to meet Moshe, our supervisor who put us to work breaking and removing rocks from fields in the kibbutz, raking leaves or picking plums . . . At 8 A.M. we ate breakfast in a just completed modern dining room. Then back to work we went until 11:30 A.M.

when we ate lunch and then worked the last stretch from 12:00 to 3 P.M. The work was exhausting with a hot sun baking us in a cloudless sky. The perspiration poured out all over my body. At 3 P.M. I had a welcomed shower and a 4 P.M. snack later. In the evenings we either rested, or played chess. Once a week movies are shown. We saw two the night we arrived, both in English with a running Hebrew translation along the side of the screen. Everyone brings their own chairs to a hillside and all sit under a cool evening night with a moon so bright it cast sharp shadows on the half lit ground. The last night in the kibbutz we went to a concert given by amateur choral groups from three kibbutzim, ours included. There I met a girl who graduated from CCNY also . . . It was interesting talking with her but she reminded me of the familiar egoism of bright independent Americans I met before. I also met with an English woman living on the kibbutz and an American from 30 Rockaway Parkway who has been here 14 years. He works in the metal barrel factory here. The kibbutz is 31 years old and rather well established but its greatest test is yet to come. Will the second generation remain here in sufficient number to prosper . . . They have neither the pioneering zeal nor the perspective acquired by the aging founders. At first the community of 600 people reminded me of a summer camp with winding paths in the woods, short pants and a casual atmosphere. The advantage of no poverty, shared wealth, few problems, good food and cleanliness recommended it but for an ambitious person the kibbutz life offers few opportunities and a rather limited choice of work and leisure. The people here are quite intelligent but of course lack this personal ambition. The children do not live at home but in classroom-homes divided by age. They can visit their parents from 5–7 pm and this retains the family ties . . . But the purpose of freeing women for other tasks actually created so many additional jobs that little has been gained in efficiency . . . Once every two years they go to a rest home for ten days and once a year they go on an ordinary six day vacation. Well, Wednesday we went to Tel Aviv and I received a pile of letters from you and Manya, forwarded from Italy. Thank you all for birthday greetings. Twenty-three already. Time certainly goes by quickly. One can almost see the decades fly by. Congratulations Elisa on your marks which make a respectable index indeed . . . I was interested in your remarks about . . . creeping age. I meet loads of girls over 18 who are not married or even planning it, so don't be concerned about it at this stage in life . . . on the Peace Corps information, I can see it is not for me. Leave the horsework to idealistic unskilled liberal arts students I say. It would be foolish to waste engineering training on such assignments . . . I am glad you are going to Spain Daddy but I wish Ma would go also since she is off cortisone and feeling better. . . .

"After Tel Aviv we headed by bus to Beersheba . . . In the morning we saw the Arab camel market and hitched to this hell hole Sodom. . . "

July 4, 1961 Tel Aviv, Israel

" . . . The latest news is that I lost my stamp album (passport) and may need another one if it is not found soon. Don't worry. It's just bothersome, not serious. After swimming in the Dead Sea, Francis and I returned to Beersheba and the next morning left our hotel to hitchhike to Elat. Conditions were bad on the road so I left poor Francis and took a bus. The road wound through parched brown and reddish wastelands, through rocky plains and sunken valleys all baking in a stagnant heat. At last the bus reached a long narrow valley and sped finally to Elat . . . At around noon I walked to a restaurant with my 'Kova Temble' hat on. The temperature was about 110 degrees and was very tiring. Every step was an effort . . . At night people fill the streets of this city walking, talking or sitting at sidewalk cafes . . . The Arab culture is dead or dying in Israel as the modern European, his clothes, his buildings and his mores invade and pervade this land. The next day it was north with a stop in Ashkelon and the Weitzman Institute. . . .

"Last night I went to a July 4th celebration. The first two hours were spent listening to American and Israeli folk songs. I was bored by the jazz and the M.C. who spoke in Hebrew to a group of which about 98 percent spoke English and 50 percent spoke Hebrew. A silly thing to do which the American Ambassador did not fail to quip about, when he rose to briefly address the group . . . I met no one and just wandered around the crowded floor, apart, with my thoughts flying far and wide. I just read that Hemingway died . . . Also Lee DeForest . . . He invented the radio tube 50 years ago . . . "

July 10, 1961 Tel Aviv, Israel

(Here I give brotherly advice to my little sister) . . . "Ma's overprotection is a problem but it is unchangeable as the laws of the Universe. Some things in life are not meant for discussion. Some things must be secrets between you and your conscience. One measure of maturity, I think, is wrestling with your own problems and actions without any advice from others. You know there were many times I went out of the house and never told or refused to tell what I had done or where I had been merely on principle and sometimes for good reasons. Shouldering the additional problem of editing your private life before your parents is part of social and personality development, your exodus to individuality.

" . . . My hotel is a fourth-class dormitory near the shore which has a young crowd of South Africans who are in various stages of military service here. I have learned a great deal about life in the Israeli army from them. The Syrian border may blow up any time now with shooting going on everyday. The young paratroopers describe their jumps, their thoughts as they leave the plane. The soldiers speak of their motivation to leave South Africa; adventure, a free passage to Israel, idealism and Zionism, dissatisfaction with apartheid. Each night I hear furious discussions over the nuances of South African government. I sit in the lounge of the Dan Hotel, deluxe class, down the street. The difference is evident not only in the . . . luxurious modernity and air conditioned plushness but in . . . the clientele. They are well heeled . . . their impressions of the Negev are from a plane at 6,000 feet. I would not trade hotels if the cost was the same and certainly not when the cost of a room is 15 times what I pay at Hotel Elat. Anyway our cockroaches are bigger."

July 16, 1961 Hotel Carmel, Safed, Israel

"Safed set almost 3,000 feet high, perched on the stony hills of Galilee, is a town steeped in the ancient Kabalist and Hasidic traditions. The synagogues painted in gaudy pastel colors enclose the drab black and brown clothed, bearded and side-locked orthodoxy. An artists' colony on a nearby slope rounds out Safed's cultural influences. But these artists are a middle aged beardless breed and not the wild bohemian types. Twenty or thirty studios and exhibitions dot the hillside town shrouded in white domed Moorish ceilings and arches of green ivy and tortured hardwood trees. The Safed streets are narrow, steep and mingle with long staircases and balconies angled off the sides. Safed is hot at midday and chilly at night. From one street I can see 15 miles . . . to Lake Tiberias, 600 feet below sea level from where I had come the day before.

"But to explain the sequence of events I should start in Tel Aviv. After leaving that city I rode by bus to Haifa. Then I visited the Bahai Temple and gardens, met some girls in the street who helped me find a cheap hotel. The next day we went to the beach outside the city where everyone was chasing 'Meduzas,' blue eerie looking crabs. I dated one of the girls, a real strange one who seems quite serious over me. We went to the movies together. I visited the Technion and got another grand tour through the electronics building. I roamed the Carmel Hills and observed the superb vistas, the long straight coastline below with the white ridges of waves rolling in from the blue and green ocean . . . I left Haifa and made a stop in Nazareth. It was hot and I felt little inspiration to climb the winding dusty streets . . . However I did bump into Mary's Well and St. Joseph's Church. The little barefoot children darting through the market and alleys were the most ill mannered I have yet encountered. They threw stones, spat, mocked, leered and sneered at strangers and beg for money just to make their impression thoroughly revolting. This is what 2,000 years of tourism can do to a quiet town . . . I hopped on a bus for Tiberias . . . I took another bus to Capernaum and their [sic] bunked down in a Catholic monastery on the site where Christ was supposed to have produced piles of food from two fish and five loaves of bread. The Father, a decent chap, gave me a mattress in a room in the motel like monastery . . . The Arabs around there liked me and I was invited to their home in the monastery where I had coffee and later a fine meal served on a straw mat. The Arabs ate squatting down on the mat. The home had dilapidated beds, no furniture outside of two padded benches but in the corner sat a . . . short wave radio . . . I hitched to Rosh Pinnas . . . later a truck took me up to . . . Safed."

July 21, 1961 Tel Aviv

"After reaching Haifa . . . I went to see Ruth, my Sabra girlfriend. It will be a very sad moment when I leave her on July 26. She is very orthodox, moody, introspective and intelligent and of course very pretty . . . Ruth wants me to fast for Tishah-b'Ab but I haven't decided. I have two days yet. It's a great moral question as well as a material one. If I do fast I know it will be for the wrong reasons, maybe even sinful reasons. Under such circumstances it may be more moral to eat, more honest to one's true beliefs. . . .

"One must travel to realize that money represents power and prestige everywhere, but most important of all money can be the tool which unshackles the chains of boredom and routine and frees one from the prison of subsistence living. With a philosophy, with imagination, money can give the freedom to explore life to its fullest, not merely to satisfy materialistic greed, but also to pursue the idealism of travel, of education and of simple curiosity. . . .

"Soon it will be good-bye to Israel, my home for almost six weeks... (Israel) is young yet it has borrowed from old cultures, from North Africa, from Eastern Europe and Asia Minor. In many ways America, older in years, is younger in spirit with its laughing immaturity, its overconfidence, its century of peace un-aged by the suffering of war at home. The contrast was symbolically dramatized the night of July 4th at the Mann Auditorium Concert. The audience rose as the *Star Spangled Banner* was played. The drums boomed, vigorously proclaiming its youth and virility. Then came the violin strains of *Hatikvah* with the ageless age [sic] of long suffering, with the weary but unbowed spirit seeking regeneration in the new body, the new land. Violins sent forth their message, their *Hatikvah* of everlasting hope. The crowd applauded and sat down. The character of the two nations could not have been more eloquently compared."

July 29, 1961 Hotel Konak, Ankara, Turkey

(After sailing from Haifa to Iskanderon on the southern coast of Turkey I journeyed north by bus) . . . "first along the coast to Adana and then north through the Toros Mountains. The road wound and climbed to about 5,000 feet with magnificent sheer rock walls and plunging valleys abounding in such grandeur that Switzerland might envy them. It grew cooler . . . I saw nomadic Turks living in teepee tents along river banks beneath the towering peaks. Their manner of living bore a great resemblance to the American Indians. We made numerous stops for drinks and food and one such stop near sunset was along a mountain stream feeding a rapid river. Then darkness fell. In the crowded bus I found some room in the back seat, curled up for a while but the sharp bounces of the bus would knock me a foot in the air and slam me heavily down again. Now we rode on a flat plain and the night was dark and cold. I vaguely remember a salt lake, some Turks singing up front, a Turk lying on the floor before me, using my pack as a pillow. At 2:30 A.M. we saw the lights of Ankara after 15 exhausting hours of the bumpiest and one of the longest continuous trips I have yet made . . . Ankara is a beautiful city set like Rome on many hills and influenced by names, buildings and statues reflecting one man, Kemal Ataturk, soldier, statesman and immortal hero of this nation . . . Turkish food I rank with French or Spanish in both its unique and fine qualities. In addition to this it is very cheap as are hotels and transportation. A fine shish kebab dinner costs about 60 cents and a room about 85 cents. The Turks seem to be quite honest. They have returned money when I gave them too much and the prices have always been reasonable."

August, 2 1961 Marmara Oteli, Istanbul, Turkey

"Today I visited the bazaar of Istanbul, a huge maze of shops and small handiwork factories. I know Ma would have been irrepressible if she saw the rugs, the metal work of brass, silver, copper and gold and the vast array of oriental curiosities. The market is enclosed in one section by a white stucco Arabic arched building. Further down the hill the shops are shaded by tarpaulins jutting out and at times completely spanning the narrow cobbled streets. Crowds mill and children run barefoot, vendors shout and beckon as this teeming bazaar moves through the day . . . Unlike Morocco, here Moslems welcome and are friendly toward tourist visits to their temples. I saw Suleyman, the Blue, the Valide and the Osman Mosques, all jewels of Byzantine architecture, which if lacking Renaissance paintings, make up for it in the grace and proportions of the buildings and minarets. On entering I removed my shoes and walked on aged carpets entirely covering the floor. Worshipers quietly bowed their heads to the mats. Overhead supported by massive columns great arched domes ascended, beautifully designed and decorated in Arabic style . . . This evening I took a bus to Galata Bridge and watched the rush hour . . . surge toward ferries which zigzagged up the Bosporus; whistles, horns boats plying every way, the multilithic crowds rushing about, the swift water . . . swirling together with the Golden Horn inlet, the city rising from its blue turbulence amid the noise and movement, the City, Istanbul. I got a 'Dolmas,' a shared taxi, and rode toward Taksim Square, center of the new section with a feeling that at last I was embracing Istanbul's immensity both physically and spiritually. . . .

"I walked to a nearby amusement park, rode a chair lift and then tried one of those physical tests of strength. It was a heavy iron sled on wheels which one must try to accelerate up a ramp to ring a bell. I asked how much and the young fellow said 50 kurus (6 cents). I paid and started warming up. A big middle aged Turk watched me, took a liking to me and started giving me advice with gestures. After failing the second time out of my allotted tries he asked me how much I paid. I said 50 kurus. Well that did it. You see the price was 25 kurus (3 cents) and the young man had taken me. Well the big Turk just 'blew his stack.' In Turkish he shouted at the young man for cheating a tourist until the poor guy thoroughly humiliated, handed 25 kurus over to me. I was elated. Justice had been served and the Turkish character redeemed."

August 5, 1961 Balkan Tourist Hotel, Sofia Bulgaria

" . . . days in Istanbul were spent walking the interesting streets, a trip by boat up the Bosporus almost to the Black Sea itself and a trip to the Princess Islands in the Sea of Marmora. At the furthest and longest of these islands, beautifully situated, set in tranquil hills and pines, without cars, I took a horse drawn carriage around the high winding road. It was nature at its perfection with the deep blue sea below, the fresh smell of pine leaf woods and the slow clippity clop of the horse pulling across the peaceful road. Yesterday I left my hotel and prepared to board the train for Sofia. And as I was buying some provisions for the 22 hour train ride an attractive Turkish girl caught my eye. Soon we were 'talking.' She bought me some buttermilk. I was touched. She spoke almost no English, we just joked around, exchanged addresses with promises to write each other. It was a crazy 30 minute romance because she had to leave for her train. My own train trip was long and grueling. First through the outskirts of the City and into sunny farmland fields and then through the black night, a tossing, cramped, bumpety night without sleep, with long stops at border posts. Twice we entered and left Turkey into Greece. At last at 4 P.M., with passport and visa I debarked exhausted to find a hotel and a welcomed bath. Sofia and the rural Bulgaria reflect a reasonable standard of living. People seem happy, not undergoing any extreme poverty and certainly do not appear to be slaves of the State. The streets, broad, cobbled and clean, meet well trimmed colorful gardens plazas, with fountains and sedate mosques or churches . . . The streets are busy with neatly dressed people coming out of stores, window shopping or waiting for street cars. Yes, it's like any other city or any other country. These are first impressions."

August 7, 1961 Balkan Tourist Hotel, Sofia, Bulgaria

" . . . Yesterday I rode a street car and then a bus to the rising slopes of Mt. Vitulla. There overlooking a flat farmland valley, with golden domed Alexander Nevsky Church gleaming in the central Sofia, picnickers spent their peaceful Sunday eating, relaxing or hiking in short pants into the higher levels of the mountain. I joined a group of Bulgarian students one with a guitar, at a cafe set on a terrace, in the open surrounded by trees and a brook. They sang folk songs of Bulgaria with the deep rich slow sad tones of sorrow. Then they sang American folk songs and rock and roll. When asked if it was 'veritable' I said 'it was American rock and roll with a Bulgarian accent.' They thought the answer was quite humorous.

" . . . Sofia is blessed with many natural springs, some hot and others cold, but all supposedly having great healing powers. In the central plaza a fountain has hot water taps for the citizens to rejuvenate their "tired blood." The magic elixir tastes just like plain hot water. The tourist items and all luxuries like rugs, woven table clothes or electrical appliances are very costly . . . It is nice though to buy meals, goods or services without fear of being cheated. After all what is the point if everyone receives salaries and personal profit is eliminated in the social picture. There is no bargaining and no shopping for bargains . . . Of course there is no tipping, a custom I heartily approve of . . . Yesterday I saw the George Dimitrov Mausoleum, with George done up like Lenin and Stalin, under glass, illuminated in black tuxedo and white pallor. The heroes of Communism remain for public exhibition after death too, to succor the last ounce of fealty from the people.

. . . In the American Legation I sat down to read the latest papers . . . A newsletter announced the Titov feat of multi encirclement of the Earth which paled the exhibition outside the legation of (our) American space capsule . . . I feel that our day will come but it may be 7 or 8 years hence.

" . . . As yet I have no plane or boat ticket home . . . My biggest and most essential dilemma is the choosing of colleges. I should like to contact ACF first and find out if a job is still waiting for me. . . .

"I am very interested in hearing about all the stories and things that have passed in the six and a half months since I left. After all I have written down in letters most of my experiences. A few are not fit for letters home of course. But within the limitations of my writing ability, the translation of reality to prose I have set down the essentials of my absence. But your activities in Brooklyn are shrouded in brief statements, hurried office memoranda, notes before rushing off on a date or a supper engagement. It is likely that on returning you all will have more news for me than I for you. So I close this letter and the last month of my adventure."

August 9, 1961 Belgrade, Yugoslavia

" . . . Soon the almost deserted train was moving out of the misty, smokey morning haze of Sofia. As the sun rose we moved through flat farmland and then later through gorges with swift mountain rivers still carving the stone. I walked through the cars to pass the time; wagon-lit sleepers with plush red carpets and private compartments, German second-class cars with pull-down seats, first-class cars with velvet seats, all empty. But in the last car I heard English and found three New England teachers who . . . were also going to Belgrade . . . The time passed quickly . . . I walked around the quiet village of Dragoman, saw chickens cross the dirt road, saw an old stout peasant woman cleaning out some blanket. (I arrive in Belgrade) After an exhausting walk up and down steep streets with a burning hot sun I found a 'hotel.' It was an old paddle wheel ferry boat sitting on the River Sava, which runs by the City. They rented out cabins below and the top deck was transformed into an evening open air restaurant with music. My cabin had just enough room for the double decker bed and a sink. Still it was home and I loved it." (I do not mention in this letter the very intimate sexual encounter which took place in my cabin. Details described elsewhere).

" . . . Yugoslavians still walk around with a jacket draped over their back with dangling empty sleeves. It is a silly custom unique to this country and unchanged since I last visited two years ago. Later I walked to the river and went to my cabin and slept. The next morning I went to the Putnik Agency and found that the Hungarian visa would take 10 days for confirmation . . . and that each day in Hungary would cost $10 for vouchers. This information ruled out travel to Hungary . . . Lately I have been giving my wash out to local people instead of doing the scrubbing myself. It is a nice feeling to have clean white laundry handed to you. It gives one a pleasant feeling of wealth and power when you put down the cash for service; a wonderful thing, money.

" . . . Tomorrow I visualize another grueling experience, 15 hours by train from 1 P.M. to 5 A.M. the next morning, to Vienna."

August 11, 1961 Vienna, Austria

"Now I sit in one of those wonderful cafés in Vienna. The people around me sit reading newspapers on wooden sticks or slowly sip coffee and eat pastry . . . Now on the horizon looms the end of this grand adventure. The day comes nearer and clearer . . . I can almost see Berlin and then Copenhagen and some point of departure and homeward; the waiting plane, the familiar faces and city. Homeward yes, glad yes but with nostalgia to return abroad. Here there is freedom, complete unbounded freedom to simply do as I desire, to let free thought and action take their course, to let my desires form my life and not my life frustrate my desires. So glad as I will be to return, so will I later be glad to once more move across the globe. This is now a part of my existence as sleeping or eating, that must find its fulfillment."

(August 12) "This morning I awoke to a rainy dreary sky which hung in an unbroken grayness over Vienna . . . Across the city from the 8th floor of the Studentenheim, the spires, slanted roofs and towers spread their disorganized way to the foothills of the Vienna forest. Bells toll and smoke slowly rises from a chimney. It will clear and be a good day."

August 12, 1961 Vienna, Austria

(I ask my father to send the following letter on my behalf to my former employer)

Mr. Auckenthaler
ACF Industries
Hyattsville, MD

Dear Mr. Auckenthaler:

Since I left ACF Industries six months ago I have decided to resume studies towards a Master's Degree at Maryland University on a half-time basis. It is my hope that a position for me at ACF is still open to fill the other half of this work- study arrangement. I write to you because I remember the sincere interest you showed in my work in those final weeks of my employment. I feel you know my capabilities and the type of job I want. Perhaps the Steam Rocket Report can aid in re-evaluating what I can do. It is my wish to work on a 20 hour per week basis in the Design Department or a department requiring electronic background. At the same time I would take 10 credits of the graduate courses, hopefully completing my degree in one and a half or two years. Since school begins in September I must know ACF's decision as soon as possible. Whether I begin is much more important now than when I begin. Thank you for your past and present consideration.

Yours truly
Jay Freeman

August 14, 1961 Vienna, Austria

"I spent one evening at the Auersperg Palace, a fabulous aristocratic mansion out of Vienna's rich 19th century. Once the gilded carved and canvassed walls served nobility as graciously as did Versailles. Now it serves ordinary people as a dance hall, restaurant and covered garden for the price of 60 cents. The ornate wood work, the artistic works of sculpture and painters adorn each room. A small orchestra played sweet music, then the irrepressible Strauss Viennese waltz brought couples to the floor, especially the older ones less self conscious, who broke the ice and started the shy ones . . . I spent (the next) evening at Augustiner Keller, a favorite haunt of mine two years ago. Arched walls, rustic Viennese atmosphere, violinists serenading with the gay lilt of waltzes, fine wine and a half grilled chicken. Feeling good I took a quick trip to Grinsing, the Greenwich Village of Vienna. I saw coffee and beer houses, singing and drinking but just as an outsider obtrusively peering in. The next day I just walked around, window shopped, saw the headlines about Berlin. I got my visa and train ticket. Now I am all excited about Berlin and the barb wire with tanks and guns and I'll be there to see it firsthand. It's perfect timing. I welcome the danger and excitement. I shall have my nose in the thick of it, you can be sure. The train will leave Vienna at 11 P.M. and will arrive in Prague at 5 A.M. After 6 hours of looking around another train will take me to Berlin at 7 P.M. . . . "

August 16, 1961 Berlin, West Germany

" . . . The ride to Prague was long, through the night, the cold night and clackety-clack of the rail coaches. Inside my compartment sat two young men, Germans also going through Prague. Using some Yiddish and some German I managed to talk about little things. Then the sky grew bright, . . . sky illuminated fields, farmlands and misty woods; the frontier and onward through Czech land. I tried to sleep in an empty first-class compartment but the car was soon to be separated from the others. In Europe you must pick the proper car and at key points locomotives juggle the wagons around and set yours on the desired track . . . By evening we reached the frontier of East Germany. Because I lacked a declaration I almost lost all the money in my wallet ($17) but the guard seeing I was just an American tourist took pity on my innocence and let me go. The smiling red faced stout Czech nearby was gleeful as the inspector left. Out of his pockets, under his coat, inside his trunk bulged cigarettes and other 'sub-rosa' merchandise. It's all a big game. Then along the Elbe River, went the train, past sheer rock mountains on both sides of the river, with quaint homes nestled in the coves and ledges, with steamers and peaceful fishing boats slowly plying their way. Then another night fell upon us and it was cold, very cold. I took out my warm flannel shirt and put it over my cotton one and then on went my jacket. Now I was wearing half my ruck sack which looked saggy and quite miserable but not as miserable as I must have looked. The East Germans left. One gave me a deutsche mark to buy an S- Bahn ticket from Ost Bahnhof in the Eastern Zone into the West. When I arrived at 1 A.M. Berlin the city was dead. The elevated train, S-Bahn was deserted and cold. The woman at the ticket window had no change but when the train approached she let me through. At Fredrickshaven Station, the frontier, I got out and walked down stairs and up the other side. The other exits had been boarded up with wood. Guards waited for me and two stopped me and asked for my passport. On the other side I rode to Zoo Station, the center of West Berlin. Deserted also but colorful with neon and a modern lively quality West Berlin felt a little more like home. A policeman outside helped me find a pension, which was nearby, across the street from the Hilton. Run by Danes it is clean with thick quilt blankets, spacious rooms, carpeted with modern furniture but it costs $2.00. Well for two days it will not ruin me financially . . . (The next day very hungry I ate three meals in the afternoon) at a place called Aschinger. This is a typical quick service restaurant where you can get served standing up or sitting down. It is efficient almost to the point of humor in contrast to the leisure of the rest of Europe. But this is West Berlin where time is money, where people rush to catch trams and buses, race cars to cross the street, where shops sell and sell. The pace is closer to New York City than any other. It is a pleasure but with all the tensions which must ensue. At 2 P.M. I saw thousands of people marching in columns in one direction. I walked with them and finding a German who spoke English I found out that this was to be a huge rally protesting the East German closure of the sector. Willy Brandt spoke to the largest crowds I have ever seen in person. Hundreds of thousands of people crowded before the Rathouse and spilled into side streets. Loud speakers echoed Brandt's fiery oration. 'We will never live as they do in East Berlin,' he said. A wave of applause swept the crowd. There was no disputing their feelings. Thick gray clouds moved swiftly overhead. The moist wind chilled the bones. Rain swept the masses and still they held shoulder to shoulder in the streets. Trams stopped, conductors climbed to the top, traffic became snarled. Angry marchers pushed cars back that had blocked the intersections by stopping in the middle. I walked towards Brandenburg Gate but 600 feet from the Gate I was blocked by guards, Only officials and the press were to be admitted I was told. It was raining and chilly now so I returned to the Zoo Station. Tomorrow I will go to the Russian Sector which may restrict picture taking. My plan is to leave Berlin tomorrow on the 10 pm train for Travemunde . . . I hope I will see the Sun in Copenhagen with many of my old friends of so long ago. Now I have just finished a fine meal with good vermouth to down it with. The lights and sparkle of night Berlin are out on Kudamm. The old Kaiser Wilhelm Church ruin now surrounded by brick and glass records in [its] ghastly destruction the ghastly past. [It was not rebuilt so that it could stand as an everpresent reminder of the war and what happened during it.] Otherwise central West Berlin presents a picture of modernity, color and vividness. . . . "

August 19, 1961 Copenhagen, Denmark

"The stage in Berlin is set for great events. In the streets outside the S-Bahn students picket against the use of the East Berlin transport system. Groups gather and vigorously agree about unity and strength against Communist aggression. 'We would suffer the destruction of World War II here in Berlin rather than submit' a student told me. Some Israeli newsmen asked us questions as we talked. They felt the U.S. would be weak as 'it always has against the Russians.' I disagreed and cited our firm stands in Formosa, Korea and Lebanon as examples. Earlier that day I went to the Eastern Sector and photographed quickly and secretly, tanks, armored cars and machine gun-carrying soldiers. I was warned a few times against it but continued anyway. You can feel tension in the air in both East and West. But in the West there is unity to defend their rights. In the East opinion differs. Soldiers are brought in from provinces and farmlands so they do not know the issues or local feelings of their countrymen in East Berlin.

" . . . (I arrive in Copenhagen by train) My heart beats fast as those old friendly streets, the Radhudpladen, the green copper clad City Hall . . . the guttural Danish sounds reappeared recalling past good times. There was the Students Klub with the same conservative leather furniture, newspapers and sedate pipe smoking readers. There was the Student Hostel same as ever. And last, most important there was Kirsten. I confronted her at the door to her home. What a surprise for her. She was thinner and quite pretty. We could hardly talk just looking at each other. But on Thursday she leaves for the United States and California to work as a mother's helper...."

August 21, 1961 Copenhagen, Denmark

"These past few days in Copenhagen have been rainy and dreary which seemed to set the mood when one tries to relive old memories. Reality never can match the aura which time bestows on the past. I felt no strong urge to revisit my old room and Mrs. Christianson or my Post and Telegraph building. I spent most of my time with Kirsten talking about the good days of years back, the future, her trip to the States. On one day we went out to a soccer game. Kirsten was the captain and I watched her team play to a 4 to 1 victory... Kirsten and I went to the War Museum to see the record of Danish Resistance. A bitter elderly Danish woman got into an argument with a German who came inside the museum. She pointed to a case showing horrible atrocities and said to him 'see what you have done.' He replied that 'he did not do this.' There are those who will never forget and those who want to.

"I shall return to Copenhagen after Sweden to pick up finally any mail. I probably will not have time to say good-bye to Kirsten who leaves on the 24th. Today I said farewell to her in a heavy rain. We shall continue correspondence as we have in the past. I read some of the letters I had sent her over the past two years. It was most interesting to see how my thoughts have developed or changed. The hostel here is filled with students from everywhere. It is crowded and noisy but has the charm of liveliness and youth, which must sound terribly 'old' of me to say but it is the way I feel at the moment, removed and objective.

"I hope Elisa is enjoying her job and her jaunt to (Cape Cod?). I think Dennis is clever and sophisticated but he is argumentative almost to the point of irritation. A discussion with him is an experience in tension... [Dennis was my sister's boyfriend at the time.]

"There must be... (a way)... to find an intelligent... set to keep Elis and me interested in the Great City. Surely there must be clubs or groups where such people gravitate, and I do not mean Hillel, Daddy. Well it shall be a new challenge which will soon face me upon my return and what looks like an extended stay in New York. I am grounded for a while but it is time that can be used effectively to consolidate past experiences, re-establish and strengthen my engineering career and plan a great new journey which will carry me to places and adventures which will shatter the imagination. I will not be deterred by the sensible pleas of parental authorities, pygmy blow guns, Arab assassins or Mau-Mau head hunters. The world is here and I plan to see it!"

August 25, 1961 Copenhagen, Denmark

"Today I returned to Copenhagen after spending three days in Lund, a university town in Southern Sweden. Four days ago I and a small group of people from the hostel decided to go to Nyhaven, the nightclub tavern . . . street in Copenhagen along one of the canals. The Vingarten Club had music, dancing, rustic atmosphere. We drank beer and talked. At 5 A.M. it closed and we went to Piccadilly's, a morning club. A Dutchman and Monica, a girl I took an interest in, and I sat half exhausted while a friendly Dane ordered beer . . . for us, on his bill. A few staggering Danes would come in occasionally. A woman wept continuously at the next table. At 8 A.M. we dragged ourselves over to the hostel for coffee. The Dutchman left and I talked with Monica. She is on the heavy side with a pretty and intelligent face, a womanly appearance of Simone Signoret at 24 years of age. She lives in Lund and attends the university. Though Swedish, Monica spoke English fluently and had an amazingly large vocabulary. She spoke deeply, probed human emotions and feelings constantly and was nervous with unstable moods. But I liked her. We planned to go to Göteborg together but I never got past Lund where we stopped supposedly just for a few hours but which turned into a most enjoyable three days . . . In Lund I did meet in a student restaurant, an English youth who spoke most eloquently at Hyde Park. I recognized him . . . For I had seen him two years ago also in Hyde Park. To my surprise I found this brilliant articulate extrovert to be only 19. A couple of evenings were spent visiting Monica's girl friends who prepared wonderful meals, tastefully set on little tables . . . (by) candlelight. The students here had their own rooms. They are self sufficient, independent and far more mature than their equivalents back in the U.S. But I noted a basic unhappiness, a boredom and lack of purpose in life that found a consistent thread in all the personalities I met. Here perhaps lies the key to the suicidal tendencies of the Swedes. If I might hypothesize I would say that when people lack traditions, have obtained materialism and a freedom to pursue basic desires, when one has tasted of life to its fullest too much perhaps, then there is no hope, no frustration, no dreams or inspiration for a better life. Under these conditions a tremendous feeling of pointlessness must overcome them. . . .

"Today I said good-bye to Monica and rode by train across flat brisk countryside. The sun was out in a cloudy crisp sky. It felt clean and rejuvenating. Once again I was alone and independent. (Back at the Hostel in Copenhagen) . . . I met Israelis . . . They like the cold climate as a welcome change from Israel. Also I see many Arabs and Southern Europeans coming up to find a free love paradise. There are turbans bobbing around tonight and Americans, some decent but many role playing. How I hate those familiar facades; the goatees . . . the ridiculous haircuts, the over serious . . . conceited faces . . . Why do so many people in their twenties gravitate to this role playing? . . . "

August 27, 1961 Train, Between Hamburg and Amsterdam

"On the bulletin board in the Student's Club I saw a note advertising a cheap ticket for sale to London by train . . . Two hours later I had in my hands the ticket and was heading for the train station for a 4 P.M. departure . . . there was the famous smorgasbord on the Gedson-Grossenbrode ferry. The sea was calm and the sun, blood red sank slowly into the horizon. The sedate crowd on deck walked and talked in the casual atmosphere of European ferry crossings. Soon the lights of the Northern German coastline appeared. By 11 P.M. I was in Hamburg. Finding a room was difficult though there were numerous pensions and hotels. At last I returned to the station and using the information service, I got a room but for $3.00. By midnight I was settled in a small hotel but since I planned to spend one night in Hamburg I made an extra effort and went out . . . I took a cab to the famous Rapierbahn district. Here bathed in multicolored fluorescence the nightlife of Hamburg paraded. There are the ubiquitous strip joints, the dance halls and sidewalk eating houses selling shashlik and sausages. But the most famous street from which the Rapierbahn draws its renown is Herbertstrasse. Behind steel wall barricades at either end, with posted notices forbidding entrance to youth, is perhaps the most famous red light alley in Europe. The first impression one gets upon entering is that of a shopping district. On either side behind quaint paned glass windows sat mannequin-like figures on little stools and chairs. The background of these showcases are red curtains and red lamps. The women, most of them obese, and plastered in make-up all leer out at the slow procession of men, as angry caged animals might. The men of ages varying between perhaps 18 to 60, some in groups, occasionally walk up to the windows, rap on the glass, which if the prostitute is interested, she opens up and a transaction proceeds. Most end negatively with the price too high. The whole atmosphere is cold, filled with antagonism and hate. The women are bitter and clearly despise the men and the men enrage the situation by smiling, laughing and bargaining over the worth of the women. The whole thing is sick and unnatural though I admit its necessity in a social order filled with human frailty. The business is so ghastly one might think the government set the street up with women actors so that the moral conscience of man might be reminded of the horrors which can befall society. But it is no act . . . The women are the dredges of society, the men seeking sex because they cannot find love. Lord knows I am no prude. My only morality is honesty and this is why I am so revolted by this. . . .

"There is another aspect of Hamburg, a brighter one that lives by the brightness and cleanness of the day. The beautiful lakes inside the city sport sailboats which can be rented and tacked back and forth across the windy waters. As I watched the white triangles gliding by, a friendly young German speaking fluent English, invited me along . . . So for 40 minutes I learned the tricks of sailboats and now I feel I could handle a small one, at least in fresh water.

" . . . I noticed a few dry leaves in the street and then I saw that the trees were beginning to take on fall colors. Here the summer is short but still the end of it marks the passage of time and the three seasons since I left home. Dry leaves, the symbol of death and the end, the symbol of the closing episode of a long and happy journey."

August 30, 1961 Bentham Hall, London, England

"Now after three days in London I feel quite settled . . . The weather is superb with sunny days and temperature in the 70s. The evening of the first day I met Linda, who I had not seen since I left London. I met her in Hillel then and seeing her again reminded me of what a beautiful girl she is. A lovely face and an hour glass body made my heart skip a beat. The first night we just walked through the streets of London till we got to the river Thames. On the other shore we could see the modern concert hall lit up . . . But I fear it is the end of our budding romance for she is leaving for Edinburgh to see the music and art festival. It was a sad good-bye at the bus stop. How often I have said sad good-byes at London bus stops. . . .

"I looked over jobs in the classified section Daddy sent me but I saw nothing that suited me. If Brooklyn Polytechnic Institute finally accepts me I will take a light program of 10–12 credits, a gradual adjustment for a heavier load.

"In my hotel the girls who cook and clean come from Madrid and I have great fun flirting with them in Spanish and talking about the evils of England in front of the old English lady who runs the place. The girls do not like England. After all [sic] in Spain there is better weather and food not to mention the congenial Latin temperament.

"Yesterday afternoon I saw *East of Eden*, one of James Dean's experiments in confusion and torment but interesting if somewhat overdrawn . . . At present I sit on a park bench along a red paved boulevard that leads to Buckingham Palace. The Horse Guards just passed mounted on shiny black steeds with black polished hooves and proud prancing gait. It is a colorful reminder of the monarchy and the traditions of England and all the more splendid on this bright and peaceful day.

"In Denmark I had a couple of hours before my train left so I ran over to a few stores, found a desk set and bought it. It should be arriving in the States in about two weeks. Of course it is modern and suits my tastes, so I hope Ma will like it. . . . "

September 7, 1961 Bentham Hall, London, England

"Still in London after ten days, this city now seems like a second home . . . Unchanged were Mrs. Brown, the grouchy battle ax who runs the place, the leather upholstered chairs and couches in the reading room and the bustle of young people . . . I met a French girl in Hyde Park and we spent an evening together. She was typically French in er thinking because previously she only spoke to boys on introduction . . . On the weekend I went out to a poor section of town to meet Abul Khan who was coming in to see me from Manchester. His sister lived in a small one room flat. I waited but he was late. We did meet the next day and spent some time together walking and talking about past adventures and plans for the future. He was the same moody Abul with an occasional flash of humor and wit which reassured me that the old spirit still burned in him. But he is basically a sad fellow.

"On Sunday I came early to Hyde Park. Later I would meet Abul there. The great tradition of Speaker's Corner has always fascinated me. In the morning crowds form in a spontaneous human reaction perhaps in the green field or on the black pavement on the Corner under the shade of aging trees. As the day wears on more speakers and crowds gather. They form pools and a constant flux of flowing humanity moves aimlessly from pool to pool searching for an interesting or entertaining speaker. The fiery black nationalist screams with angry eyes from his high ladder platform. He yells invective and insults, scorn and hatred at Englishmen, at white men and proclaims the violent conquest of the enemy by Black Africa. The English . . . look upon him with humor, tolerance and mild antagonism. He is too insane to be taken seriously. Nearby the oily Socialist argues his scientific politics. His semantics are sound. He has all the answers. He views world politics as a realist but seeks power as an idealist. Then come the ex burglars and safe crackers speaking for contributions. And then there the Christians; the Catholic Evidence Guild, with their angelic types, the cross and the Bible, seeking lost souls, the Salvation Army singing hymns and relating personal miracles, the kneelers who pray on the sidewalk oblivious to the noise of traffic and the skeptical curious, the Latter Day House of Israel with bearded Jewish types proudly preaching conversion, the Watch Tower crowd with their eternal doomsday predictions. Then there are the assorted crackpots, individuals preaching against sin or for it, against religion or for it, singing loudly or heckling pointlessly. I did some heckling too, just for the experience. The Ban the Bombers sometimes start talking rockets, bombs and guidance systems. They soon go above their heads in technical terms and are ripe for a good authoritative technical explanation on just what they are dealing with. . . . The evening approached. As the sun went down on an orange sky Hyde Park became a study in silhouettes, orators with arms pointing here, gesturing with vigor above the heads of the crowd, smoke rising in the air beneath the darkening shadows, the misty fields growing cold, flashing eyes, white teeth, anger and hatred, salvation with hymns and prayers on the pavement behind double decker buses and glaring city lights. All the turmoil, all the fears and desires of the human spirit are exposed in this bazaar of speakers and listeners. As the evening grows older the crowds gradually diminish. By midnight the Corner is quiet. Street lamps illuminate black pavement and a few scraps of newspaper tumble in the chilly breeze; all that is left to mark the fury and temper which held sway during the day.

" . . . At Bentham hall I met Lillian, a cute little girl from Wales. She spoke Welsh before English but said that today this local condition exists only in rural areas and Welsh is dying out. I loved her interesting British accent. Mrs. Brown the house mother told me to leave because the place was booked up. After a few days of avoiding her she finally put her foot down. Grudgingly I left and used the chance to take my bags to the airport on a standby basis. There were planes but they wanted $250 and I have a chartered flight lined up for $130 . . . So I shall remain in England a little longer. BPI, the Draft Board, the electronics industry, family and friends will have to wait a little longer. Now I am staying at Hillel House. . . .

"I put in an order for an MG Midget, a smart English sports car. The order is meaningless until I send money but placing it here can save me $400 on the final cost. The total price after taxes and shipping runs to $1570 while it sells for $1950 in the States. But I must be subsidized since I am low on money. . . . "